FORENSIC HANDWRITING
IDENTIFICATION

Other related books

Questioned Documents: A Lawyer's Handbook

Jay Levinson

FORENSIC HANDWRITING IDENTIFICATION

IDENTIFICATION

FUNDAMENTAL CONCEPTS AND PRINCIPLES

Ron Morris

ACADEMIC PRESS

A Harcourt Science and Technology Company

San Diego San Francisco New York Boston
London Sydney Tokyo

ACADEMIC PRESS
A Harcourt Science and Technology Company
Harcourt Place, 32 Jamestown Road, London NW1 7BY, UK
http://www.academicpress.com

ACADEMIC PRESS
A Harcourt Science and Technology Company
525 B Street, Suite 1900, San Diego, California 92101-4495, USA
http://www.academicpress.com

ISBN 0-12-507640-1

A catalogue record for this book is available from the British Library

Typeset by Kenneth Burnley, Wirral, Cheshire
Printed in Great Britain by The Bath Press, Avon
00 01 02 03 04 05 BP 9 8 7 6 5 4 3 2 1

CONTENTS

*This book is dedicated to
the memory of a good friend,
Harlan Forbes III*

FOREWORD

Since the beginning of time, man has relied upon markings and some sort of writings to either send messages or to record history. With the evolution of time, the sophistication of man and growing technology, such markings have obviously evolved as well. They are now manuscripts, negotiable instruments and legal documents, to name a few. Their purpose and use has also reached unimaginable proportions. Unfortunately, so has the unlawful use of such instruments. Hence, the need for forensic analysis of questioned documents and a good understanding of handwriting.

Modern man has learned to write and use characters as a general rule in the classroom. Today, children begin to write and are taught writing styles based on the language, culture or standards of learning set forth by their particular school system or teacher. This becomes a very relevant factor when one studies and understands how a person writes or even attempts to disguise their writing. The individuality in one's writing takes on such characteristics as noted in detail in the chapters to come. Often, these patterns are the very element which allows a trained eye to detect and or understand their writer.

As we embark on the new millennium, the cyber/computer age is also revealing to us an even greater vulnerability to the unlawful use of data and documents. In many cases this can be identified as electronic-type fingerprints.

Criminologists, forensic document examiners, investigators, and others have long been tasked to use inscriptions and markings as clues to identify their writers. It may be to validate the authenticity of the marks and signature, or to identify sources, location or an actual person. Furthermore in many cases, as our book will reference, it may be to identify "the criminal".

Questioned Document Examiners have become, over the past decade, the integral keys to successful investigations, which involve the need for such forensics. The courts, generally speaking, do not solely rely on the testimony of the investigator. They require additional scientific evidence to support the charges or claims against those accused.

This text is designed to be a working handbook for professionals in and related to this field of expertise. It is a very basic guideline to assist you in successful evidence gathering and to afford a better understanding of the relevance and importance of such scientific evidence.

JERRY IANNACCI
Catoctin Consultants
February 2000

ACKNOWLEDGEMENTS

I have learned that when entering upon a project such as writing a book there are a lot of people involved who assist the author in many ways. I would therefore like to acknowledge some of them, and their contributions, at this time. First, my wife who never had to look far for me because I was sitting in front of the computer instead of doing the many things on her "honey do" list. Second, my publisher Mr Nick Fallon who kept the pressure on, in a nice way, and helped to provide the extra motivation I needed to get the book written. Third, all of the FDEs with whom I worked over the years who had a profound influence on me during my training period, who contributed of their time and talents to help me learn how to be an FDE. They will always be remembered for their effort and patience. Fourth, Ms Sharon Barber for her invaluable services as editor of this work before I turned it over to the publisher. The greatest compliment I received from her was when she said she understood what I was writing and learned a lot that she never knew before. Thank you, Sharon, for all your help; without you I could not have done it. Fifth, Mr Jerry Iannacci, with whom I have written another book, for his contribution to this book by writing the foreword and guide to use. He has been a good friend for many years, a professional investigator, and is a respected criminologist who runs his own company, Catoctin Consultants, LLC located in Frederick, Maryland.

Thank you all for your assistance. Without your help and encouragement, this project would have been impossible.

ABOUT THE AUTHOR

Ron Morris is President of Ronald N. Morris & Associates, Inc. Certified by the United States Secret Service Forensic Sciences Division and the American Board of Forensic Document Examiners, he has worked as an examiner of questioned documents for the Metropolitan Police Department, based in Washington DC, the United States Secret Service and the US Treasury Department.

Educated at George Mason University, Fairfax VA, he has attended and instructed training courses at the US Treasury Department, the US Secret Service, Georgetown University, and numerous professional organizations such as the American Academy of Forensic Sciences, The American Academy of Questioned Document Examiners, the International Association of Credit Card Investigators, the Mid-Atlantic Association of Forensic Sciences, the Southwestern Association of Document Examiners etc.

Ron Morris is a member of the American Academy of Forensic Sciences, The International Association of Financial Crime Investigators, formerly the International Association of Credit Card Investigators, the Mid-Atlantic Association of Forensic Scientists and the Canadian Society of Forensic Sciences.

He is co-author of the book *Access Device Fraud and Related Financial Crimes* (CRC Press, Boca Raton, 1999) and numerous reports and technical papers on a wide range of questioned document topics. He has testified as an expert witness in numerous federal, state, local and military courts – along with courts in the District of Columbia.

ABOUT THE
CONTRIBUTING AUTHOR

Jerry Iannacci is a criminologist and is the current CEO of Catoctin Consultants in Frederick, MD. He is a recently published expert on financial crimes and access devices (*Access Device Fraud and Related Financial Crimes*, CRC Press, Boca Raton, 1999). His background includes being a law enforcement officer in Long Island, NY; Director of Safety and Security Operations in Washington, DC, for a major hotel corporation; and an executive with a major financial corporation, serving as its Deputy Director for Investigations. In this last capacity, he was assigned to the US Secret Service Task Force in Washington DC, to help organize one of the world's most successful cooperatives between the government, public, and private sectors receiving the Attorney General's award for their successes.

Iannacci has been president of the International Association of Financial Crimes Investigators (Mid-Atlantic States), in addition to being a member of the organization's National Board of Directors and serving as the Training and Education Chairperson. He was a special advisor to the Pentagon during the Gulf War and has lectured internationally on Task Force Cooperatives on the importance of joining forces in fighting crime and related problems.

A few years ago, Iannacci decided to apply his investigative experience to look at criminal activity and organized groups that involve youth. When he joined Catoctin Consultants, his goal was to help the Maryland State Police introduce before the Maryland General Assembly a bill on Child pornography and Internet-related crimes, which did happen in 1998. Then, in 1999, he was requested by the Maryland Senate to help pass the Fraud Identity Takeover Act.

INTRODUCTION

Many books and technical papers have been written on the subject of questioned documents. Some are better than others when dealing with the many, and varied, topics a Forensic Document Examiner has to deal with. Most of the books have sections on handwriting and hand printing identification and the material covered is usually general. Recently, there have been several books written that deal just with handwriting identification; however, none of them deal with the topic of exactly how a person learns to write, how their fingers, hand, wrist, arm, etc. move and the resultant pen direction when writing. There have been many technical papers written that are based on studies of letterform patterns and their frequency of occurrence in writings of particular groups, for example a study just completed on "The Frequency of Round Handwriting in Edmonton, Alberta Schools" (Crane 1999: 169–74).

A lot of technical papers have been written about the elements of disguise writing, the effect of physical and emotional illness on handwriting, and the effect of transitory factors such as disguise writing under the influence of drugs and alcohol, writing with the unaccustomed hand, etc. Writing is a dynamic activity. The writer's fingers, hand, wrist, arm, etc. are in motion. There is variation in movements based on normal variation and the many influences that can affect how a person writes.

The purpose of this book is to review the basic concepts that affect a person's writing. Because writing is a dynamic activity, the Forensic Document Examiner (FDE) must understand how the writer holds his pen, positions the paper, moves his fingers, hand, wrist, etc. when examining a writing. He should be able to visualize the movements of the writer, evaluate pen direction, and determine the significance of factors, such as relative relationships between the various parts of a writing, the influence of writing on paper having and not having a pre-drawn baseline, etc. He should also know the importance of systems of writing and how they influence the writer during his formative years and even as a graphically mature writer.

This book covers many of these subjects. It has numerous illustrations that are explained in some detail, but it also encourages the reader to study them and find other important factors that affected or influenced the writer. The book is practical in approach and is designed for the investigator who must rely on handwriting comparison to assist him in his investigations, the attorney who retains the services of an FDE or has to use his services during a trial. It can also be used by trainees of the profession to further understand the basic principles behind the movement of the writer's hand and how the dynamics of the act of writing influence the resultant pattern left on the paper by the writer.

Pattern recognition is the beginning process of handwriting identification. It has long been known that just because two or more writings look alike and have the same patterns, it is not necessarily true that they are by the same writer. The FDE must go beyond simple pattern recognition to accurately determine that the writings are of common authorship. This book and the principles and examples covered in it should be of great assistance to the reader in learning how to properly evaluate the patterns, qualities, and features of a writing and how to begin attaching significance to them for identification purposes.

It takes years of specialized training to become an FDE. Anyone who thinks they can pick up a book like this or a more complete text on questioned documents, read it and become an FDE has the wrong impression of the profession. This book is designed as an aid to be used by professionals who want to learn more about the subject of handwriting, not to make them an FDE. This topic is covered in more detail later in the book. The author hopes that the reader will profit from this book and be better able to understand the concepts behind handwriting and hand printing identification.

REFERENCES

Crane, A. (1999) "The Frequency of Round Handwriting in Edmonton, Alberta Schools," *The Canadian Society of Forensic Science Journal*, 32(4), December.

The text of this book can be of significant assistance to several professionals who have the need to understand handwriting and questioned documents. Here are some examples and facts to consider.

LAW ENFORCEMENT INVESTIGATOR

Whether you are a police officer, constable or special agent, the relevance of this topic is paramount to any successful document-associated examination. Forensic Questioned Document Examination, although not a new field, is relatively new to most. Properly used, it can also help in the preliminary stages of an investigation. It may also help to confirm investigative intuition.

Let's review it in a quite practical way. What follows is a short case study.

You are assigned to investigate a credit card or access device fraud case. You interview your complainant and gather all the required information. It is determined during the course of your investigation that the following facts exist:

1   The victim whose credit card was used unlawfully is a respected law-abiding member of the community – a medical doctor by profession. The doctor noticed several thousand dollars in charges on his monthly statement from his Visa credit card that were not familiar to him. He disputed the charges with his bank and assures he did not make these purchases.

2   He has always been in possession of his credit card and had never left it behind anywhere. The only persons who were aware of his card number were his wife and office manager who paid his bills. It was determined that the wife would have no motive and that no outside sources were a factor or suspect in the matter.

3   All the credit card vouchers totaling over $12,000 were obtained for evidence, from local merchants. The handwriting appeared disguised but could have been written by the same writer.

4   What would be the investigator's course of action? How would his/her knowledge of handwriting further the investigation?

The Answer

Your new understanding of handwriting, complemented by your basic investigative skills, should lead you to this most appropriate course of action: which is to obtain handwriting samples from the office manager. This would include *original copies* of her office work and properly gathered handwriting specimens which could be used to match against the questioned handwriting.

This would help the Forensics Questioned Documents Examiner establish pattern base lines from original writings as well as to be able to do the comparative study with your newly obtained specimens. Provide the examiner with specimen writings of the victim as well as the suspects.[1]

[1] *For those who read this text, another key factor is that you should be able to provide the examiner with exactly what they need, not withstanding the ability to interpret their findings.*

This method or scientific approach to your investigation lends far more credibility to your case than would an interrogation (hoping for a confession). Ideally, when you have some hard evidence in your hands, depending on your venue, you may only need to have the examiner's opinion and related cause to indict or arrest your suspect.

PROSECUTOR/SOLICITOR/ATTORNEY

Regardless of whether or not you are the defense attorney or prosecutor, it is extremely relevant to understanding the findings of the examiner/investigator. It is very difficult, if not impossible, to successfully prosecute or defend such a matter without a complete understanding of such expert opinions.

1   How were the specimens obtained?
2   What is the expertise of the examiner?
3   What comparative studies were completed to identify the writer?
4   How many specimens were taken and what are the results of all suspect forensics?
5   What requests did the investigator make to the examiner?
6   How were the steps used in the comparative study and what factors were considered by the examiner?

TRAINEE FORENSIC QUESTIONED DOCUMENT EXAMINER

This book fulfils several functions for the trainee:

1   It is a working text for study and reference.
2   It helps the examiner understand the philosophy of writing.
3   It emphasizes the need for understanding systems and qualities of forensics.
4   It helps to ascertain how to determine significant features of handwriting.
5   It mandates the importance of writing clear and concise reports.

Use the science of Forensic Questioned Document Examination to your best advantage. As I mentioned earlier, it affords credibility and may reduce the risk of your making costly mistakes. Use the book as a reference text after your initial course of instruction. Most of the methodology will remain consistent and will prove to be an excellent guideline for your handwriting and questioned document related cases.

CHAPTER 1

THE PHYSIOLOGY OF WRITING

HANDWRITING RULES OF EXECUTION

"Handwriting" is not handwriting. Most people write with their hand, but there are a substantial number who are not able to use their hand so they write with their foot, mouth, etc. Writing is actually a brain function and the hand – foot, mouth, etc. – is merely a device with which to carry out instructions sent to it by the brain. For the purpose of this book, it is assumed that handwriting refers to hand writing. However, virtually all of the concepts presented and discussed throughout this book also apply to writing done with the foot, mouth, etc.

The individual develops writing skills in the following manner:

- The infant learns to clasp round objects like a finger or stick with his hand by grasping the object in the hollow of his hand and wrapping his fingers around the object to keep it in place.
- The preschooler learns to make random movements and markings with his arm while holding a crayon. Some children hold the crayon in their hands in the way that a toddler holds onto a finger, and are begin to hold it with their fingers like an adult holds a pen. Regardless of how the child holds the crayon he leaves a record of his random movements by a series of lines on the paper.
- The youngster learns to color within the preprinted lines of the picture while manipulating the crayon with finger, wrist, and arm movements.
- The young student learns to make individual letters by drawing them one line at a time. For example, the "A."

Line one   Line two   Line three   The complete letter

The arrows on the completed letter show the stroke direction called for by the copybook to make the letter.

A pre-printed set of model letter forms, referred to as a writing system or copybook is placed before the student and he is asked to draw the individual letters by following the instructions of his teacher and book.

- The older student learns to connect individual letters while maintaining legibility. This is not an easy task for him to accomplish. In part, the success of this exercise depends upon the handwriting system, his attention to detail, and many hours of practice to master the task. Over time the act of writing individual letters and connecting strokes becomes habitual, and the writer finds his writing speed increasing while retaining legibility.

- The more skillful writer develops a series of combined finger, wrist, and arm movements usually associated with "graphic maturity" (Saudek 1978: 381). At this level, he establishes a pattern of movements required to make letter shapes, connecting strokes, and other writing movements repeatedly. Wilson R. Harrison refers to this concept as the writer's "master pattern" (Harrison 1966: 306). The writer does not produce a letter or group of letters exactly the same way every time he writes it. There is some normal variation expected in every writer's writing. A more in-depth discussion of this concept will be covered later in the book.

Writing skill and "graphic maturity" are concepts that will also be covered later in more detail. For the purposes of this discussion, experience teaches that the majority, if not all, of the physiological principles of handwriting apply to all writers, regardless of the writing system learned.

Robert Saudek studied the writing act, how people learned to write, how they actually wrote, made letters, connected them together, etc. Even though he studied the writing of the people of England, where he lived, he also studied the writing of people from Europe. He had writers perform a series of experiments from which he derived a set of principles that are as valid today as they were then. If anything, experience has shown that his principles are scientifically sound and most important of all, reproducible (Poulin 1963).

The following material is a paraphrased/edited version of some of the principles from his book, *Experiments with Handwriting* (Saudek 1978). Paraphrased/edited material from other topics in his work will also be included in this book. When the paraphrased/edited material is used in this book, there is a reference to the source of the original work at the end of each chapter.

SEVEN PHYSIOLOGICAL PRINCIPLES OF HANDWRITING (Saudek 1978: 96–98)

Handwriting is usually done with the fingers and hand, connected to the writer's body by his arm. Like the fingers and hand, the wrist and arm contain many nerves and muscles that can affect the writer before, during, and after the act of writing. Therefore, it is necessary to examine the physiological principles of writing as summarized in the following seven principles.

Principle No. 1

Handwriting is a form of self-expression and for the graphically mature writer the various movements involved are habitual. The muscles of his fingers, hand, and arm react to brain instructions communicated through the nerves. In most writers the fingers, hand, and arm then move with a rhythmical and unrestricted action to accomplish the brain's instructions. This *natural* act of writing by the writer can provide him with a certain amount of pleasure. If he is a "graphically mature" writer, as will be defined in this book, he is able to concentrate on the content of what he is writing and not on how each pen movement is supposed to be made. This is true regardless of whether the mature writer uses his fingers, hand, and arm separately or in some combination. The same applies to the toes, foot, leg, hip, mouth, etc.

His brain knows each movement necessary to write a letter, combinations of letters, connecting strokes, etc., and how they are supposed to look after being written. When finished with all of the writing, he consciously or unconsciously compares each mental image with what he actually wrote. Occasionally, he may go back to a stroke, letter, or combination of letters and make corrections to clarify the written image on the paper so it conforms more closely to his mental image. This activity is referred to as patching or retouching of the writing for the purpose of clarification.

Principle No. 2

The hand muscles function best when making rhythmical contraction and relaxation movements. They become fatigued when either movement dominates. Therefore, *normal, natural* writing occurs when the muscles are not fatigued, but are functioning in a rhythmical fashion. This topic will be covered again with the discussion on unnatural and disguised writing.

Contracting muscle actions are usually more developed than are relaxing muscle actions. Because they are, the writer's grip on the pen is more forcible on downstrokes than upstrokes when the writer is holding the pen in what some call a normal writing position. As the writer increases the "grip pressure" (Saudek 1978: 378) and moves the pen toward him, he gradually applies more force on the pen point in the direction of the paper, resulting in the writing of a darker line. When upstrokes are written, his "grip pressure" gradually decreases, the pen point is not forced against the paper surface with as much pressure, so the written line is lighter.

There are exceptions, but they are not the result of any exception to this concept. Some writers write upstrokes that are darker than downstrokes. Remember the phrase above, "when the writer is holding the pen in what some call a normal writing position." What happens to the darkness of the line when the writer, either right- or left-handed, holds his hand in the "flexed wrist or hooked wrist position? . . . The pencil can be held in a variety of grasps with the wrist flexed or bent. This is more typically seen with left-handed writers but is also present in some right-handed writers." (Alley: 2–3). The palm of the writer's hand rests on the paper above the writing, his wrist is flexed, or bent, so the fingers and hand point toward the writer. With the hand in this position, the "grip pressure" is greatest as the pen is moved away from the writer. When the muscles contract, the pen is pulled away from the writer, and when they relax, the fingers and hand move toward the writer. In this situation the writer's upstrokes are darker and the downstrokes lighter.

Figure 1.1

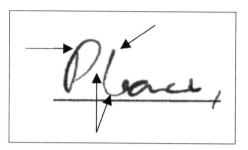

The writing of the "P" and "l" in "Place" shows the heavy upstroke on the back of the "P" and the light downstroke on the clockwise oval or right side of the letter. The "l" also shows the variation in pressure as the muscles in the fingers relax when the pen is moved toward the writer and contract as it moves away from the writer.

There are a number of other ways for writers to hold the writing instrument. Kathy Alley describes them very well, as follows:

Functional Grasp Patterns
- *Tripod grasp with open web space:* The pencil is held with the tip of the thumb and index finger and rests against the side of the third finger. The thumb and index finger form a circle.
- *Quadrupod grasp with open web space:* The pencil is held with the tip of the thumb, index finger, and third finger and rests against the side of the fourth finger. The thumb and index finger form a circle.
- *Adaptive tripod or D'Nealian grasp:* The pencil is held between the index and third fingers with the tips on the thumb and index finger on the pencil. The pencil rests against the side of the third finger near its end.

Immature Grasp Patterns
- *Fisted grasp:* The pencil is held in a fisted hand with the point of the pencil on the fifth finger side on the hand. This is typical of very young children.

■ *Pronated grasp:* The pencil is held diagonally within the hand with the tips of the thumb and index finger on the pencil. This is typical of children ages 2 to 3.

Inefficient Grasp Patterns
■ *Five finger grasp:* The pencil is held with the tips of all five fingers. The movement when writing is primarily on the fifth finger side of the hand.
■ *Thumb tuck grasp:* The pencil is held in a tripod grasp but with the thumb tucked under the index finger.
■ *Thumb wrap grasp:* The pencil is held in a tripod grasp but with the thumb wrapped over the index finger.
■ *Tripod grasp with closed web space:* The pencil is held with the tip of the thumb and index finger and rests against the side of the third finger. The thumb is rotated toward the pencil, closing the web space.
■ *Finger wrap or Interdigital brace grasp:* The index and third fingers wrap around the pencil. The thumb web space in [is] completely closed. (Alley: 2–3)

Principle No. 3

Usually, the relaxing of a muscle requires more time than its contraction when the writer is fatigued, because relaxation becomes more difficult. Contraction of fatigued muscles does not appear to be as affected in the short run, because the muscles are stronger. Over time though, contraction is also affected.

Principle No. 4

If the ability to relax a finger muscle is lost, but not the ability to contract it, the finger is usually cramped, and it may become spasmodic. This spasmodic condition can cause the finger to randomly strike the pen. If this condition occurs in the index finger, resulting grip pressure variation can cause unusual occurrences of light and dark lines in a single writing stroke.

Principle No. 5

During the act of writing, spasmodic fatigue (writer's cramp) may be localized as stated in Principle No. 4 or the fingers, hand, and arm may be involved. It does not occur during the constant rhythmical alternating of contracting and relaxing muscles, except after very prolonged periods of writing. This ideally controlled rhythm affects "grip pressure" on the pen and writing pressure simultaneously. It does not affect the writing impulse, merely its fulfillment. When spasmodic fatigue occurs, one or both of the pressure habits may be affected.

Principle No. 6

When the first signs of cramping or fatigue occur, the writer usually makes some kind of adjustment. He may alter the way he holds the pen, change its angle, etc. Any change he makes affects the writing.

Principle No. 7

It is necessary to study the manner in which muscular tension and relaxation succeed one another. When the contraction and relaxation are rhythmical, the writing is more likely to be normal. If they are not, we can decide if attention is being diverted, even if only momentarily, from context to the mechanical details of writing in the writing of a graphically mature writer.

FACTORS INFLUENCING LETTER FORMATION

A writer learns to write by the "impulse method" (Saudek 1978: 38–40). This method will be covered more fully when we study speed of writing; but for now, a brief explanation is given as background for this section. The different writing impulses are as follows:

- *The stroke impulse:* the writer learns to write by drawing individual lines, which, when connected together, make a letter (ibid: 389).
- *The letter impulse:* he writes whole letters as a single writing act (ibid: 381).
- *The syllable impulse:* he writes syllables or several letters connected together.
- *The word or name impulse:* he writes complete words or names as a single act of writing (ibid. 394).
- *The sentence/phrase impulse:* when he reaches "graphic maturity," he thinks and tries to write sentences/phrases as a single act (ibid: 388).

To summarize, after practicing letter formation by using a series of individual strokes, the writer's writing speed increases. He learns to write complete letters, then several letters in combination, words, and finally sentences or phrases without thinking about how to draw each stroke of each letter.

According to Saudek, the following twelve factors seem to influence letter formation (Saudek 1978: 235):

- The mechanical means. For example, pen, ink, writing material, writing surface, etc.
- The writer's degree of graphic maturity.
- The writer's relative speed of writing.
- The system of writing learned.
- The writer's nationality.
- The writer's degree of visual sensitivity and impressionability.
- The writer's power of graphic expression.
- The writer's characterological factors, vanity, affectation, and desire to imitate others, etc.

- The writer's knowledge of foreign languages, special training, etc.
- The writer's physiological condition.
- Chronic physical impediments the writer may have.
- In addition, whether the letter form stands alone, or at the beginning, middle or end of a word.

Overlapping and further explaining these twelve factors are the following sixteen transient factors tending to influence not just letter formation, but writing in general (ibid.).

WRITING INSTRUMENTS AND MATERIALS

Except in extreme cases the writing instruments and materials – pen, ink, paper, writing surface under the paper, etc. – usually will not make writing unidentifiable. A writer using satisfactory writing instruments and materials, together with a smooth writing surface, should be able to write in a normal and natural manner. On those rare occasions when one or a combination of these factors is unsatisfactory, the act of writing can be affected. How much depends upon the type of problem encountered, and how the writer compensates for it.

For example, if he uses a defective ballpoint pen, he will stop, if only shortly, to clear ink and paper residue from the ball housing or to try to correct an ink flow problem. If he uses a nib pen and a paper fiber catches in the nib, he will eventually stop writing to remove the fiber. In either case, his writing speed slows before the problem is fixed, and when it does, line quality deteriorates because of the writing instrument problem and the reduction in writing speed. After correcting the problem, he again starts to write, but it will take him a brief amount of time to return to his normal writing speed before the disruption distracted him.

If the pen is about to run out of ink, the ink line will start getting lighter. When the pen runs out, the writer may find another pen and continue writing. With his new pen, he may even overwrite some of the previous material before resuming his normal writing. The overwriting in this situation is natural rather than unnatural.

If he is writing on a rough surface, he may stop, find a smoother surface, and begin again. If the writing surface is unusually rough and he is forced to continue writing on it, the written line will contain tremor caused by surface roughness. Examination of the back of the sheet of paper will help detect whether the writing surface was the problem.

THE SCHOOL COPY FROM WHICH WE LEARNED TO WRITE

There exists a natural conflict between writer and system. The effect of the writing system he learned is not always so decisive as many suppose. Most systems are formulated with more consideration being given to the reader than to the writer. He wants to economize movement, increase speed, and yet he must maintain legibility.

Many educators and penmen express a great deal of concern over the deterioration of handwriting. For them good handwriting is related to legibility. They maintain that one reason is because handwriting is not emphasized as much during a student's formative years.

Many Internet web sites provide services to correct what is perceived to be a serious problem. A few of these sites cover such topics as:

- Rules for good handwriting (www.argonet.co.uk/users/quilljar/rules.html)
- Handwriting initiative (www.argonet.co.uk/users/quilljar/init.html)
- Kate Gladstone's handwriting problems
  (www.global2000.net/handwritinggrepair/KateHwR.html)
- Letter formation (www.drewcrpcler/cp./cmcjpst/cp./alley/let-for.html)

In addition, there are many, many more.

THE WRITER'S DEGREE OF GRAPHIC MATURITY

As a writer matures, he departs from the system or copybook style of writing and incorporates more individuality into his writing. The concept of individuality is covered in detail later. Regardless of whether the writer slavishly adheres to the system or writes with a great deal of individuality, he is governed by the requirement for legibility. Ultimately he wants to be able to communicate with the person who must read what he wrote, so what he writes must be legible.

There are different levels of "graphic maturity," each governed by a number of different factors working together. The impulse system outlined above is a basic concept in understanding "graphic maturity." An immature writer, i.e. a child learning to write, uses separate pen strokes to draw a letter. As his "graphic maturity" level increases, he goes from writing with a stroke impulse to writing with a letter impulse. At this level, each letter is written as a complete unit, because he has no doubt about what it is supposed to look like or how it is to be made.

The next levels are the syllable and word impulse levels. Here, he knows how to write combinations of letters as a single unit. Eventually he learns how to write complete words and a limited combination of words. He knows how to spell the word and the combination of letters necessary to write it. He writes them comfortably and without hesitation, because he does not have to think about what letters make up the syllable or word, or how to write them.

The highest level is the sentence/phrase impulse level. As the name implies, the writer at this level thinks and attempts to write in complete sentences or phrases. However, he finds that his thoughts are ahead of his pen. According to Saudek, the following eight conditions must be satisfied before it can be said that a writer is writing naturally and automatically at this level.

He can write a letter fluently, easily, and automatically only under these conditions:

1   When there is *no* doubt, whatsoever, as to what the letter form looks like or how to write it. That is, when the mere sound of the letter is enough to evoke its graphic image in the writer's mind.
2   When the writer has unimpeded control of the writing instrument.
3   His ability to write is free from any sort of physical or mental impediment.

When he can write a word automatically, and only when the following condition is added to the three already defined:

4   When the writer has no doubt about the spelling of the word, its sound, or the thought it evokes, together with its complete graphic image.

Because not all people think in images, the second part of this principle cannot be considered a universal statement of truth.

He can write a sentence automatically only when the following conditions are added to the four that are already defined:

5   The writer is so intent on the content of the sentence that he no longer pays attention to the details of the act of writing nor is he conscious of problems relating to the physical act of writing. For example, he is in no doubt about the following:
    (a) The legibility of the writing. This is particularly true in rapid writing where the details of the individual features do not conform to the copybook standard.
    (b) The beauty of the letter forms.
    (c) The distinctness of the horizontal spacing between sentences. Some writers may connect two or more words or sentences without lifting the pen.
    (d) The symmetry of the writing's general spacing.
6   When the writer is completely at home with the language he is writing. It is rare to find anyone who can succeed in writing both his native and a foreign language automatically and equally as well within the same body of writing.

7   When the writer does not suddenly change from one language to another within the text. Even if he is perfectly at home in both languages, there is a sudden hesitation when passing from one language to another.

8   When the writer no longer believes there is a basic difference between the meaning of the spoken and written word (Saudek 1978: 40–41).

Note that it is not always possible to determine from the writing itself whether the cause of the retardation is a faulty writing instrument, physical or mental impediment, or nervousness. Sometimes it becomes necessary to investigate the background of the writing by other means. For example, asking questions about the writer, such as his age, physical condition, the circumstances under which the writing is produced, etc.

The writer who meets or exceeds the criteria described above is considered a "graphically mature" writer. Whether his writing is legible or not has little or nothing to do with "graphic maturity." ". . . legibility is sometimes unrelated to the artistic quality of the script, for many an elegant and fluid handwriting will prove difficult to decipher; whilst another, which is irregular and lacking in rhythm, may be read with ease, although it may afford little pleasure to the eye of the beholder" (Harrison 1966: 308). Legibility is a measure of whether and with what ease a reader can read the written material.

Although he does not use the term "graphic maturity," Ordway Hilton sums it up this way: "Writing is far from a lifeless form. Every specimen reveals animation individual to its writer and reflects the pen movements that have produced it. At one extreme is a smooth, continuous, rhythmic, rapidly executed writing, filled with grace and poise, and artistically shaded with points of emphasis, displaying a freedom of motion characteristic of a highly skilled penman. In direct contrast is a hesitant, interrupted, halting, laborious, slowly executed writing with an uncertain hand, showing irregularities typical of one to whom writing is a hard physical or mental task. There are still other qualities of writing movement. The strokes may be precise or careless, or they may be reworked or retouched in an effort to perfect and improve the legibility" (Hilton 1982: 154). He goes on to say: "The animation in writing is closely related to the physical processes involved. Depending on the skill and training of the writer, as well as his natural inclinations, writing is executed by movement of the fingers, the wrist, and the arm, either individually or more generally in varying combinations" (ibid.: 155).

A primary indicator of unnatural or disguised writing is wavering or broken strokes, but it is also a natural accompaniment of immature writing. Such writing must be examined carefully to ascertain the cause of the slow writing. If the cause is a *low level of "graphic maturity,"* the writing is in all probability naturally written; and if it is due to a *deliberate* reduction in "graphic maturity," the writing is disguised. A transitory factor, such as an injury, being out in cold weather, the effect of a drug, etc., can also cause a decrease in the writer's level of "graphic maturity." More about this area later.

TEMPORARY OR PERMANENT PHYSICAL DISORDERS

It is not always possible to distinguish, from the writing alone, between permanent and temporary impediments. After a time, the central nervous system adapts itself to a loss of a hand or eyesight, etc. Some temporary impediments may affect writing more than permanent ones, but it depends upon the writer and the nature of the temporary impediment.

THE DEGREE OF WRITING ROUTINE

The amount of time a person spends writing may determine his general "graphic maturity," skill level, and relative speed of writing. Some people write so infrequently that when they do, they struggle with the task. They may write slowly because they are not familiar with the spelling of and the words they are trying to use.

Further, it must be noted that manual skills in various activities not connected with writing does not necessarily improve one's writing skill. Just because someone engages in activities that cause him to contract and relax the same muscles he writes with, does not mean that his level of "graphic maturity" is going to be higher or even increase.

The amount of formal education he has is not necessarily related to his level of "graphic maturity." For example, a person may have a job that requires him to write a lot, yet he has little formal education. His level of "graphic maturity" may actually be greater than the writer who has a PhD in economics, physics, etc. who may not write as much because they use word processors and mainly sign their name.

THE SPEED OF WRITING

It is not possible to write rapidly under the majority of systems. Most systems call for uniform writing pressure. When a writer increases his speed of writing he finds that he cannot write up and down strokes with uniform pressure. An increase in writing speed typically results in relative pressure habits. Relative pressure habits are the difference in writing pressure between up and down strokes. They are the result of the normal rhythmical alternation between contraction and relaxation of muscles. Relative pressure habits are not part of most handwriting systems. Furthermore, copybook letter forms are such that most of them cannot be made without stopping at some point during the writing of a letter or retracing a stroke that is already written. Whenever a writer stops or retraces a line, it takes time.

"... Not everyone writes at the same rate, so that consideration of the speed of writing may be a significant identifying element. Writing speed cannot be measured precisely from the finished handwriting but (it) can be interpreted in broad terms as slow, moderate, or rapid" (Hilton 1982: 21). Since the concept of speed of writing is to be dealt with in greater depth in Chapter 12, nothing more will be said about it at this time.

THE SENSITIVENESS OF THE EYESIGHT

A writer knows how a letter or combination of letters is supposed to look after he writes them. His eyesight confirms that the image on the paper conforms to the one in his mind.

If a person is able to see during his formative years, reaches "graphic maturity" and then looses his eyesight, for a time he may still write at his achieved level. As the writer ages, gradually loses his eyesight, and is no longer able to match what he writes with his mental image, his writing will change. Other factors in the aging process will also affect his "graphic maturity."

A number of technical papers have been written about the handwriting of the blind and how a person's writing changes with age. Because these topics are beyond the scope of this book, the reader is referred to the technical literature.

MEMORY FOR FORMS

This topic overlaps with the one above. When a writer observes a letter or its embellishments, and wants to adopt them into his writing, the better his memory of forms the more accurate will be his writing of them.

Writers are influenced by the handwriting of other people. For example, a son may like the shape of a letter written by his father so he practices making that letter until he thinks it is like his father's. When he is satisfied with the way he writes it, how it looks (because it is like dad's), he will begin to write it without paying further attention to its details. He has mastered the writing of the letter.

A writer then, even with a letter impulse level of skill, knows how to write a letter and what it is supposed to look like. It does not have to be like its copybook equivalent, it can be some variation of it depending upon how he individualizes it and how it conforms to the writer's graphic image of that letter or combination of letters.

The better his memory of forms and the more time he spends practicing how to write a form he wants to adopt, the more habitual his movements become and the closer the new form will be to the model. That is not to say that he will write the new one exactly like the model; it only says that what he produces will more closely resemble the model. If the new form is very simple, then at some future time it may not be possible to determine which of the writers wrote it. The better his memory of forms the closer he may come to repeating what he saw.

PREVIOUS AND PRESENT ENVIRONMENTS

As stated previously, some writers, consciously or otherwise, imitate letter forms they have seen that strike them as pleasing. Previous and present environments, therefore, do have an influence on the way a person writes. When handwriting is studied for identification purposes, the examiner must always ask if it is possible that the feature being examined could have been influenced by the writer's past or present environment. The following are some examples of the environmental influences upon a writer:

■ Different nationalistic styles of writing. Let's assume that a child who is learning to write moves from the US to Europe. There he is enrolled in a school that teaches a different writing system than the one he was learning in the US. Some features of the letters and numerals may be very different from those he had practiced while some are not that different. For example, let's assume he learns to write the number "1" in the US as follows:

$$1$$

Moreover, after he moves to Europe he is taught to write the same number as depicted below:

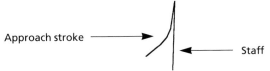

In making the approach stroke he is taught to make it longer, at a steeper angle and slightly curved, and closer to the staff than the one he first learned to write. As he begins to write these new features, he also incorporates them into his writing habits. Notwithstanding his having to learn these new system features, he is still influenced by the previous system features and his writing may very well become a combination of the two. How much of a combination depends upon the set of writing habits he develops.

■ Professional environment. Mathematical equations consist of both letters and numerals. It is necessary to distinguish between them because the letters may represent constants like "pi" (a Greek character) which is equal to 3.14 . . . or as an electronic engineering problem some letters are used in equations that can have more than one meaning. For example, the letter "Z" can represent any value the engineer wants. However, if he is working the equation using pencil and paper, depending upon the speed with which he writes the number "2" and the letter "Z," they look very much alike. So much so that he must be able to distinguish between the two characters. One way would be to put a short horizontal line through the angular part of the letter "Z" as follows:

or a line through the zero, "0":

$$\emptyset$$

to distinguish it from the letter "O." Added features such as these are carried over from technical writings to everyday writing because they become a part of the writer's writing habits and are not necessarily dependent upon technical context.

FORMAL EDUCATION

A writer's level of formal education or professional training may not have much of an influence on his ultimate level of "graphic maturity." Since this subject already has been touched on, nothing more will be added to the topic at this time.

GENERAL INTELLIGENCE

A person's intelligence is not derived solely from his formal study of books in a structured college or university program. While that type of intelligence is important, there is also the intelligence a person acquires by virtue of life experiences. Intelligent people frequently show a propensity to write with a sentence impulse even when their level of formal education would suggest they write with a lower level of "graphic maturity." As a rule, the more intelligence a writer has the more he concentrates on subject matter when writing than on the act of writing itself.

   Some people might be classified as partially illiterate but are intelligent, even though they have not mastered the spelling of words in their own language. Sometimes these people can demonstrate a tendency to write at a high level of "graphic maturity." They do so in spite of their self-invented, phonetic spelling. The essential element is that they are more interested in content than in mechanics.

CONCENTRATION ON THE SUBJECT MATTER

This topic has been covered sufficiently already. It is listed here only because it is a separate factor that must be considered.

CONCENTRATION ON THE CALLIGRAPHY

Calligraphy is defined as "the art and manner of writing with beauty and grace" (Roman 1968: 65). It is also defined as "1. fancy penmanship or the art of writing beautifully. 2. handwriting; penmanship" (Random 1992). Today, calligraphy remains an art form. When a person is writing calligraphy, he will, of necessity, concentrate on how each letter is made and connected. The more proficient he is with calligraphy, the less attention he pays to the writing act. Since the goal is to write as closely as possible so the final product closely resembles the model, more attention must be paid to the act of writing than to content, and this necessarily slows the writer.

In normal writing, whatever he writes must resemble the writing system he has learned. Regardless of how artistic the writing, the only way he has of communicating is assuring that whatever he has written will be recognized and understood by the reader.

CHARACTEROLOGICAL FACTORS

Although the FDE does not try to determine the character or personality of a writer, based on handwriting characteristics, personality and character can influence how a person writes. For example, self-assurance, sincerity, carelessness, imagination, aesthetic taste, etc., can all have an impact on the artistic nature of a person's writing. Some examples of this are stylized signatures, drawings, embellishments, detail in writing individual letters to insure legibility, etc. A prime example is the signature of "John Hancock" on the Declaration of Independence.

PSYCHOPATHOLOGICAL FACTORS

A writer who suffers from a severe psychopathological problem may produce writing that contains characteristics and elements that have meaning only to him; for example, his drawings, unusual and even bizarre text formats and letter forms, unusual punctuation, etc. Each writing must be examined individually, and under very controlled circumstances, incorporating the scientific method of research. If after a long period of research, study, and evaluation some general statements about the relationship between his personality and writing characteristics can be made, they would apply only to that writer.

For example, I remember one writer who used rectangular boxes – "■" – for I-dots and punctuation symbols as follows:

The i-dot   The colon   The semi-colon

As the reader understands, the use of such diacritics and punctuation marks is unusual. The psychopathological reason for this writer using these boxes in this manner is known only to her.

Because further discussion of this topic is outside of the scope of this text nothing more will be said about this topic. Should the reader wish to peruse this topic further, he is encouraged to search what recognized scientific literature there may be on the subject.

TEMPORARY EMOTION OR EXCITEMENT

When a person is temporarily excited or under emotional stress, his writing can be adversely affected; to what extent is dependent upon the individual. Usually when a person is excited, he does not have the same level of control over the pen as when he is not excited and the writing appears more random, larger, and possibly not as legible. The conditions under which he is writing can also be a factor just as they are when he is not as excited. When the situation changes again and he is back to a more normal emotional state, his writing should return to its normal appearance.

While this list is not all inclusive, it does provide some information about transient and even permanent factors that can and do influence writing. The greater the number of factors operating which affect a person's writing, the greater the possible variations the features of his writing may take.

PRINCIPLES OF THE WRITING MOVEMENT

Are there principles of the writing movement that can be relied on? Yes! If something is classified as a principle, it means that whatever statement is made will usually be true. A rule, as defined in the *Random House Webster's Electronic Dictionary and Thesaurus*, College Edition, is as follows:

1. A principle or regulation governing conduct, procedure, arrangement, etc.
2. The customary or normal circumstance, occurrence, practice, quality, etc. the rule rather than the exception. . . .

16. To exercise dominating power or influence; predominate.

17. To exercise authority, dominion, or sovereignty.

18. To make a formal decision or ruling, as on a point at law.

19. To be prevalent or current.

Idiom

21. <as a rule> generally; usually.

For normal, natural writing, the following rules of execution fit within the scope of the definition. As the reader will soon see, they are also an integral part of the physiology of writing. This will become clearer as each rule is integrated into future topics as follows (Quirke 1930: 21–28)

1   Every writer has adopted a relatively constant and distinctive average degree of slope in his writing. This slope may change within narrow limits.

2   When the average angle of slope is altered beyond certain limits, the following may happen:
    (a) Symmetry of curve structure is impaired.
    (b) Uniformity of letter size may be destroyed.

3   Every writer has a normal mean speed of writing. He can change this normal mean speed arbitrarily, but his handwriting will reveal traces of the fact that the normal writing speed has changed.

4   Artificially induced *slowness* is betrayed by a less firm and harmonious execution of the writing act. One indication of this change is in the size of recurring examples of the same letter. This variation in the height and width of letters will probably be outside of the norm for a particular writer.

5   For a given set of writing conditions, every writer has an absolute mean size of letter formation. He usually does not deviate from this mean size without a deliberately conscious effort and the decreasing of his writing speed.

6   Any attempt at deliberate variation of the absolute and/or mean size of a letter formation is accompanied by inconsistency in the size of successive examples of the same letter.

7   The *greater* the speed of writing, the greater the difficulty forming acute angles between two successive strokes executed in nearly opposite directions.

8   For every writer, the localization of relative pressure points is involuntary.

9   No writer can deliberately alter the localization of his relative pressure habits *except* at the expense of writing speed, symmetry, and line quality.

What these rules teach is that when a writer makes any changes in his normal writing habits, there will be a corresponding effect in the writing. Because writing is habitual, a writer desirous of deliberately changing his writing will generally fall back into his normal writing habits. This will occur over time and is a function of the writer's ability to maintain the changes he has made. More about this later as we cover subsequent topics.

NATURAL AND AUTOMATIC WRITING

What is normal natural writing? " . . . no amount of practice can be counted on to ensure that any particular individual will eventually be capable of writing a smooth, fluent, and rhythmic hand" (Harrison 1966: 295). This being the case, then whatever level of skill and "graphic maturity" he reaches, is not that his natural and automatic writing level? Yes! Natural and automatic writing is any writing "executed normally without an attempt to control or alter its identifying habits and it's usual quality of execution" (Hilton 1982: 20).

The eight conditions that must be met before a writer can write naturally and automatically are listed in the section above on the writer's degree of graphic maturity. The reader is encouraged to review them at this time. To obtain a better understanding of what makes writing natural and automatic, we must first examine the systems of writing taught in school. Systems provide the student with model letter forms he must learn to write and repeat sufficiently so the action of writing them becomes a natural activity regardless of his ultimate level of skill or "graphic maturity."

In summary, "graphic maturity" is reached when the following conditions are met:

- The writer has no doubt about the form and movements necessary to write a letter.
- The writer has complete control of the pen and writing surface and there are no mechanical problems offered by either of them.
- There is no transitory, or permanent factor, affecting the writer's ability to write.
- There is no doubt on the part of the writer as to the legibility of the writing, relative pressure habits used to write the letters, relative spacing habits between letters, words, sentences, lines, paragraphs, the size and shapes of margins, etc.
- The writer is comfortable with the language and writing system he is writing.
- He does not change from one language or writing system to another within the text he is writing.
- In summary, any act or occurrence of anything or event on the writer that causes him to pay more attention to the way he is writing than what he is writing will affect the writer's level of graphic maturity (Saudek 1978).

REFERENCES

Alley, Kathy, "Pencil Grasp", obtained from Internet site,
www.drewcrocker.com.cnchost,com/alley/pencl.html

Harrison, Wilson R. (1966) *Suspect Documents Their Scientific Examination*, 2nd edn,
London.

Hilton, Ordway (1982) *Scientific Examination of Questioned Documents*, revised edn, New
York.

Poulin, Gilles (n.d.) "The Influence of Writing Fatigue On Handwriting Characteristics In A
Selected Population, Part One: General Considerations," an undated paper presented at
the 1993 Annual Meeting of The American Society of Questioned Document Examiners,
Ottawa, Ontario.

Quirke, Arthur J. (1930) *Forged, Anonymous, And Suspect Documents*, London. Full credit
for the principles and concepts behind the paraphrasing/editing of his work belong to
and is the intellectual property of Mr. Arthur J. Quirke and his sources. My only purpose
here is to try to simplify and consolidate some of those principles and concepts, putting
them in language more easily understood in our time.

Random (1992) *Random House Webster's Electronic Dictionary & Thesaurus*, College
Edition, Reference Software International.

Roman, Klara G. (1968) *Encyclopedia of the Written Word*, New York.

Saudek, Robert (1978) *Experiments With Handwriting*, Sacramento, CA. First published in
Great Britain by George Allen & Unwin.

CHAPTER 2

HANDWRITING SYSTEMS

DEFINITION OF HANDWRITING SYSTEMS

"Languages are systems of symbols; writing is a system for symbolizing these symbols. A writing system may be defined as any conventional system of marks or signs that represents the utterances of a language: . . . , it was once generally held that all writing systems represent some stage in a progression toward the ideal writing system, the alphabet. The accepted view today is that all writing systems represent relatively optimal solutions to a large and unique set of constraints, including the structure of language represented, the functions that the system serves, and the balance of advantages to the reader as opposed to the writer" (*Encyclopaedia Britannica*).

Handwriting is taught to, and learned by, a person using either a copybook letter form, or observing and adopting a letter, combination of letters, or symbol(s) as written by someone else. What is a copybook letter form? Hilton defines copybook form this way: "The design of letters that is fundamental to a writing system. This term is derived from the old methods of teaching handwriting from a copybook containing engraved script printed on each page for the student to imitate" (Hilton 1982: 18).

Instead of copybook form, Harrison (1966: 288) uses the terms "style characteristics" and "national characteristics" (ibid: 289). He defines "style characteristics" this way: "These are taught to the child when learning to write. The style of handwriting which is acquired by the learner is that which is fashionable at the particular time and place" (ibid: 288). He describes "national characteristics" this way: "Although many countries employ written alphabets which derive from a single source from, for example, the block capitals of Roman times, few have identical letter designs. This means that although style characteristics are useless for the identification of a handwriting, they may be used to determine the nationality of the writer, or, more correctly the country where he was taught to write" (ibid: 289). This may have been true to some extent in 1966, but it is no longer an accurate statement.

Because of the large influx of immigrants into the United States and the integration of many cultures at every level of the American society, people are adopting many aspects of each other's culture. Writing is just one area. The student, and to some limited extent the more mature writer, while learning to write is influenced by copybook forms, his schoolteacher's writing, and his fellow students. For example, with the integration of schools in the 1960s many white and black students began attending the same school. Before that time there was a letter form frequently found in the writing of African Americans and rarely, if ever, found in the writing of other racial groups. At the time the letter was known as the "3W," or "black W." It was written is such a way that the left side of the "W" was shaped like a "3" and the balance of the letter was a normal "W."

Figure 2.1
The "3W" letter form.

The "3W" letter form is not taught in any copybook that the author is aware of and the origin of this letter form is unknown. However, its use by writers of different races is now much more commonplace, not only in the handwriting of whites but also of Hispanics and other ethnic groups whose members have been exposed to and have adopted it.

Of what value are handwriting systems? Handwriting systems are valuable because people who speak a common language also want to be able to communicate by the written word. To accomplish this, they must have a common alphabet of mutually recognized symbols. Over time, many handwriting systems have been developed and intermingled. Many of the letter forms we use today are common to much of the western world.

In the Asian region of the world, a language's written form is very different from the Roman system used in many western countries and is frequently unique to a particular country or ethnic group. In 1994 S.C. Leung, in the abstract of an article entitled "The Scientific Examination of Chinese Handwriting", made the following observation: "The Chinese character, invented about 4,000 years ago, was based on an idiographic concept, eight basic strokes arranged two dimensionally forming the essential building components of the character. As a result of the complex structure, there are many different ways of writing a Chinese Character. . . . There are generally three common styles of Chinese handwriting: the regular style; the running style; and the cursive style, which can either be written in the orthodox form or the simplified form. On the other hand, individual or personal characteristics can be categorized into measurable parameters and qualitative parameters. Apart from these, there are complications involving the writer himself" (Leung 1994). A casual glance at Chinese writing confirms how different it is from the Roman system used in most western countries; and their letter/word forms are very different from those used in Japan, Thailand, etc. The Arabic form of writing is also very different from systems used in Japan, China, Thailand, and the western world.

Notwithstanding all of these different systems, for the FDE handwriting systems provide a foundation upon which people learn to write the language of their culture. No matter what the system, the forms dictated by it provide a reference point from which the writer may slightly deviate; but when he does so, his writing becomes more identifiable. The concept of individuality is covered later.

During the act of writing, the writer experiences a natural conflict. He must adhere to the copybook form(s) and its legibility requirements, and yet he wants to write faster and faster. Handwriting systems coupled with the departure from the copybook forms, known as individuality, combine to form the "master patterns" Harrison talks about in his work. Further, without systems and copybook forms, there is no frame of reference to distinguish between class and individual handwriting characteristics resulting from this natural conflict experienced by the writer.

When the word foundation is used, it usually means a base or footing upon which something is built. Well that is what a system of writing is. It is a foundation, base, or footing for a particular culture's alphabet and written word. There are rules that "apply to all Western handwriting, regardless of the so-called copybook style" (Jarman). These rules are as follows:

1　Good writing is based on a pattern of ovals and parallel lines.

2　All small letters start at the top.

3　All the downstrokes are parallel.

4　All similar letters are the same height.

5　All downstrokes are equidistant.

6   The space between words is the width of the small letter o.

willoyou be mine

7   Ascenders and descenders are no more than twice the height of small letters, preferably less.

h g l p d

8   Capital letters are no higher than the ascenders, preferably less.

Ch Br Dl Ph

9   Lines of writing are far enough apart for ascenders and descenders not to touch.

you go joy get pit
home back doll

10   Letters which finish at the top join horizontally.

o r v w l f

11   Letters which finish at the bottom join diagonally.

a c d

12   Letters which finish on a stroke moving left, are best left unjoined. (Jarman)

b g j p s y

Christopher Jarman has classified these as rules that "apply to all Western handwriting regardless of the so-called copybook style." The question that must be asked though is, is this an accurate statement? The answer is a qualified, yes. They are if the writing is more of a manuscript style of writing and for some letter forms found in the D'Nealian system. If the system is more like the Palmer or Zaner-Bloser system, then the answer is, the rules do not necessarily apply.

The Palmer system is a cursive form of writing and the letters have more detail than the letterforms shown in the rules above. It is not a system that allows the writer to write rapidly. The letters (f, g, j, p, q, y, and z) all have looped lower projections. Therefore, Rule 12 does not seem to apply to these letters because the writer must complete the lower loop by returning the pen to the baseline of the writing. In the case of the lower projection on the "f," he must move his pen first to the right and then to the left as he brings it back toward the baseline. Some of the letters have movements to the left, such as the upper projections on the (b, d, f, h, k, etc.). The leftward movements are opposite to the direction of writing. In the Roman system, the writer moves from left to right; so when he writes rapidly, any movement to the left takes up needless time.

Figure 2.2
The Palmer system.

When the student is learning to write a copybook system, he is instructed on how to move his pen. The following example, Figure 2.3, shows a page from a copybook with letterforms that have each of their component parts or lines numbered. The student is instructed to draw line one first, line two second, etc. After each line is drawn, their combination should represent the finished letter form. Of course, the ultimate goal in the exercise is legibility.

Figure 2.3

A page from a student's copybook showing how he should draw or write each part of a letter. (From an uknown source. It is typical of those found in many handwriting primers.)

One of the more important things this illustration does is confirm the impulse concept discussed in Chapter 1. Notice that the student is taught to make each line with a single movement. Over time, it will not be necessary for the student to concentrate on each individual line or pen movement. Rather, he will concentrate more on the shape of each letter, then several letters in combination, etc., until he reaches his highest level of graphic maturity.

In summary, there are many handwriting systems. Each is a function of a culture's desire to communicate by the written word. The handwriting system allows this written communication to take place. Students first learn to write as the system dictates by slavishly copying model letter forms. Soon they vary from the system to some extent or they practice writing letters as they are written by someone they admire who lives in that society.

For the examiner of questioned documents, systems are a foundation upon which people learn to write. He knows that writers will not slavishly adhere to those systems for very long because they are impatient and want to complete the writing task as soon as possible. In doing so, their writing takes on a special uniqueness known as individuality.

EXAMPLES OF THE DIFFERENT SYSTEMS

A couple of examples of the different handwriting systems have already been discussed: the manuscript style and the Palmer system. There are many other systems taught in the schools of this country. In 1993, the American Society of Questioned Document Examiners conducted a "Handwriting System Survey" (ASQDE 1993) to try and determine which systems were taught in the United States. Some results of that survey are as follows:

- Some states teach multiple systems. Alabama, for example, utilizes a textbook list of systems and leaves it up to each school to choose which system they will teach.
- Some public schools use different systems than those used by their private school counterparts.
- A number of states recommend no specific system. The schools are free to choose their own system.
- Numerous states recommend the use of the Zaner-Bloser, D'Nealian, Palmer, McDougall Littell, etc., systems and a few mandate which system will be required for their schools.

Regardless of which system is taught to and learned by the student, they all have the following things in common:

- Many of the letterforms are similar in shape and details.
- The student is instructed to write each letter using the impulse method (described in Chapter 1).
- Most important of all, each system produces a recognizable text that can be read by anyone who can recognize and read the language that system represents.

Some foreign countries also use some of these same systems. A paper written by Julio H. Bradley (1993) that was presented at the same ASQDE meeting as the survey showed that over the years a number of systems similar to those taught in the United States were also taught in Argentina and in other Latin American countries. Another study presented at this same ASQDE meeting, entitled "Class Characteristics of Latin American Hand Printing" (Berthold and Wooton 1993), sought to develop a method for identifying class characteristics in Latin American hand printing. In an undated paper, the Australian Federal Police Document Examination Branch produced a paper showing the "Handwriting Systems 1900 to 1990" used in Australia. It can be seen for these few examples that the study of system writing is very important to the FDE.

THE TEACHING OF SYSTEMS AND THEIR INFLUENCE – RESULTS OF A STUDY

In June 1960 a study was issued by the Committee on Research in Basic Skill, University of Wisconsin, Madison, WI. The study was conducted by Virgil E. Herrick, Professor of Education, with the assistance of several assistants. Excerpts of the conclusion of his research are reproduced here because of their importance to understanding the influence of handwriting systems on handwriting identification. Also included are tables and keys to letter forms of the systems of writing his research covered, some of which are still used today. This information will be of assistance to the reader in understanding how handwriting systems and learning them are important in establishing writing habits that make handwriting identifiable.

> ... The commercial systems for the most part are in common agreement on legibility as the overall objective in handwriting instruction. Legibility is frequently defined as writing which is easily read and easily written. Since there is no standard alphabet, letters advocated for use in manuscript and cursive writings are those which are simple, distinct and easy to execute.
>
> Handwriting is generally regarded as a tool for communication; it is a means for recording and conveying thoughts. Its primary role is, therefore, one of function; handwriting instruction should fulfill the communication needs of children in school as well as out. Handwriting is not considered, therefore, as an isolated skill without content; it is closely correlated with reading, spelling, language arts, arithmetic and social studies. Some systems regard that the true test of handwriting instruction is the quality of students' writing in meeting standards of legibility and appearance in other instructional areas aside from the handwriting period.
>
> While the commercial systems state that content is more significant than mechanics of writing, nevertheless handwriting is essentially a skill which demands knowledge and practice for adequate or optimal development. The handwriting act is regarded as a complex of motor and perceptual skill which need to be developed formally and

systematically. The writing act should become automatic and proper writing habits established early so that writing becomes an efficient vehicle for expressing ideas.

Initial considerations advocated by commercial handwriting systems in developing motor skills in handwriting included good body posture, correct placement of paper, proper arm position, correct holding of pencil or pen and proper combinations of shoulder, forearm and finger movement so that greater control of the writing movement as well as a free, relaxed writing mood are secured. Movement of the arm rather than finger actions are desired to achieve fluent writing (reasonable speed). As arm movements are made, a rhythm in writing is developed as the students swing along from one pause to the next.

Necessary to this motor skill is the concurrent development of perceptual skills which may involve proper visual, auditory, tactile, and kinesthetic-sensory images of the letter forms. It is stated that writing is basically reproducing these mental images on paper through the process of recall. Systematic procedures in the learning process devised by some systems advocate seeing the letter or word, hearing it as it is said aloud, tracing the letter in the air to tell how the letter is made and finally writing it on paper, using the movement of the hand. These procedures appear to constitute the psychological rational for introducing letter forms to children . . .

The handwriting systems indicate that handwriting skill demands systematic practice. Such practice can only evolve from definite formal instruction. Although the commercial systems may emphasize different specific objectives in the instructional period they contend that practice ought to be purposeful. The purposes for the handwriting activity proposed by the systems are varied. They . . . ; or the specific objective may be supplied by a technique in legibility (slant, spacing, size, alignment, and line quality) or a particular stroke to be learned. In beginning writing, when new letters are presented, the teacher analyzes the letter structure so that students learn the parts of the letter; they learn to recognize its shape and appearance so that they may distinguish it likenesses and differences from other letters. It is evident that writing develops from an initial drawing phase to the formation of specific letters. In learning to write, students are frequently asked to draw circles and practice vertical and horizontal strokes and later make them into small and capital letters of the alphabet. . . . To facilitate learning of the letter forms some systems present a list of generalizations. The following are illustrative of some of them:

In manuscript writing:

1. All letters are composed of straight lines, ovals (almost circles) or parts and combination of straight lines and ovals.
2. In general, the strokes begin at the top and are made downward; other strokes are made from left to right.
3. Raise the pencil at the end of each stroke.
4. Leave spaces as wide as an "o" between words, half as wide between letters.

In cursive writing:

1. Letters are joined by short connecting strokes.
2. A medium uniform forward slant, conductive to maximum legibility and speed is recommended.
3. Pen or pencil should move forward in a series of looping swings and continuous strokes until the word is finished; then, if they are present, "t" is crossed and "i" is dotted.

While there is a common recognition that correct letter formation is the most significant aspect of legibility, the systems disagree as to how the letter forms should be taught. They vary from approaches which employ a stroke by stroke presentation to those which introduce letters and integral parts of words or present such letters as they are needed. The formatter approach groups letters according to basic strokes or similarity in characteristics. For instance, . . .

The Zaner-Bloser system groups cursive small letters in the following manner:

1. Under turn group: i, u, w, c, e.
2. Hump group: h, m, n, u, x, y, z.
3. Oval group: a, d, g, q, o.
4. Upper loop: l, b, f, h, k.
5. Lower loop: j, q, p, y, z.

These principal or controlling strokes determine the sequence and continuity in the instructional pattern in handwriting. Here strokes are combined to form individual letters; letters are grouped into words, words into sequences. . . . While these systems predominantly use this part to whole basis in their stroke by stroke presentation of letters, they may concurrently employ other logical bases in their instruction. Other bases proposed for the introduction of letters are the simple to the complex, ease or difficulty of mastery, frequency of use, space relationship (height), size and movement. In cursive writing letters are characteristically grouped according to beginning or ending strokes . . .

Diametrically opposed to the stroke by stroke presentation are the systems which propose that children should not be led to practice at great length on separate letters of "meaningless" parts of letters but rather on words and short sentences. The "word approach" is meaningful and rational to students, because this is the context in which children characteristically use letters. As was stated earlier, however, most systems recommend that in practice a combination approach to teaching letters in beginning handwriting be followed: a combination of letters taught one at a time, in meaningful words, and in phrases or sentences . . .

While the systems use handwriting scales in comparing the quality of students' writing with standardized norms, much greater emphasis is placed upon self-evaluation by students of their own writing. Children should be taught to analyze and criticize the results of their handwriting to discover possibilities for improvement. The identification of specific errors defines the kinds of practice which are needed and pupil progress is measured in terms of improvement over past achievement. Students are thus made aware of their responsibilities for their own growth in handwriting.

The handwriting systems also make a careful study of nature of the learners taught – their capacities, needs and interests in handwriting so they will be able to achieve independent as well as optimal writing. It is stated that there is no expectancy of a uniform degree of skill in the classroom. There is awareness of wide range in students' abilities in writing so that lesson plans are based upon group and individual instruction rather than upon mass instruction. The basis for such grouping may be the writing needs of students and special interests in handwriting.

. . . There is also some encouragement to students to develop their own individual style of writing provided they do not distort its legibility (Herrick 1960: 104–111).

The following tables and keys are also a part of Herrick's work and serve as a guide to how letters are written and their features. Some overall patterns are found in different systems as the tables show. Although some modifications have been made to systems such as the Palmer and Zaner-Bloser over the years, the basic features shown in the keys still serve as a guide for differences in systems.

REFERENCES

American Society of Questioned Document Examiners (1993) "1993 ASQDE Handwriting Systems Survey," presented at the ASQDE Meeting, 18–22 September 1993, Ottawa, Ontario, Canada. Author(s) unknown.

"Australian Handwriting Systems/1900 to 1990." Compiled by the Australian Federal Police, Document Examination Branch. Author unknown.

Berthold, Nancy N. and Wooton, Elaine X. (1993) "Class Characteristics of Latin American Hand Printing," presented at the ASQDE Meeting, 18–22 September 1993, Ottawa, Ontario, Canada.

Bradley, Julio H. (1993) "Handwriting Systems Used in Argentina and Other Countries of Latin American," presented at the ASQDE Meeting, 18–22 September 1993, Ottawa, Ontario, Canada.

Encyclopaedia Britannica 98 CD, Multimedia Edition.

Harrison, Wilson R. (1966) *Suspect Documents Their Scientific Examination*, 2nd edn, London.

Herrick, Virgil E. *et al.* (1960) *Comparison of Practices in Handwriting Advocated By Nineteen Commercial Systems of Handwriting Instruction*, Committee on Research in Basic Skills, University of Wisconsin, Madison, WI.

Hilton, Ordway (1982) *Scientific Examination of Documents*, revised edn, New York.

Jarman, Christopher, "12 Rules for Good Cursive Handwriting," Rules for Good Handwriting (http://www.argonet.co.uk/users/quilljar/rules.html).

Leung, S.C. (1994) "The Scientific Examination of Chinese Handwriting," *Forensic Science Review*, 6(2) December.

The A.N. Palmer Company, 1901, 1908, 1913, 1915, and 1931, New York.

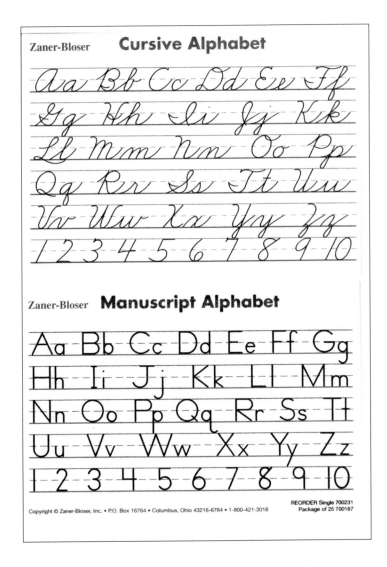

Figure 2.4

The latest version of the Zaner-Bloser Cursive and Manuscript Alphabet systems. Students today will be modeling their writing against this system assuming it is the one they learn during their formative years. Compare the model letters in these with their counterparts in the Herrick study shown in Tables 2.1 to 2.5 (Zaner-Bloser, Inc.).

Table 2.1

Differences in forms of lower case manuscript symbols.
Below: Key to Table 2.1.

Handwriting company	a	b	c	d	e	f	g	h	i	j	k	l	m	n	o	p	q	r	s	t	u	v	w	x	y	z
American Book Co.	o	o	o	o	x	o	o	x	x	x	x	x	x	o	x	o	x	o	o	x	x	x	o	x	o	#
Beckley-Cardy	o	o	x	o	x	o	#	x	x	x	x	x	x	o	x	o	o	☆	@	x	x	x	o	x	x	o
Benson	x	x	x	x	#	x	x	x	x	o	x	x	x	x	o	x	x	x	x	o	#	#	x	o	o	x
Economy	x	x	x	x	x	o	x	x	x	o	x	o	x	o	x	x	x	x	x	x	o	x	x	x	x	x
Hackman	o	#	x	@	o	x	o	o	x	o	#	o	x	o	x	☆	@	x	x	o	x	o	x	@	x	
Hall & McCreary	x	x	x	x	x	x	x	x	x	o	o	x	o	x	o	x	x	x	x	o	x	o	x	x	x	x
Harlow	o	o	x	o	x	x	o	x	x	x	x	x	o	x	o	x	o	@	x	x	o	x	o	x	☆	o
Laurel Book Co.	#	x	o	x	x	@	@	x	x	o	o	x	x	x	#	$	o	o	#	o	x	o	#	o	#	o
Noble & Noble	x	x	o	x	o	x	☆	x	x	o	x	o	x	o	x	#	o	x	#	x	o	o	x	#	x	x
Palmer	x	x	x	x	x	x	x	x	x	x	o	x	x	x	x	x	#	#	x	x	x	x	o	x	x	o
Peterson	No complete manuscript alphabet given																								
Pitman	No manuscript																								
Public School Pub. Co.	No manuscript																								
Scott, Foresman	x	x	x	x	x	x	x	x	x	o	o	x	x	o	x	x	x	#	o	o	x	x	x	o	x	o
Scribner	x	x	x	x	x	x	x	x	x	#	x	x	o	o	x	x	#	#	o	x	x	x	@	x	o	o
Seale	x	x	x	#	x	o	x	x	x	#	@	x	o	x	x	@	x	x	#	x	o	o	x	x	x	@
Steck	o	o	x	o	x	#	o	x	x	#	x	x	x	o	x	o	o	o	o	x	x	x	o	x	x	x
Harr Wagner	No manuscript																								
Zaner-Bloser	o	o	x	o	x	o	o	o	x	x	x	o	x	o	x	x	o	&	x	o	x	x	o	x	x	x

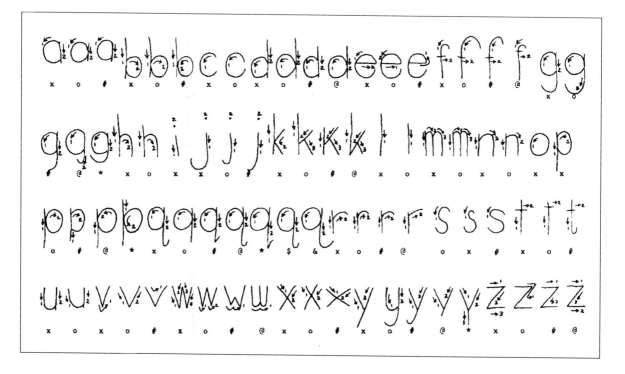

Table 2.2

Differences in forms of upper case manuscript symbols.
Below: Key to Table 2.2.

Handwriting company	A	B	C	D	E	F	G	H	I	J	K	L	M	N	O	P	Q	R	S	T	U	V	W	X	Y	Z
American Book Co.	o	x	@	x	o	o	o	o	o	x	@	o	☆	o	x	x	x	o	x	o	@	o	o	#	#	o
Beckley-Cardy	x	x	x	o	x	x	x	o	o	x	x	x	x	#	x	x	x	x	x	o	x	x	x	x	x	x
Benson	x	x	o	x	@	x	o	x	x	x	@	o	@	x	x	x	o	o	x	x	x	o	o	x	#	#
Economy	#	o	x	x	o	x	x	x	#	x	o	x	o	x	x	x	x	x	x	o	x	x	x	x	x	x
Hackman	x	x	#	o	#	x	#	o	x	o	x	x	x	o	x	x	x	x	x	x	o	o	x	x	o	x
Hall & McCreary	#	x	#	x	o	x	x	x	o	x	o	o	o	x	x	x	x	x	x	x	xo	x	x	x	x	x
Harlow	o	x	o	x	o	o	o	o	o	x	@	o	x	o	x	x	o	x	o	x	o	o	o	o	o	#
Laurel Book Co.	x	o	#	o	x	x	@	x	x	x	o	o	#	@	o	x	#	#	o	x	x	o	#	@	#	#
Noble & Noble	x	o	x	o	☆	#	#	x	x	x	#	#	x	x	x	x	#	x	x	x	#	x	x	x	x	x
Palmer	x	x	x	x	#	x	x	x	x	#	o	x	o	x	x	x	x	x	x	x	#	x	x	x	x	x
Peterson	No complete manuscript alphabet given																									
Pitman	No manuscript																									
Public School Pub. Co.	No manuscript																									
Scott, Foresman	#	x	x	o	#	o	x	x	o	x	x	x	o	x	x	x	x	x	x	o	x	x	#	x	x	x
Scribner	x	#	o	#	x	x	o	x	x	o	#	o	#	x	x	x	o	o	o	x	x	#	#	o	x	#
Seale	x	x	x	x	x	x	x	x	x	x	x	x	x	x	x	x	x	x	x	x	x	x	x	x	x	x
Steck	o	x	x	o	x	x	x	x	x	#	#	x	x	x	x	x	x	x	x	x	x	x	x	x	x	x
Harr Wagner	No manuscript																									
Zaner-Bloser	x	x	x	x	@	x	x	x	#	x	x	x	x	x	x	x	x	x	x	o	o	x	x	o	x	x

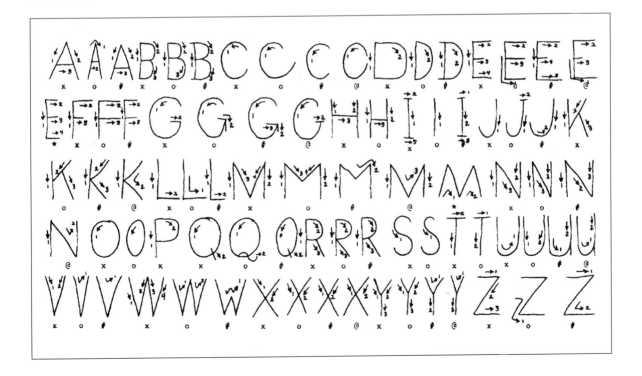

Table 2.3

Differences in forms of manuscript and cursive numerals.
Below: Key to Table 2.3.

Handwriting company	Manuscript numerals										Cursive numerals									
	1	2	3	4	5	6	7	8	9	0	1	2	3	4	5	6	7	8	9	0
American Book Co.	x	x	☆	☆	o	o	@	#	x	o	x	–	&	x	x	x	x	#	x	x
Beckley-Cardy	x	x	x	@	o	#	x	@	x	o										
Benson	x	o	x	x	o	x	o	x	x	o	x	–	x	☆	x	x	o	#	o	x
Economy	x	$	@	x	x	o	#	o	x	x	x	x	o	x	x	o	o	@	x	x
Hackman	x	@	#	x	x	$	#	o	o	x	x	+	#	#	o	o	o	x	o	x
Hall & McCreary																				
Harlow	x	#	x	#	o	#	o	#	x	o	x	x	=	o	x	x	x	x	x	x
Laurel Book Co.	x	o	o	#	x	x	o	x	x	x	x	x	o	x	x	o	x	x	x	x
Noble & Noble	x	x	x	o	o	x	x	x	x	x	x	#	&	x	x	x	#	x	x	x
Palmer	x	o	o	#	x	☆	x	x	o	o	x	x	x	x	o	x	@	@	o	x
Peterson											x	x	x	o	#	x	#	x	x	x
Pitman											x	@	x	x	x	o	x	x	o	x
Public School Pub. Co.											x	☆	x	o	x	x	@	x	@	x
Scott, Foresman	x	x	x	o	x	@	x	x	o	x	x	&	☆	#	o	x	o	#	x	x
Scribner	o	☆	x	x	x	x	x	x	o	x	x	ç	x	@	o	x	x	o	o	x
Seale	x	o	o	x	#	x	o	x	x	x	x	$	x	o	o	x	x	o	#	x
Steck	x	x	x	o	x	x	x	x	x	x	x	x	o	x	o	x	#	x	x	x
Harr Wagner											x	@	☆	x	#	o	#	x	x	x
Zaner-Bloser	x	x	o	x	@	x	#	o	x	x	x	+	#	x	o	o	o	@	x	x

Key to Table 2.3.

Table 2.4

Differences in forms of
lower case cursive symbols.
Below: Key to Table 2.4.

Handwriting company	a	b	c	d	e	f	g	h	i	j	k	l	m	n	o	p	q	r	s	t	u	v	w	x	y	z
American Book Co.	x	o	#	x	x	o	@	#	x	o	x	x	x	x	x	#	x	x	x	x	x	#	x	o	#	x
Beckley-Cardy	o	x	o	o	x	x	o	x	x	x	x	x	x	x	#	x	#	x	x	x	x	o	x	x	x	x
Benson	x	x	@	x	x	o	x	x	x	x	x	x	x	x	x	x	o	x	x	x	x	x	x	x	☆	x
Economy	x	x	#	#	x	x	x	x	x	x	x	x	x	x	x	x	x	x	x	x	x	x	x	x	x	x
Hackman	x	x	o	o	x	x	o	x	x	x	x	x	x	x	x	o☆	#	o☆	x	x	x	x	x	x	x	x
Hall & McCreary	x	x	x	x	x	x	x	o	x	x	x	x	x	x	x	o	x	☆	x	x	x	x	o	x	x	o
Harlow	o	#	o	o	x	x	o	x	x	x	x	x	x	x	#	#	#	$	x	x	x	x	x	x	x	o
Laurel Book Co.	x	x	$	x	x	x	x	x	x	x	x	x	x	x	x	x	o	x	x	x	x	x	x	x	x	x
Noble & Noble	x	x	x	x	x	x	x	x	x	x	x	x	x	x	o	x	o	x	x	x	x	x	x	x	x	x
Palmer	x	x	#	@	x	x	x	x	x	x	x	x	x	x	x	x	x	o	x	x	x	x	x	x	x	o
Peterson	o	x	o	o	x	x	o	x	x	x	x	x	x	x	#	x	o	#	x	x	x	x	x	x	x	x
Pitman	x	x	x	x	x	#	x	x	x	x	x	x	x	x	x	o	x	#	x	x	x	x	x	x	x	x
Public School Pub. Co.	x	o	o	o	x	x	x	x	x	x	o	x	x	x	x	x	x	#	x	x	x	x	x	x	x	x
Scott, Foresman	x	o	x	x	x	x	x	x	x	x	x	x	x	x	x	x	x	x	x	x	x	x	x	x	x	x
Scribner	x	#	☆	x	x	x	☆	x	x	o	o	x	x	x	x	@	x	@	x	x	#	o	#	#	o	#
Seale	x	x	#	x	x	x	x	x	x	x	x	x	x	x	x	x	x	#	x	x	x	o	x	x	x	@
Steck	x	x	@	x	x	x	#	x	x	x	o	x	x	x	x	x	x	x	x	x	x	o	x	x	x	x
Harr Wagner	x	x	@	x	x	x	x	x	x	x	x	x	x	x	x	x	x	x	x	x	x	o	x	x	x	x
Zaner-Bloser	x	x	x	x	x	x	#	x	x	x	x	x	x	x	x	x	x	o	x	x	x	x	x	x	@	x

Table 2.5

Differences in forms of upper case cursive symbols.
Below: Key to Table 2.5.

Handwriting company	A	B	C	D	E	F	G	H	I	J	K	L	M	N	O	P	Q	R	S	T	U	V	W	X	Y	Z
American Book Co.	x	&	o	x	#	#	@	o	x	o	x	☆	x	x	x	+	x	o	@	o	x	#	o	o	x	o
Beckley-Cardy	o	#	o	@	o	x	o	x	o	x	x	x	o	x	x	☆	x	x	o	x	o	x	x	x	x	o
Benson	x	x	o	x	x	$	x	o	o	x	x	x	o	x	x	x	x	@	o	☆	x	x	x	x	x	x
Economy	x	@	o	☆	#	x	x	o	x	x	@	x	x	x	x	@	x	+	x	x	x	x	x	o	x	x
Hackman	#	x	#	x	x	&	x	$	x	x	☆	@	x	o	x	x	$	@	x	$	$	o	☆	@	#	@
Hall & McCreary																										
Harlow	x	&	x	x	o	+	o	o	&	o	x	x	x	x	x	o	x	x	o	x	x	x	x	x	x	x
Laurel Book Co.	x	x	x	@	x	o	o	o	@	x	x	x	x	x	x	x	#	o	o	x	x	x	x	x	x	x
Noble & Noble	x	x	x	x	o	ç	x	x	@	x	x	x	x	x	x	x	x	#	x	=	x	x	x	x	x	x
Palmer	o	x	x	x	x	@	o	x	$	x	o	x	x	#	x	$	☆	☆	x	#	o	x	x	x	x	x
Peterson	#	#	x	x	o	x	x	x	☆	x	x	x	x	x	x	o	x	x	x	x	x	x	x	o	x	x
Pitman	x	o	#	o	x	#☆	#	☆	#	x	x	o	x	x	x	x	☆	$	#	o☆	☆	☆	@	#	☆	#
Public School Pub. Co.	x	$	o	x	o	x	x	x	x	o	x	x	x	x	x	x	☆	@	=	x	x	x	x	x	x	x
Scott, Foresman	x	x	#	x	x	=	o	@	o	x	x	x	x	o	x	x	$	@	o	&	@	o	$	☆	☆	@
Scribner	o	☆	@	#	@	#	#	#	#	#	#	o	#	@	o	#	o	#	#	@	#	@	#	#	o	#
Seale	x	#	o	o	o	o	x	x	o	o	x	#	x	x	x	☆	#	x	x	x	x	x	x	x	x	x
Steck	x	@	o	x	o	o	x	x	x	x	x	x	x	x	@	x	+	x	x	x	x	x	x	x	x	x
Harr Wagner	x	x	x	o	x	☆	#	o	@	x	x	x	x	x	x	x	=	ç	o	x☆	x	x	o	x	x	x
Zaner-Bloser	x	#	x	o	o	x	o	x	o	x	x	x	x	x	x	o	☆	x	o	x	x	x	x	x	x	x

CHAPTER 3

CLASS CHARACTERISTICS

DEFINITION OF CLASS CHARACTERISTICS

What is a "class" characteristic? There are a number of definitions:

- Ordway Hilton defines it as: " . . . Not all characteristics encountered in document examination are peculiar to a single person or thing, and one that is common to a group may be described as a class characteristic" (Hilton 1982: 15).
- A feature of writing that approximates the form and details of the copybook letter.
- In a paper entitled, "Handwriting Identification for the Investigator," the definition is, "Class characteristics belong to the system or style of writing the person learned. They may also be forms or features added to letters by environmental or cultural influences" (Morris 1995: 15).

Everyone's writing consists of a combination of "class" and "individual" characteristics. To what extent and in what combination is dependent upon the individual. This is one of the basic reasons why handwriting is identifiable. The literature on handwriting identification has not defined the population size of writers who learned a particular handwriting copybook system and who use common variations of system letter forms frequently found in random writings, features adopted from other writers etc. What is known is that most system writing taught in the western world today is based on Roman letter forms. Notwithstanding its common source, the greatest differences in today's systems seem to be in letter details – approach and ending strokes and how letters and letter combinations, and their features, are written. These differences are the result of the aesthetic preference and belief of the system's originator that the letter is easier to write.

We are also certain that when a letter or letter combination is written legibly, conforming to the copybook, the person reading what is written is in no doubt about what the letter(s) represent. The interpretation and meaning of the specific combination of words is a subject certainly beyond the scope of this text.

Class characteristics learned by the writer are important because they, in part, determine, or certainly have a significant influence upon, how a person writes. In Chapter 2 there is a detailed discussion on how the student learns to write copybook forms. The objective of the current chapter is to go into more detail about the fundamentals of class characteristics and their relative importance in handwriting identification.

A person may write with his right or left hand, foot, mouth, etc., as discussed in Chapter 1. A part of this discussion will deal with how left-handed writers write. Because their population is large and getting larger, it is necessary to focus on this group because some of the features of their writing are different from those written by a right-handed writer. Their writing offers certain challenges to the Forensic Document Examiner, not because it is easier or more difficult to identify – it is not! When making some letters or parts of letters, some left-handed writers use different stroke directions and relative pressure habits from right-handed writers. For example, some left-handed writers make ovals that are misshapen because of the way they hold their pen, upstrokes that are heavier than downstrokes, etc.

One important area in the examination and evaluation of a writing for identification purposes is to determine stroke direction of a handwriting feature, or that used in making the whole letter, particular combinations of letters, etc. More about this topic in Chapter 13, when the process of comparison will be discussed. In this chapter, stroke direction is considered to be a class characteristic because the copybook shows the student how to make each letter and what direction to move his pen.

HOW ARE LETTERS CONSTRUCTED?

How are letters constructed? The impulse theory of writing was covered in great detail in Chapter 1. Briefly restated, its elements are as follows:

- *The stroke impulse:* the writer learns to write by drawing individual lines, which when connected together make a letter (Saudek 1978).
- *The letter impulse:* he writes whole letters as a single writing act (ibid: 381).
- *The syllable impulse:* he writes syllables or several letters connected together.
- *The word or name impulse:* he writes complete words or names as a single act of writing (ibid: 394).
- *The sentence/phrase impulse:* when he reaches "graphic maturity," he thinks and tries to write sentences/phrases as a single act (ibid: 388).

How are letters constructed? They are constructed in accordance with instructions given in a copybook (as in the example below) the teacher's instruction, influence on the student by friends and family members, etc. As you can see, the student is influenced by many different sources and frequently tries to satisfy each of them.

Figure 3.1 illustrates how the "stroke impulse" method of learning how to write letters is used in a copybook. Each letter of the alphabet – upper and lower case, numeral, and connecting stroke between letters – are demonstrated in the copybook as shown in the figure. There are exercises for the student to perform to reinforce each lesson.

Figure 3.1

Enlargement of a page from a handwriting primer used to teach youngsters how to write.

This illustration clearly demonstrates the application of the stroke impulse method of writing. As the student writes more and faster, he will eventually learn to write letters as letters without thinking about how to draw each line of the letter. As shown in Figure 3.1, the student learns to write the "W" using four separate strokes of the pen (McDougal 1990: 77).

The numbered line with the arrow shows the student the correct sequence and direction of pen movements to write each line of the letter. Making a letter, following these instructions, teaches the student how to write the copybook style – "class" characteristic – way of writing. The letter "3W," shown in Figure 2.1, is also a "class" characteristic of writing, because it too is written by a large number of writers. The population of the group is larger today because this letter form is now also found in the writings of African Americans, whites, Hispanics, etc, due to society being more homogeneous than it used to be.

One question that comes to mind is will the "class" characteristics of a copybook form of writing by a right- and left-handed writer be the same? Or, are there "class" characteristics associated with left-handed writers that are not typically found in the right-handed writer?

Statistical studies show that approximately 15% of the population are left-handed and that that percentage is increasing (Hackney: 1). Teaching the left-handed student to write, especially if the teacher is right-handed, can be challenging. One handwriting system, Zaner-Bloser, has published a series of papers and training aids on their Internet site to aid teachers in working with left-handed students.

The following is a series of excerpts from those papers.

Positions for Writing:

■ Paper Position: For manuscript writing, the left-hander should position the paper with the lower corner a little to the left of the midsection. For cursive writing, the paper is slanted less, with the lower right corner pointing toward the midsection or just a little to the right of it. The strokes are pulled down toward the left elbow, whether manuscript or cursive is being written. (ZB, hwresearch2: 1–2)

■ Pencil Position: The writing instrument is held between the thumb and first two fingers, about an inch above its point. The first finger rests on the top of the pencil or pen. The end of or the bent thumb is placed against the writing instrument to hold it high in the hand and near the large knuckle. The top of the instrument points in the direction of the left elbow. The writing should take place within the left half of the desk surface, i.e., to the left of the midline of the body. (ZB, hwresearch3: 1)

■ Special Provisions: . . . It is often helpful for the left-hander to hold her or his pencil a little higher than the right-hander. The pencil points toward the left elbow, not toward the shoulder as the right-handers do." (ZB , hwresearch4: 1)

■ Special Problems: The Hooked Position: The hooked wrist is caused by incorrect paper position. . . . twisting of the hand or wrist can be detrimental to legibility and fluency. (ZB, hwresearch3: 1)

■ Special Problems: Reversals: The problem of reversals is common to the left-handed child. Most errors result from confusion between the lowercase manuscript d and b and p and q. Awareness of the problem and concentration of the formal teaching of left to right progression and forward and backward circles before introduction of the teaching of the manuscript letters b, d, p, and q result in fewer reversals of these letters. (ZB, hwresearch3: 1)

From these excerpts, it is evident that the left-handed student has special needs that require a teacher's attention. If those needs are not met, or if there is any inconsistency in teaching penmanship to a left-handed student during his formative years, what should be a "class" characteristic in his writing can become an individual characteristic.

Part of Zaner-Bloser's research involved the selection process for finding a handwriting program to teach all students. They developed "six questions educators should ask before choosing a handwriting program" (ZB, hwresearchreview1: 1). Before asking these six questions, there is a discussion that must take place on whether a vertical or slanted handwriting system should be taught to a student. After many years of research and study, Zaner-Bloser found some surprising answers to the questions that are the basis for the following six questions:

1. Which alphabet is developmentally appropriate? Farris (1997) maintains, "By age 3, children produce drawings that are composed of the same basic lines that constitute manuscript letters: (1) vertical lines, (2) horizontal lines, and (3) circles . . . Because of such early experience, most 6 and 7 year-olds can create these vertical and horizontal lines more easily than the relatively complicated connections associated with D'Nealian manuscript up-and-down motion and horizontal lines by a left-to-right motion, they rely predominately on already acquired gross motor skills." (p. 344) . . . Children who learn to write using a slanted alphabet must learn three times as many strokes as children who learn to write using a vertical alphabet. (ZB, hwresearchreview1: 1–2)

2. Which alphabet is easier to write? . . . the vertical manuscript alphabet is a direct result of its being an easily learned system that relates closely to initial learning. Because there are only four simple strokes that make up the vertical manuscript alphabet, writing the letterforms is quickly mastered by young children. . . . Slanted manuscript, however, was created to be similar to cursive. Because of this, children must learn 12 different strokes. . . . The writers of the slanted alphabet "produced more misshapen letters, were more likely to extend their strokes above and below the guidelines, and had greater difficulty maintaining consistency in letter size" (Graham 1992: 7). (ZB, hwresearchreview2: 1)

3. Which alphabet is easier to read? Vertical manuscript letterforms are more easily read than other styles of writing. . . . Because italic writing is more difficult to read, it interferes with comprehension and speed." (ZB, hwresearch2: 1–2)

4. Which alphabet is more easily integrated? Handwriting is not an isolated part of the language arts. Letter recognition is the first step, and when the letters children are learning to write are similar to those they use in reading and spelling, success in all three skills comes more easily. (ZB, hwresearchreview3: 1–2)

5. Which alphabet is easier to teach? Graham (1992) states "Before starting school, many children learn how to write traditional (vertical) manuscript letters from their parents or preschool teachers. . . . The vertical manuscript alphabet is easy to teach because there is no reteaching involved." (ZB, hwresearchreview4: 1)

6. Does slanted manuscript help with students' transition to cursive? . . . Graham (1992) finds no evidence substantiating claims that using a slanted manuscript alphabet enhances the transition to writing with cursive letters. (ZB, hwresearchreview4: 1)

There is a reference page of studies for these six questions found at their web site, http://zaner-bloser.com/html/hwresearchreview5ref.html. The reader is encouraged to visit the web site for a detailed listing of those sources.

In addition to research papers, there are a number of handwriting activities the teacher can draw upon for assistance when teaching left-handed students. These activities are designed to reinforce the lessons of proper penmanship and legibility.

One "class" characteristic of a system is the writing direction; not stroke direction, which has been covered, but the direction the writer wants to go as he writes. Does the writer move the pen, hand, and arm from left to right because that is how writing and reading is done, or does he move from right to left as in the Arabic and Hebrew writing systems? The answer to this question can help the examiner establish the significance he must attach to the various features of writing. If the writer deviates from his normal writing direction or the "class" characteristics required to write letters and symbols of the system, that deviation may be individual to that writer.

Another copybook feature that is also a class characteristic is the length of the lower extenders or projections. Some copybook systems state that lower projections should be approximately two-thirds the height of the upper projections, as in Figure 3.2.

Figure 3.2

The lower projections in this system are approximately two-thirds the length of the upper projections as measured from the pre-drawn baseline. (Source unknown.)

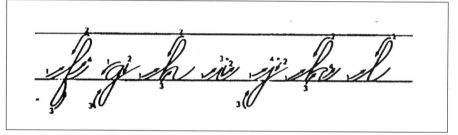

In another copybook the length of lower projections is the same as the height of the lower case letters having upper loops, such as the "h" in Figure 3.3.

Figure 3.3

(McDougal 1990: 36.)

In Figure 3.3, the total space between the two dark lines is divided into three equal parts. The student who learns to write using this copybook would make the upper and lower projections of equal distance. For the purpose of establishing a common reference in this illustration, the upper and lower projections start at the foot of the left side of the "h" in "together," and the length of the lower projection of the "g" begins at the top right of the oval of the "g" in "together."

HOW ARE LETTERS CONNECTED?

How are letters connected? Typically, letters are connected by underhand (garland), overhand (arch), or compound curve strokes. Underhand strokes are typically used between letters like, "de," "er," "es," etc.

Figure 3.4

The use of underhand and compound curve connecting strokes between letters (McDougal 1990: 48, 49, 52).

Figure 3.4 shows three types of connecting strokes between letters. A simple underhand stroke is used between the "de," "er," "bu," and "ow" letter combinations. A compound curve consists of an under and overhand stroke combination, as used between the "ea" and "ma".

Connecting strokes and how they are made is important. They can be made in any combination of the following ways:

- Uniform writing pressure on the pen resulting in a line written on the paper that is of uniform width.
- Sometimes they are barely perceptible because they are written with little writing pressure and only a trace of ink remains on the paper as the pen moves over its surface.
- There is a "tick" mark on the letter preceding and following the pen's direction. The connection of two letters is made by an air-bridge. The pen leaves the writing surface after the first letter is made, travels to the next letter just above the writing surface, and is re-applied to the surface at the beginning point of the next letter. The point where the pen left the paper and where it is re-applied usually will have a "tick" mark.

SYSTEM INFLUENCE

Some of the other features of writing influenced by the system are as follows:

- The placement of letters with respect to the baseline of the writing. Students are taught to write all letter and letter combinations so the base of each letter rests on the baseline. The lowest point of the connecting stroke between letters such as "mu" or "es" is also to touch the baseline. This general rule of baseline placement applies even if there is no pre-drawn baseline on the paper.
- The spacing between letters is to be uniform and approximately the width of an "o."
- All small letters such as the "a," "c," "m," "s," etc. are to be of uniform height and approximately one-third to one-half the height of the tall letters, such as the "l," "t," etc.

- All tall letters and the upper projections of letters such as the "b" are to be the same height. The oval of the "b" or arch on the "h" are to be the same height as the small letters. In some systems, the upper projection of the "t" is not supposed to be the same height as the other upper projections. Its height is supposed to be approximately two thirds the height of the other upper projections.
- The distance between the legs of the "m" and "n" are supposed to be uniform.
- The overall slant of the writing is to be uniform and the same as the slant of letter components such as the legs of the "m" and "n." The overall slant of the writing means that the slant of tall letters, small letters, and components of individual letters are to be uniform.
- All loops are to be open. Letters such as "e" and "l," upper projections on the "h," and "f," and lower projections on the "f," and "g," their loops, when written as cursive letters, should be eyelet shaped and opened. Some copybook systems teach that upper projections on the "d" and "t" are closed and are written as retraced lines.

NON-SYSTEM INFLUENCE

What are some non-system influences? Several have already been discussed, but they will be listed here as a review along with others not previously discussed. A writer is influenced by one or more of the following:

- Teachers. Teachers may be required to teach a system that is different from the one the writer learned to write in school. When instructing young students teachers may write a letter or feature of a letter differently from the way it is written in the book. The student may like what the teacher wrote better than what is in the book and practice making that feature, thus incorporating it into their writing habits.
- Parents and other family members. Like teachers, these writers, when helping the student with their homework or just in the normal course of their writing, may write a letter or feature that the student adopts.
- Friends. Friends of the student also influence the student's writing in the same way the teacher and family members do.
- Exposure to multiple writing systems. If the student has learned to write more than one system, his concept of letter forms and their features is influenced by the similarities and differences of the letters in those systems.
- The writer's own concept of how a letter form and its features should look. If his teacher allows him to deviate from the copybook form then as he matures as a writer he will depart even more from the copybook forms. His idea of how letter forms and features should look and be written eventually leads to further departure from the system toward a more individual writing.

Of all the non-system influences, the last is extremely important. It is primarily from this last one that the writer's handwriting individuality is derived. In Chapter 4 the subject of individuality is covered in greater detail.

REFERENCES

Hackney, Clinton, "The Left-Handed Child in a Right-Handed World," and article from Zaner-Bloser at their Internet site http://zaner-bloser.com/html/hwresearch1.html

Hilton, Ordway (1982) *Scientific Examination of Documents*, revised edn, New York.

McDougal, Littell (1990) *Handwriting – Brown Level*, McDougal , Littell & Company, New York.

Morris, Ronald N. (1995) "Handwriting Identification for the Investigator," Unpublished paper.

Saudek, Robert (1978) *Experiments with Handwriting*, Sacramento, CA. First published in Great Britain by George Allen & Unwin. (Full credit for the principles and concepts of Mr Saudek's work belongs to, and is the intellectual property of Mr Saudek and his sources. My only purpose in paraphrasing his work here is to try to simplify and consolidate some of his principles and concepts, putting them in language more easily understood in our time.)

Zaner-Bloser, Handwriting research web sites as follows:
 http://zaner-bloser.com/htm/hwresearch2.html
 http://zaner-bloser.com/htm/hwresearch3.html
 http://zaner-bloser.com/htm/hwresearch4.html
 http://zaner-bloser.com/htm/hwresearchreview1.html
 http://zaner-bloser.com/htm/hwresearchreview2.html
 http://zaner-bloser.com/htm/hwresearchreview3.html
 http://zaner-bloser.com/htm/hwresearchreview4.html

CHAPTER 4

INDIVIDUALITY AND
INDIVIDUAL CHARACTERISTICS

DEFINITION

Random House Webster's electronic dictionary defines "individuality" as: "1. the particular character, or aggregate of qualities, that distinguishes one person or thing from others" (Random 1992). Hilton defines individual handwriting characteristics as: " . . . more or less peculiar to a specific writer. . . . constitute the backbone of an identification, . . . " (Hilton 1982: 160). While Harrison does not offer as clear a definition, he does say: "In spite of the fact that millions are taught to write from identical copybooks, it should now be apparent that, from the standpoint of letter design alone, there is ample scope for individuality in handwriting" (Harrison 1966: 305). "In spite of this severe limitation to the number of different handwritings which are theoretically possible, there is no doubt that on the basis of letter design alone, the number of distinguishable handwritings is virtually unlimited for all practical purposes."(ibid: 307).

"In contemporary handwriting, employing something like forty distinct letter formations, considering capital letters as distinct from their lower case counterparts, and neglecting such uncommon letters as 'X,' 'Z,' 'x' and 'z,' the number of distinct and distinguishable handwritings which are possible on the basis of letter design alone must reach astronomical proportions" (ibid: 305–306).

Osborn wrote, "Any character in writing or any writing habit may be modified and individualized by different writers in many different ways and in many varying degrees, and the writing individuality of any particular writer is made up of all these common and uncommon characteristics and habits. As in identifying a person, . . . it always is the *combination* of particulars that identifies, and necessarily the more numerous and unusual the various elements and features the more certain the identity" (Osborn 1929: 251).

Saudek views individuality as part of a writer's rhythm and associates it with the development of his graphic maturity. "The rhythm of a handwriting is characterized by the individually formed variations between movement and immobility during the act of writing. . . . In our terminology a movement-unit means the track which the pen covers between pause and pause" (Saudek 1978: 223).

"Between pause and pause," in Saudek's work, is the pen movement that takes place between two directional changes of a pen. This concept is easily illustrated by the reader performing the following experiment, take a pen and put two dots on the sheet of paper, one on the left side and one on the right as in Figure 4.1. Place the pen point on the left dot. Now, move the pen to the right, stopping on the right dot. At this point, reverse the writing direction drawing a line from right to left as shown in Figure 4.1. Note that the following occurs as you write this line. After moving the pen off the left dot you begin to increase its speed. At some point between the two dots the pen will be moving at its maximum speed and then you will start to slow down as you approach the dot on the right until the pen comes to a complete stop at that point. (The concept of speed of writing will be covered in more detail in Chapter 8.) After stopping on the dot at the right, again change direction and move the pen back to the left stopping on the dot you started from. The same increase and decreasing of speed will occur in this direction. Repeat this action several times trying each time to start from, and stop on, each dot. In a more rapid writing act the pen will not come to a complete stop before changing direction. More about this later; however, it should be noted here that when the writing direction is changed, whether at a point or on a curve, the point at which the directional change takes place is known as the "pause" point.

Figure 4.1

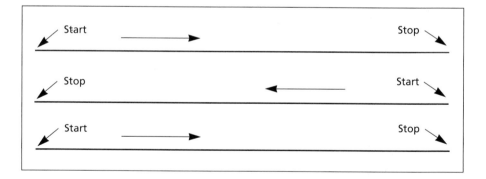

Figure 4.1 graphically shows the movement of the pen from the left, where it starts, to the right where it stops, reverses direction moves to the left, again reverses direction and once more moves to the right. The movements are shown as separate lines for illustration purposes. The writer does not remove the pen from the paper, and then reapply it; rather his writing is one continuous act of back and forth movements between the two defined points on each side of the paper. The starting and stopping points in this example are the pauses, because it is at these points that the writer pauses before reversing direction. The same principle applies if the lines are written vertically or on some angle.

The same principle applies if the writer slows the pen while making a turn on either side of the paper, reversing direction without coming to a complete stop.

The wider the turn the less the pen movement is slowed, the tighter the turn, the slower the pen movement in the turn.

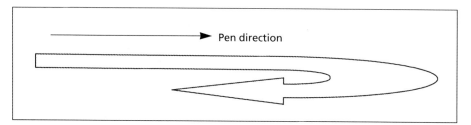

Figure 4.2

Figure 4.2 graphically shows the movement of the pen as it slows to change direction from right to left. On a turn, such as the one illustrated here, the pen never comes to a complete stop on the right before changing direction, as in Figure 4.1.

Regardless of writing direction, or the location of pauses, an opportunity exist for the writer to introduce his own individuality in the connecting line between two pauses – Figure 4.1 – or when gradually changing writing direction, as in Figure 4.2. A few simple experiments by the reader will confirm this concept.

Experiment No. 1: Take the pen and draw a series of underhand – counterclockwise – elliptical motions at your normal relative slant – that is, whatever angle of slant is comfortable to you when writing. Next, move the pen over and repeat this experiment, but this time vary the angle of slant to the left, and then to the right, as far as you can through a series of gradual angle changes, and note the effect on the lines and their shape.

Experiment No. 2: Repeat the experiment using overhand – clockwise – pen movements. In both of these experiments change the relative angle of the oval from right to left and observe the changes that take place.

Experiment No. 3: In the same way make a series of infinity formations beginning with a formation that is parallel to the horizontal, as in the example in Figure 4.3. Write the connected ovals while moving them counterclockwise until they are vertical. Continue the movement of the symbol until the series is again horizontal, 180° from the starting direction.

Examine the results of these experiments and try them again to see if the results are any different. Have other writers also try them and see how their results compare to yours. Remember; experiment continuously to verify principles and techniques.

Figure 4.3

Simple experiments.

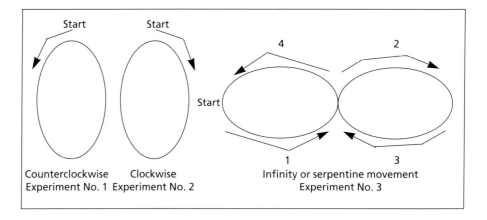

Individuality is also related to the writer's level of "graphic maturity." This does not mean that in every case the higher his level of "graphic maturity" the more individuality he has in his writing. While there is a relationship between the two, a person with a low level of writing skill can have as much, or more, individuality in his writing than the writer with a higher "graphic maturity" level. A person who writes at the highest level of "graphic maturity," the "sentence/phrase impulse level," must write with some degree of legibility or his writing will consist of a series of meaningless lines and pen movements.

The classic example of this is the old story about the physician's prescription slip. The pharmacists must be able to read what is on the prescription slip or he will have to call the physician to find out what medication the patient is supposed to receive. To make sense of what is written, the writer must include some legible letter forms, etc., so the reader can at least have some idea of the context of the material.

Even though Saudek's conclusions are valid, a more modern view of individuality is being developed that reflects these concepts as quoted at the beginning of this chapter. Individuality, as the dictionary definition says, is the "aggregate of qualities" (Random 1992) of the writing and not necessarily those limited to a single written line between two "pauses" in pen movement. It must be remembered, what occurs between "pauses," either as a pair or collectively as a series of pauses, is what the modern and classical definitions of individuality are addressing.

One definition of individuality, proposed by the Scientific Working Group on Documents (December 1998: 2), describes it as: "Identifying characteristics: marks or properties that serve to individualize writing, such as, formations and relative sizes and heights of letters." In an earlier version of their work (August 1997: 4) individuality was defined as: "Characteristics of writing which are unusual or rare and have great significance in determining whether two bodies of writing were prepared by the same person." Both definitions address individuality from a broader perspective than just what occurs between two pauses. However, it also allows for what happens between those two pauses, because what happens between them can be significant in identifying the writer.

In a training text, written by the author, individuality is described as:

> . . . handwriting features and characteristics that are a departure(s) from a norm. Some reasons for the departure(s) are as follows:
>
> - A deliberate action on the part of the writer to change a feature, or combination of features, in his writing because of individual preference.
> - The writer's perception of a characteristic feature(s) or letter-form(s), and how he imitates it with the writing instrument given his level of graphic maturity, and manual dexterity.
> - His occupation or profession that may require the use of an alternate letterform or feature that over time becomes part of his regular writing. For example, the "0" with an angular line through it to distinguish it from the letter "o", or the letter "Z" with a short horizontal line through the angular line connecting its top and bottom horizontal lines, to distinguish it from a "2" in a mathematical equation, etc.
> - Influences on his writing during his maturing years by teachers, family, and friends, and even the current lack of emphasis on penmanship in the schools (Morris 1999).

What is meant by " . . . departure(s) from a norm?" Norm is defined as "a standard, model, or pattern" (Random 1992). Norm, then, can be any – or any combination – of the following:

- Copybook letter forms.
- Letter designs and other features dictated by the writer's culture apart from copybook forms.
- Generally, accepted letter designs and features, apart from the copybook designs, used by a large percentage of the population in which the writer learned, and continues to write.

As he matures, the writer departs from the use of some of the *class characteristics* he learned and introduces into his writing his own *individuality*. This departure can begin as early as the 3rd or 4th grade of school (Ramsey 1998: 36, 38–39). Over time, these individual characteristics become a natural part of his writing because his arm, hand, and fingers are repeating movements that are becoming habitual. It is the combination of these two, the class and individual handwriting characteristics, that makes handwriting identifiable.

If a writer exclusively writes copybook letters, at the "impulse" or "letter" skill level, it is unlikely that he will ever be identified as the author of what he writes. The assumption made here is that between "pauses" he introduces no individuality into his pen – writing – movements, or letter formations and other features that are individualistic to him; however, if this writer introduces sufficient individuality between the pauses in the writing of individual letters, his writing could be identifiable to some degree of certainty.

The argument can be made that the number of writers who do not depart significantly from a copybook style is very small. Therefore, their writing should be more easily identified because they are members of a smaller population of writers. While not without some merit, this argument is not completely valid. Writing a copybook style is an activity most people can perform by slowing their writing speed and using copybook letters as a guide for drawing each letter. Frequently, he can do the same thing by recalling copybook letters from memory and attempting to write them as he did when a young child.

If individuality is so important in handwriting and hand printing identification, then why is it important to have a working knowledge of handwriting systems? Because, without that knowledge, letters and features that should be given the weight of a class characteristic may mistakenly be given the importance due an individual characteristic. For example, unknown to the FDE, a writer may have learned and retained some of the influence of a foreign handwriting system he learned as a child. Without some knowledge of handwriting systems, and possibly even some background information on the writer, such as where and what systems he learned to write in school, the FDE could assign more significance than he should to what is a foreign handwriting system characteristic.

From this discussion, it can be seen that individuality is not limited to just a single feature of handwriting. At this point, individuality as it relates to three features (beginning and ending strokes, letter construction, connecting strokes, etc.) of writing will be discussed. Individuality is also present in the relationship between the letters and the baseline, spacing habits, relative height relationships, etc. These will be discussed in more detail later.

INFLUENCE ON LETTER CONSTRUCTION

What influence does individuality have on letter construction? As we have seen, individuality and the act of writing are inseparable. Not all writings have a high degree of individuality, such as a signature, but the vast majority of writings do have at least some perceptible amount. In handwriting and hand printing identification, the job of the FDE is to determine which features, when taken collectively, comprise the individuality of the writer. How the writer constructs his letters is one characteristic that must be considered. Is the letter legible or does the reader have to guess what letter the writer wrote based on its context?

Legibility is defined as: " . . . capable of being read or deciphered, esp. with ease, as writing or printing; easily readable" (Random 1992). Signatures, as written by some writers, are frequently thought of as illegible, but very distinctive or individualistic. Just because writing is legible does not mean it lacks sufficient individuality to be identifiable. Legibility is a reading factor, not a measure of a writer's level of graphic maturity or individuality.

Occasionally, the FDE will determine that a feature, or combination of features, is an accidental rather than the normal writing by the writer. "Accidentals are isolated, brief, or temporary digressions from normal writing practices" (Huber and Headrick 1999: 46). The level of proof necessary to establish that a feature is an accidental is extremely high. It cannot be assumed that just because a feature is found in the questioned writing and not in the specimens, even though every other significant feature is in absolute agreement, that the feature not in absolute agreement must be an accidental. Such an assumption significantly increases the possibility of error in reaching the conclusion that two writings are written by the same writer. The assumption that the differing features could be by another writer must always be considered first.

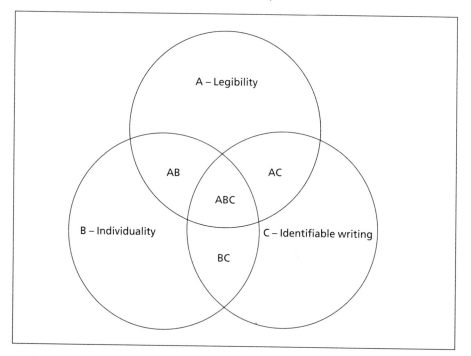

Figure 4.4

Figure 4.4 is a diagram illustrating the relationship between legibility, individuality, and identifiable writing. Each circle represents a particular feature of writing:

- Circle A – legibility (illegibility is discussed shortly)
- Circle B – individuality
- Circle C – identifiable writing

There is a relationship that exists between these features as shown in the areas where the circles overlap. For example:

- The overlapping portion of A and B, designated by the area and text box "AB," represents all legible writing that also has individuality.
- The overlapping portion of A and C, designated by the area and text box "AC," represents all legible writing that is identifiable.
- The overlapping portion of B and C, designated by the area and text box "BC," represents all writing that has individuality and is identifiable.
- The overlapping portions of A, B, and C, designated by the area and text box "ABC," represent all legible writing that has sufficient individuality to be identifiable. An analysis of the remaining relationships is left to the reader.

Legibility, individuality, and establishing the identity of a writer are key elements for the FDE. Individuality is often thought of as being more pronounced in a signature than a characteristic of extended writing. Actually, both can have a great deal of individuality; and frequently an extended writing is more identifiable than a signature because there is more opportunity for the writer to demonstrate his individuality. As the overlapping circles illustrate, just because writing has individuality does not mean it is always identifiable. For example, take a signature that is very individualistic but consists of a series of numerous random lines. Such a signature may not have a sufficient combination of legibility and individuality to make it identifiable.

Extended writings can be legible, have a great deal of individuality, and be identifiable. There are many more opportunities to incorporate individuality into the features of an extended writing than may not exist in a signature. However, not all writing, even extended writing, is legible. If Circle A represented "illegible" writing, then it becomes obvious that some "illegible" writing is not only identifiable, but has individuality. The overlapping area "ABC" represents such writing.

A practical illustration of how this applies to handwriting is found in Figure 4.5. Figure 4.5 shows two names written by the same writer. Note, the capital letters, "F" and "P." Each letter begins with a down stroke, a clockwise spiral movement up and to the left forming the left side of the letter. At the top of each letter the clockwise spiral movement continues downward, only for a short distance in the case of the "F," where it ends at the top of the retraced stroke extending from the left shoulder of the lower case "r." On the "P," the pen

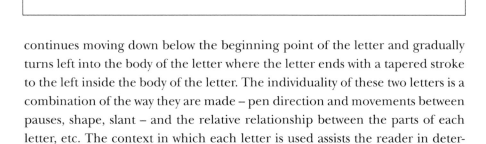

Figure 4.5

continues moving down below the beginning point of the letter and gradually turns left into the body of the letter where the letter ends with a tapered stroke to the left inside the body of the letter. The individuality of these two letters is a combination of the way they are made – pen direction and movements between pauses, shape, slant – and the relative relationship between the parts of each letter, etc. The context in which each letter is used assists the reader in determining that they are different letters.

A further analysis of the two names, as written by this writer, is as follows: the letter "r" in "Frank" is not connected to the "F" or to the "a" following it. The "r" has a tall, retraced line extending, slanted to the left of vertical, from the left shoulder of the letter. The top of the letter is written with an underhand, counterclockwise motion, and the letter has a short retraced line, slanted to the right, extending from the right shoulder of the letter. The "a" is not connected to the "r" preceding it. The "a" has an elliptical shape oval to the left of the retraced vertical line forming the right side of the letter, and the letter appears to be connected to the "n" following it. The "n" has a retraced line on the left side, a "v" shaped formation to the left of the tent-shaped formation on the right side of the letter. The "n" does not appear to be connected to the last letter of the name, "k." The "k" has a tall staff on the left side of the letter with a "c" type formation on the right of the staff. The beginning of the "c" formation consists of a tapered stroke and the end of the formation is directed up and blunt.

The "a" in "Paul" is similar in shape to that in "Frank," but wider. It appears to be connected to the left side of the "u" at the top of the retraced line. Notice the narrowing of the connecting stroke between the "a" and "u" as the pen gets closer to the latter.

Some other features of these two words that can be thought of collectively as examples of this writer's individuality are as follows:

"Frank"

1. The small spacing between the "F" and "r."

2. The tall left shoulder on the "r" extending up and to the left of vertical.

3. The narrow spacing between the "r" and "a."

4. The separation between the down and up strokes on the left side of the "n;" and the rising baseline, the bottom of the left side is lower than the ending stroke on the tent formation, or right part of the letter.

5. The tangent point of the right curved side of the "k," the length of that stroke above and below the tangent point, and its blunt ending.

"Paul"

1. The absence of space between the "P" and "a."

2. The tall left and shorter right side of the letter "u."

3. The wide spacing between the "a" and "u" compared to that between the "P" and "a."

4. The wide bowl of the letter "u," the tall left and short right side of the letter, and the connecting stroke connecting the "u" and "l" at the top of the letters right side. The smaller spacing between these two letter's than between the "a" and "u."

5. The width of the "l" compared to its height and the bluntness of the ending of the stroke.

INFLUENCE ON CONNECTING STROKES

A connecting stroke best illustrates Saudek's observation that individuality can occur in a written line connecting two "pauses." The shape of a connecting stroke is governed by the letter just written, the letter about to be written, and the writer's habits when writing letters that stand alone, are the first letter in a name or word, if the letter is within a word and between two other letters, or if it is the last letter of a word.

Since handwriting movement(s) is a habitual activity, the writer's writing habits govern how a letter is made and how it is connected. Depending upon these habits, connecting strokes can be individualistic or very common and can take on many forms that fit within the following general categories:

- The movement may be a straight line, a curved line, or a compound or serpentine movement.
- A continuously written line, where the pen remains on the paper surface at all times while the stroke is written.
- A broken line because the writer stops the writing act, raises the pen from the paper bluntly, or gradually lifts the pen off the paper leaving a tapered ending stroke on the letter just written, and reapplying it gradually to the paper forming a tapered beginning stroke for the next letter.

In some literature, the term to describe the motion of the hand between the time it leaves the paper and its reapplication is referred to as an air bridge. The difference between a connecting stroke and a beginning and ending stroke on a letter is sometimes difficult to interpret when the letters are within a word. There is no mistaking them if the letter is the first letter of a word or when it stands alone. The confusion usually occurs when the writing is a manuscript style.

There may be a complete starting and stopping of the pen during the writing of connecting strokes. These complete start and stop actions result in blunt endings on the stroke before the pen is raised from the paper, and where the pen is reapplied before the writing act resumes.

- Some writers connect the last letter of a word with the first letter of the next word, even though they were taught not to. The system the writer learned may have called for the connecting of these letters, the writer's relative writing speed is such that the pen is not completely raised off the paper between the last letter of a word and beginning letter of the next word.
- The style of writing (cursive, printing, manuscript, etc.), in part, determines whether connecting strokes are called for between letters. Cursive writing usually calls for connecting strokes while manuscript writing has connections between some letters and not others, and true printing uses no connecting strokes between letters. Some systems teach that leaving out connecting strokes between two letters, the latter beginning on the right (i.e. "*a*," "*c*," "*d*," etc.), is acceptable to help improve the speed of the writing without sacrificing legibility.
- True printing does not call for connecting strokes between letters.

Connecting strokes, like letter formations, have master patterns. The following questions help illustrate this point: What is the style of the writing? What two letters are being connected together? Does the letter combination "call for" a connecting stroke? If so, how should it be made? If the style of writing is cursive, then by definition, most of the lower case letters should be connected and some of the upper/lower case letter combinations will also be connected. Some exceptions are typically those letters beginning on the right side of the letter form, particularly if the letter form is lower case, such as the "*a*," "*c*," "*d*," etc.

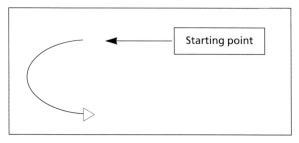

Figure 4.6

Figure 4.6 illustrates how letters beginning on the right side have their starting point at the top of the letter and a spiral motion to the left and down toward the baseline of the letter to make its left side.

INFLUENCE ON BEGINNING AND ENDING STROKES

Beginning or initial strokes are called for in many of the copybook standards. As written by the individual writer they can be very plain or embellished. Embellishment of beginning strokes is usually not something a writer learns in school from the copybook. It is a developed habit governed by the writer's individuality and the context within which the embellishment appears.

Usually, when people think of embellished writing they think of signatures, like the one in Figure 4.7. In this instance, the first letter of the name should be an "L" but because of the embellishment of the writing it is not possible to determine what letters make up the name, whether it is just the first and last name of the writer or the first, middle initial, and last name.

Figure 4.7

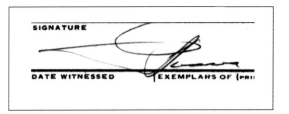

The embellishment may be a long approach stroke as in 1 through 3, loops as in 4 through 6, retraced lines as in 7 through 9, two-part forms as in 9, small hooks as in 10, and what appears to be multiple formations, such as the "3W," in 11. See Figure 4.8.

Figure 4.8

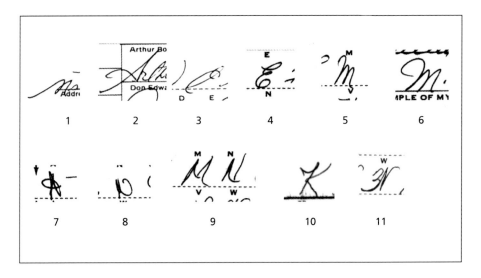

Embellishments are also found on the end of letters. Figure 4.9 shows several examples of letters with embellishments on the end of the letter.

Figure 4.9

How a writer embellishes a feature, letter, combination of letters, words, etc. is as varied as the number of writers. One of the important things is how consistent those embellishments are and when they are used. Remember that a person is not a machine that writes nearly the same way each time, that he does write around a "master pattern" within a given context. It is important therefore to duplicate the context when obtaining specimens for comparison purposes.

If the writer uses a tapered beginning or ending on his embellishment, the FDE knows that the pen was in motion before it made contact with the paper. (See Figure 4.10.)

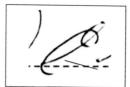

Figure 4.10

If the writer has the pen in motion before making contact with the paper and then once he does make contact he stops the pen to change direction, there is usually a tick mark at the very beginning of the approach stroke on the "K" and "W," as in Figure 4.11.

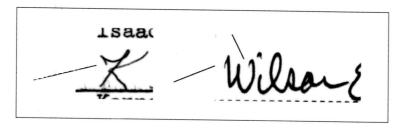

Figure 4.11

The same feature appearing on the terminal stroke of the letter shows that the writer stopped the pen before raising it from the paper; and when he did, the direction of the movement off the paper is recorded as the tapered tick mark, shown on the "W" in Figure 4.11.

The direction of the pen's movement before making contact with the paper can be determined regardless of whether the approach or terminal strokes are long and tapered, embellished or not. They provide the FDE with invaluable information about how the writer moves his hand. However, as Harrison observed, " . . . the fact that one specimen of writing is completely devoid of initial strokes does not mean that it cannot have been written by the author of another specimen which is liberally garnished with abnormally long examples of this formation" (Harrison 1966: 315). For ending or terminal strokes, he observed that " . . . If a writer is found to use long spurs to these letters, then similar long spurs are almost certain to be present in every contemporary specimen of his handwriting. A similar constancy is found in the use of the more rarely encountered short spur, which approximates to little more than a 'tick.'" (ibid) Further, he found that terminal strokes, primarily those on the " . . . letters, 'o,' 'w,' and the arcade form of 'r' . . . " are more consistent in length than on other letters (ibid).

SUMMARY

Individuality is an extremely important concept and part of the handwriting identification process. By properly evaluating the significance of each feature, based on its rarity – or frequency of occurrence in random writings – and establishing the collective importance of those features when combined with the class characteristics of the writing, the FDE is satisfied that the significance of the combination is unique enough to separate that writer from all others. Once that level of certainty has been reached, then he can safely conclude that the writings are by the same writer. This statement assumes the following:

- That the writings, both questioned and specimen, are the normal, natural writing of their writer.
- That the probability of another writer having exactly the same combination of individual and common features is so small that for all practical purposes it does not exist.
- Even though truly individual, hence significant, characteristics usually occur on those letter forms and combination of letters that are complex in their design and execution, individuality can also occur in a line between two pauses and give it sufficient significance for identification purposes when it is given proper weight.
- That there is a sound basis for concluding that any accidental feature present in the questioned writing was written by the writer of the balance of the material. Further, that the specimen writer wrote the questioned writing, including the accidental feature, if the evidence of authorship is sufficient to conclude that he wrote the questioned material.

Individuality and its significance is the central element for the identification of handwriting and hand printing.

REFERENCES

Harrison, Wilson R. (1966) *Suspect Documents Their Scientific Examination*. London: Sweet & Maxwell Limited.

Hilton, Ordway (1982) *Scientific Examination of Questioned Documents*, revised edn, New York: Elsevier North Holland, Inc.

Huber, Roy A. and Headrick, A.M. (1999) *Handwriting Identification: Facts and Fundamentals*, New York: CRC Press.

Morris, R. (1999) "Handwriting and Hand Printing Identification for Investigators," unpublished; a study guide written for use as a text when teaching the fundamentals of handwriting identification to investigators.

Osborn, Albert S. (1929) *Questioned Documents*, 2nd edn, Albany, NY: Boyd Printing Company.

Ramsey, Sandra L. (1998) "A Study of the Evolution of Handwriting from Grades Three to Six," *Journal of the American Society of Questioned Document Examiners*, 1(1) June.

Random (1992) *Random House Webster's Electronic Dictionary and Thesaurus*. College Edition, Reference Software International.

Saudek, Robert (1978) *Experiments with Handwriting*. Sacramento, CA. First published in Great Britain by George Allen & Unwin.

SWGDOC (formerly) TWGDOC (1998) SOPs and Terminology Draft Guideline (#9).

TWGDOC SOP Subcommittee Suggested QD definitions.

CHAPTER 5

FEATURES OF WRITING

DEFINITION

The word feature is defined as:

1   a prominent or conspicuous part or characteristic . . .
2   something offered as a special or main attraction.
3   to be a feature or distinctive mark of.
4   to delineate the main characteristics of; depict.
5   Informal. to conceive of; imagine; fancy.
6   to play a major part.
7   being or offered as a highlight; featured . . . (Random 1992).

No better definition of features of writing has ever been given than the one by Ronald M. Dick in a paper he wrote for the US Secret Service, Office of Training, Handwriting Course for Investigators. He defines features of writing this way: "Features of writing could be defined as those characteristics that are peculiar to the writing of a particular individual and which constitute his writing habits" (Dick: 4). They consist of both conspicuous and inconspicuous characteristics. By inconspicuous, the author does not mean that they are latent or otherwise invisible, he is referring to those features of the writing the average person may not notice, or even knows exist, and what significance they have for identification purposes.

The FDE places a good deal of significance on both the conspicuous and inconspicuous features of writing when determining whether two or more writings are of common authorship. One of the major reasons for errors in handwriting identification is basing an opinion on a few similar features of the writing and ignoring or not attaching the proper significance to the dissimilarities and differences indicative of another writer. Just because conspicuous features have pictorial similarity and the inconspicuous features appear to be the same does not necessarily mean the writings are of common authorship. This topic is covered more thoroughly in the chapter dealing with opinions.

The thing to remember is that variation in writing around some "master pattern" is extremely important. The concept of variation applies to every quality and feature of writing. It can be the result of any number of factors, including but not limited to the writing instrument used, writing surface, position of the writer when writing, the purpose of the document on which the writing is placed, nervousness, illness, use of drugs and intoxication, intentional disguise, etc.

WHAT ARE THEY?

What are the features of handwriting? Most of them are self-explanatory or are explained in detail in other sections of this book. Therefore, a detailed explanation of each one will not be given in this chapter. Some of the features of handwriting are:

- The overall size of the writing, the overall and the relative height relationships between letters, words, etc.
- Letter formation and how it is written; i.e., upper v. lower case letters, manuscript v. cursive or script, cursive v. printed letter usage, etc.
- The relative relationships of writing, such as slant, spacing, pressure habits, attention to baseline (both pre-drawn and imaginary), spacing habits, height relationship between letters, component parts of letters, letter combinations, words, etc.
- Line quality resulting from the relative speed of the writing or some transitory factor affecting the writer's ability to write.
- The curvature of pen strokes, lines, etc.
- Flourishes and embellishments on letters or in the writing of various features, including the direction of pen movement in making beginning and ending strokes, etc.
- The connecting strokes between letters – usage, curvature, direction of pen movement, etc.
- Pen lifts within and between letters, etc.
- Abbreviations of letters and words.
- Punctuation marks – how they are made, and used.
- The placement of marks, such as punctuation marks, i-dots and t-crosses, etc.

This list is not meant to be a comprehensive list covering all the features of writing. Rather, it is a list of some of the more common features. When performing a handwriting examination and comparison, it is essential that the FDE carefully consider *all* qualities and features of the writing because it is the agreement in their combination that enables a FDE to distinguish one person's writing from another.

REFERENCES

Dick, Ronald M. (n.d.) "The Identification Of Handwriting – A Brief Discussion." A paper written for and used as part of the US Secret Service Office of Training Course in handwriting for investigators.

Random (1992 and 1999) *Random House Webster's Electronic Dictionary and Thesaurus* College Edition, Reference Software International.

CHAPTER 6

QUALITIES OF WRITING

DEFINITION OF QUALITIES OF WRITING

The word quality is defined as:

1. an essential characteristic, property, or attribute . . .
2. character or nature, as belonging to or distinguishing a thing . . .

The quality of writing is an essential characteristic for the consideration of the FDE. Its importance in assisting him to establish the following cannot be over-emphasized:

■ A writing's naturalness and ultimately the significance that should be attached to its features.

■ Whether the writing is a simulation, tracing, or unnaturally written and therefore suspect.

■ Distinguishing between similarities and differences in the writing and whether all of the writing features are within the writer's normal range of variation.

Quality of writing is defined by Ronald M. Dick as: ". . . the overall reflection of writing skill, and is governed largely by the movement through which the writing was produced" (Dick: 3). Writing quality is the result of a number of physiological factors that affect it, such as how the writer holds the pen, the combination of movements by fingers, hand, wrist, and arm, etc.

EXPLAINED WITH EXAMPLES

Some of the basic factors denoting the quality of writing are:

■ The rhythm of the writing, not just the rhythmical contraction and relaxation of the muscles, but also the rhythmical alternation between movement and pausing after completing the movement. Rhythm is affected by both the physical and mental aspects of the writer and has an influence on the range of variation around a feature's "master pattern."

- The relative speed of the writing.
- The roundness or angularity of the writing.
- The smoothness or jaggedness of the writing.
- The legibility of the writing.
- The artistic-ness of the letter forms and overall writing.
- The awkwardness of letter forms, connecting strokes, etc.
- The relative pressure habits of the writer.
- The presence or absence of exaggerated features.

The quality of a writing may vary from the smooth, free-flowing movements of the pen resulting from the normal contraction and relaxation of muscles producing good relative pressure habits, a normal range of variation, etc., which are characteristic of a skillful writer, to the slow, uniform writing of a less skillful writer using a stroke of letter impulse.

The combination of writing qualities and features is what constitutes individuality. That individuality consists of elements such as:

- The type of writing instrument used – pencil, ball-point pen, fountain pen, roller ball pen, etc. – and how comfortable the writer is with each one.
- How the writer holds the writing instrument.
- How the pen is moved across the writing surface by the interaction of the fingers, hand, wrist, and arm.
- The texture of the writing surface – smooth, uneven, rough, etc. – the writer is writing on at the time. The choice of writing instrument and surface can either allow the writer to write normally, rhythmically, or serve as a transitory factor affecting the writing.
- The writer's writing position, comfortably sitting at a desk, standing at a counter, writing using someone else's back or his own hand as a writing surface, sitting in a car, etc.
- The level of skill possessed by the writer.

The writer's rhythmical writing patterns are extremely important in handwriting identification. Their importance to assessing the significance of writing features cannot be over-emphasized.

Figure 6.1 illustrates the writing of good quality, certainty on the part of its author to know what and how it should be written. The writing is rhythmical and demonstrates that the author is comfortable with the writing instrument and how to use it.

Figure 6.2 illustrates the writing of a person having less skill, poorer overall quality, etc. than the writer in Figure 6.1. Notice the greater angularity of the writing, more uniform relative pressure habits, etc. displayed by this writer.

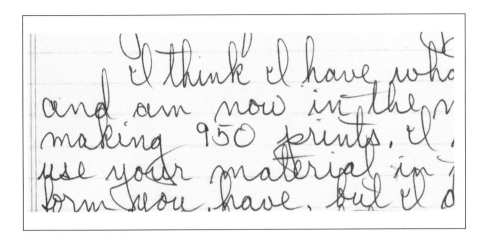

Figure 6.1

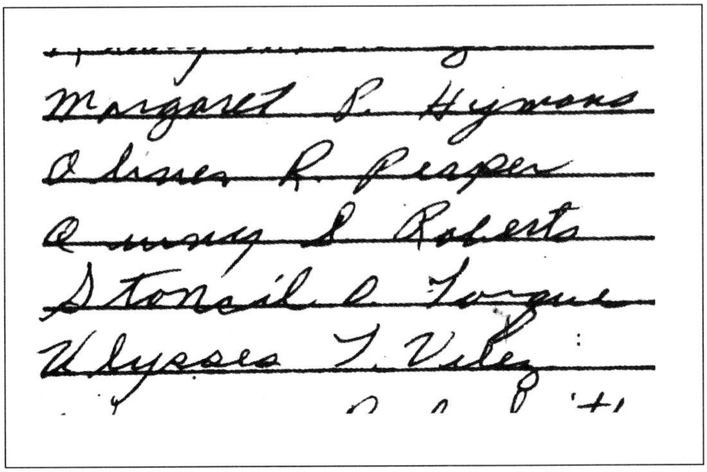

Figure 6.2

No examination is complete until the writing's quality and features are given their proper significance and due consideration. When the FDE forgets, or does not perform this step in his examination of the writing, he will surely err in determining the authorship of the writing.

REFERENCES

Dick, Ronald M. (n.d.) "The Identification Of Handwriting – A Brief Discussion", A paper written for and used as part of the US Secret Service Office of Training Course in handwriting for investigators.

CHAPTER 7

LINE QUALITY

DEFINITION

Quality is defined as:

1. an essential characteristic, property, or attribute . . .
2. character or nature, as belonging to or distinguishing a thing . . .
3. character with respect to grade of excellence or fineness . . . (Random 1992)

Line quality is "an essential characteristic, property, . . . " of writing. Line quality is an important characteristic of writing when properly evaluated in conjunction with all the other qualities and features of the writing. It conveys to the FDE a great deal of information about the writing, such as the writer's skill level, whether the writing is unnaturally written or possibly disguised, the possibility of the writing being an attempted simulation or tracing, etc.

EXPLAINED WITH EXAMPLES

Line quality can take on a number of different forms and is in large part governed by the impulse level at which the writer writes. A written line can contain varying amounts of tremor from a great deal to no tremor; it can be of average quality – smooth, written with uniform writing pressure, consist of good relative pressure habits – light up and heavy downstrokes, etc.

The impulse level at which the writer writes is very significant in determining the amount of tremor that can be introduced into the writing. The impulse levels of writing are as follows:

■ *The stroke impulse:* the writer learns to write by drawing individual lines which, when connected together, make a letter (Saudek 1978: 389).

■ *The letter impulse:* he writes whole letters as a single writing act (ibid: 381).

■ *The syllable impulse:* he writes syllables or several letters connected together.

■ *The word or name impulse:* he writes complete words or names as a single act of writing (ibid: 394).

- *The sentence/phrase impulse:* when he reaches "graphic maturity," he thinks and tries to write sentences/phrases as a single act (ibid: 388).

By way of review, write every letter in the alphabet, both upper and lower case, *using the stroke impulse level of writing*. When you have finished, examine each letter with a magnifying glass, and observe the following.

Since each line or part of a letter is made with a single movement, you were forced to write slower than your normal writing speed, and line quality was compromised. For example, in Figure 7.1, each part of the letters is written with a single pen movement, or stroke impulse, and the line quality is marginal to poor with varying amounts of tremor.

Figure 7.1

Figure 7.2

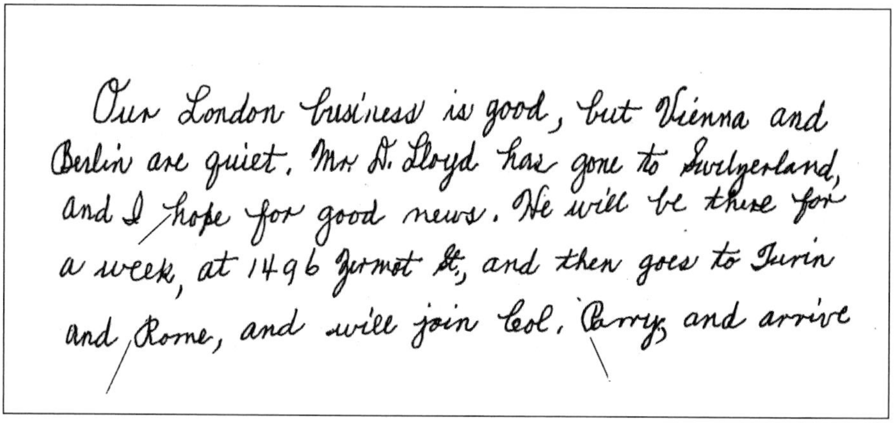

Figure 7.2 illustrates cursive writing having a marginally poor to average line quality. Notice the tremor in the written line, frequent directional changes of the pen and pen adjustments. These are all indicators of a slow writing act. Now look at Figure 7.3.

Figure 7.3

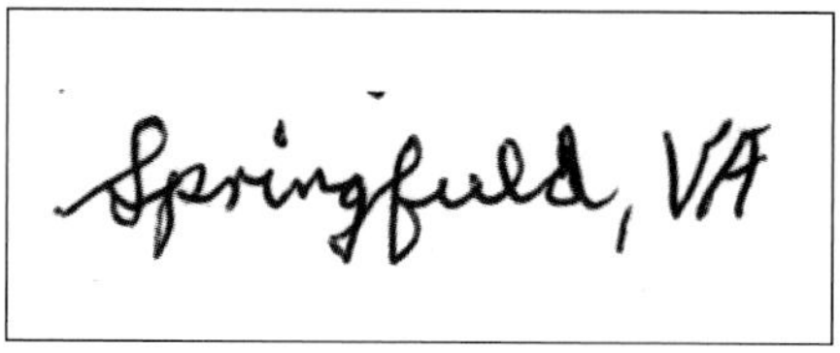

The line quality of this writing is very close to that of the writing in Figure 7.2. Notice the use of some common letters, such as the speed "r," by both writers. Although the line quality of the writing in Figures 7.2 and 7.3 is similar to that in Figure 7.1, the former are more consistent with writing at the letter/syllable impulse levels. They are also consistent with finger writing, which is written slowly, with relatively uniform pressure, awkward movements having frequent and often abrupt changes in pen direction, blunt beginning and ending strokes, etc. typical of the stroke, letter/syllable impulse levels of writing.

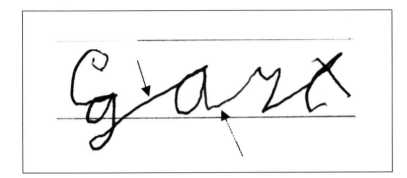

Figure 7.4

Figure 7.4 is an enlargement of another writing with line tremor, as indicated by the arrows. The line connecting the lower projection and the letter "a" does not have as much tremor as the line connecting the foot of the staff on the right side of the "a" and the top, left, shoulder of the "r." This writing is slightly different than the previous two examples, because of the presence of relative pressure habits by this writer. The connecting stroke between the "a" and "r" consists of two parts; first, the line extending from the top of the "a" down its right side to a point just above the pre-drawn baseline. The connecting stroke from that stopping point to the top of the left shoulder of the "r" is written with less writing pressure than the connecting stroke between the foot of the right side of the "r" and the top of the "t" staff.

Figure 7.5 illustrates an enlargement of a writer writing at the word/name impulse level. The line quality is excellent, the writer has good relative pressure habits, there is no tremor in the line, and the locations where the pen changes direction are smooth and rounded, not angular.

This is line quality usually associated with natural writing; but if this writing is natural writing, then is the writing in Figures 7.1 through 7.4 unnatural writing? No! The level of writing skill as evidenced by line quality indicates that some writers are less skillful with a pen, they write more slowly, change pen direction more frequently, and the line quality of their writing is not as good. However, their writing is as natural for them at their skill level as it is for the writer at the sentence/phrase impulse level. That is the importance of the impulse system,

Figure 7.5

because it provides part of the framework of principles within which the FDE determines whether or not writing is natural or unnaturally written.

Figure 7.6

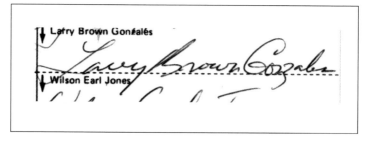

Figure 7.6 illustrates writing by the writer with sufficient confidence that he is in no doubt as to what the letters are supposed to look like, if they should be connected, etc.; and the writing is with sufficient speed that some of the letters are not recognizable were it not for the context in which they appear. Another example of this style of writing is seen below in Figure 7.7.

Figure 7.7

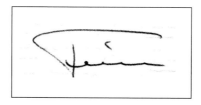

This writing illustrates the highest impulse level, the sentence/phrase level. Again, the writer is in no doubt how the name is to be written, what the letters are suppose to look like, etc. This writer is very skillful with a pen. The line quality is excellent; there is no evidence of tremor or any indication of hesitation, etc.

SUMMARY

Figure 7.8

| Questioned No. 1 | Specimen | Questioned No. 2 |

Figure 7.8 will be discussed in greater detail in Chapter 12, where it is Figure 12.4; but for this discussion, the Questioned No. 1 writing has very poor line quality because it is a tracing of the specimen name. Questioned No. 2 also has poor line quality because it is a simulation or drawing of the specimen. Notice that they have many of the qualities of a writer with a low level of skill, that is because the writer has reduced his skill level in order to copy someone else's handwriting habits. This figure helps to illustrate the importance of line quality as an indicator of the writer not writing with his normal writing habits. A further and more detailed explanation will be given in Chapter 12.

Line quality is important. It, like all of the other qualities and features of a writing, must be weighed and the proper significance attached to it in the examination being conducted.

REFERENCES

Random (1992 and 1999) *Random House Webster's Electronic Dictionary and Thesaurus*, College Edition, Reference Software International.

Saudek, Robert (1978) *Experiments With Handwriting*, Sacramento, CA. First published in Great Britain by George Allen & Unwin.

CHAPTER 8

RELATIVE SPEED OF WRITING

DEFINITION

Relative speed of writing. What is it? Does it mean the writer is writing at one mile per hour then increases his writing speed to five miles per hour, etc.? No! Relative speed of writing is not a measurement of how fast the writer is writing at any given point in time. Rather, it is the result of an analysis of the psychological factors affecting handwriting.

Huber defines writing speed as: "The rate of line generation, sometimes wrongly regarded to be the rate of word generation, that varies with the size of the writing" (Huber and Headrick 1999: 411). Hilton observed that: "Not everyone writes at the same rate, so that consideration of the speed of writing may be a significant identifying element. Writing speed cannot be measured precisely from the finished handwriting but can be interpreted in broad terms as slow, moderate, or rapid" (Hilton 1982: 21).

How can we interpret the relative speed of writing from what is written? To answer this question we must first turn to a basic law of physics, momentum, as it applies to handwriting. Momentum – (mass)(velocity) – as defined by Sir Isaac Newton, is the "rate of change of 'motion.'" (Miller 1977: 115). Velocity is a vector quantity, so momentum is the movement of a mass – the pen and hand – in any direction at some speed. In this case, the velocity of the pen varies according to the normal muscular interaction of contraction and relaxation by the writer.

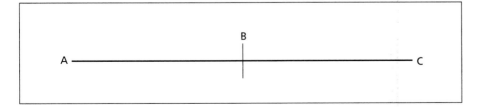

Figure 8.1

Figure 8.1 is a horizontal line divided by the vertical line at "B." For purposes of this discussion, let's assume that the writer places the point of his pen at "A." He begins moving the pen from point A toward C. As he moves the pen from point A, he gradually increases its speed until he reaches point B, where he begins reducing its speed until the pen comes to a complete stop at point C.

Figure 8.2

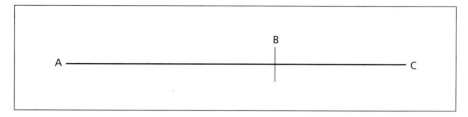

Figure 8.2 is a line of the same length, as in Figure 8.1, but the location of B has been moved so it is closer to point C. In this situation, the writer's pen has a longer distance to travel to get up to a maximum speed and a shorter distance to return to a full stop. If the location of B changes, its location will determine the amount of time the pen accelerates and decelerates for any given writer. Only in the first example, Figure 8.1, is the acceleration and deceleration constant. In the second example, it varies depending upon the distance between A and B, and B and C. The distance the pen travels between pauses, points A and C, is very important. Of equal importance is the shape of the line between the two points. More will be said about this as we go on.

What does this simple example tell us about the relative speed of writing? From this example and additional experiments, the following general principles concerning relative speed of writing can be derived.

- Every writer writes longer lines at a greater speed than shorter ones.
- Every writer varies his writing speed when writing a straight line between pauses or stops.
- Every writer writes in such a way that the speed of his pen is constantly varying over the length of its movement.

These principles apply to a straight line. But what happens if the line is not straight, for example the line in Figure 8.3?

Figure 8.3

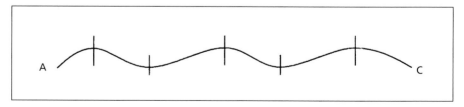

There are five places, between point A and point C in Figure 8.3, where the writer alters the direction of the writing. From the demonstration above, we know that every time the writer approaches one of these directional change points his speed of writing is reduced. After the directional change, he begins increasing his relative speed until he approaches the next directional change, at which time and at some point between the two lines, he again slows his writing. From this example the following principles are derived.

■ When writing a line where the pen changes direction, as in Figure 8.3, the speed of the pen varies at each directional change point.

■ If the directional changes are smooth, rounded curves, like those in Figure 8.3, and not blunt or sudden changes, even though the speed of the pen changes while writing at the directional change point, the pen is never brought to a complete stop.

What if the directional change is sharp, as in Figure 8.4? The pen is brought to a complete stop at points B and C so that its direction can be changed. Hence the principle, when writing a line and the writer wishes to change direction (at point B), the pen must come to a complete stop before the movement between B and C can begin.

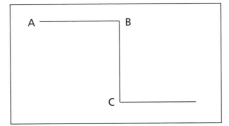

Figure 8.4

Another principle is derived from Figure 8.4: "The laws of inertia will prevent any writer from bringing the movement of his pen to a standstill in accordance with his intention of the moment. If we apply this doctrine to the simplest of all graphic formations, namely, the dot, it means that no one is capable of making a dot when writing at a high rate of speed which actually has the form of a full-stop, but that he will instead of this produce a form which, when examined through the microscope, and often with the naked eye, has the form of a comma or accent" (Saudek 1978: 64). As a follow-up to this principle, if a writer is writing rapidly he cannot place an i-dot directly over its staff without first coming to a complete stop. And by definition, if a writer is writing rapidly, he is incapable of writing a tremulous line, because such a line requires him to write slowly, while frequently changing pen direction, as in Figure 8.4.

These principles are directly related to the writer's impulse level of writing.

■ *The stroke impulse:* the writer learns to write by drawing individual lines which, when connected together, make a letter (Saudek 1978: 389).

■ *The letter impulse:* he writes whole letters as a single writing act (ibid: 381).

■ *The syllable impulse:* he writes syllables or several letters connected together.

- ■ *The word or name impulse:* he writes complete words or names as a single act of writing (ibid: 394).
- ■ *The sentence/phrase impulse:* when he reaches "graphic maturity," he thinks and tries to write sentences/phrases as a single act (ibid: 388).

These impulse levels serve as a good measure to describe the relative speed of the writer. Saudek explained why relative speed of writing occurred using his impulse level principles of writing, while Hilton described the general pictorial nature of relative speed by describing it " . . . in broad terms as slow, moderate, or rapid" (Hilton 1982: 21).

TENDENCY TO THE RIGHT/TENDENCY TO THE LEFT

Returning to the physical concepts that apply to the relative speed of writing, there is one that has a profound impact on how a person writes: it is the concept of inertia. "A first and basic attribute of matter is that any piece of it, which we call a 'body,' tends to resist any change in its motion. This attribute of matter is called *inertia*" (Miller 1977: 15). As has already been noted, when a person is writing and wants to abruptly change the direction in which the pen is moving, he brings it to a complete stop, then begins moving it in a different direction. If he wants to change direction more slowly, he writes a curved line, like that in Figure 8.3, but does not have to bring the pen to a complete stop.

So, what does the concept of inertia have to do with handwriting and what the FDE observes on the paper? Usually, writers in the western world write from left to right. This means that in order to write rapidly – at the sentence/phrase impulse level – they must keep the pen moving to the right. When writing letters, such as the lower case "m," "n," "r," etc., for example, they will usually be tent-shaped with rounded, rather than pointed, tops that require the writer to stop, then change direction. This tendency to the right can also be found in the separation in the arches of the "m" and garland shape "w." Another indication is the direction of the pen when ending a letter or word, for example, the direction of the terminal stroke at the bottom of the lower projection of the "J" in Figure 8.5. Here the writer is moving the pen rapidly and wants to go to the "o" as soon as he can.

Figure 8.5

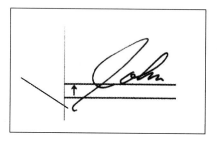

If the writer has a strong tendency to the right, he will frequently neglect the vertical parts of letters because his preference is to move the pen from the left to the right as quickly as possible without interference. Vertical movements and details of letters called for by many systems are an impediment to the rapid writer, because they are a distraction from the normal flow of the writing. Figure 8.6 shows the directional tendencies a writer is influenced by when writing. In every writing there is this combination of tendencies to the right and left plus the relative slant of the writing influencing the writer while he is writing. The hooked lower projection on the "J" in Figure 8.5 is an illustration of tendency to the right while the terminal stroke of the "s" in "wings," in Figure 8.7, is an example of tendency to the left.

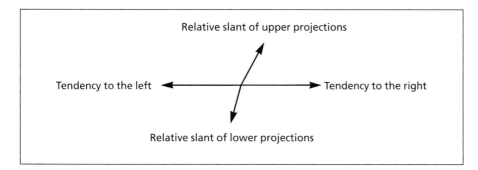

Figure 8.6

Another way of looking at this is to think of the writer writing a paragraph. After he has composed what he wants to write in his mind, he must then put it on paper. He picks up the pen and begins to write; but when he does, where are his thoughts? Not where the pen is on the paper! He is thinking of what he is going to write, say four lines ahead of his pen. He wants to get through where he is actually writing as quickly as possible. In his haste the signs of tendency to the right will frequently be more pronounced in his writing because he is not able to write as fast as he can think or quickly put together the concepts and ideas he wants to get on paper. Also in his writing will be a tendency to write wide letters and upper and lower projections consistent with speed of writing.

What happens when he reaches the right margin or edge of the paper? There, his strong tendency to the right is limited only by the amount of writing surface remaining. If that amount of space is small and he still has a lot to write, he is forced to bring the pen back to the left margin and begin to write anew.

Figure 8.7 further illustrates pen direction and speed by the tick marks at the end of the "m" in "them" and the "n" in "then," the first two words in the last line. This writer makes the t-cross after writing the whole word. Note the tick marks to the left at the bottom of the right side of each letter. On the first t-cross there is a small hook on the left side of the t-cross pointing in the direction of the terminal hook on the "m." These show that the writer started the word by

Figure 8.7

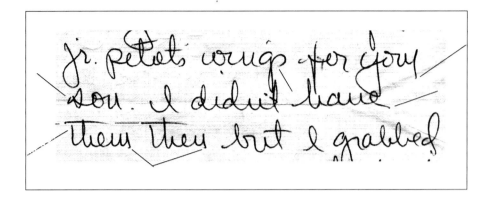

making the t-staff with a downstroke and placed the t-cross over the staff while moving the pen from the terminal of the "m" to the t-cross.

The short line between the end of the tapered t-cross of the first word and the t-staff of the second word shows the movement of the pen between these two points. Note also that after the pen made contact with the paper, the writer's hand was still moving to the right; hence the bow to the right of the t-staff.

Notice also how this writer varies the writing speed, relative speed of writing.

Figure 8.8

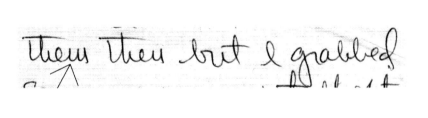

Figure 8.8 shows the writer varying the speed of writing for each part of a letter. The light upstrokes and heavy downstrokes are evidence of normal muscular interaction between contraction and relaxation, and the point at which the writer reapplies pressure on the pen as it is brought back toward the body is very clear. On some upper projections the writing act is stopped and there is a pause before the pen direction is changed – the "t" in "didn't," the "h" in "have," the "h's" in "them" and "then," in Figure 8.7 – etc. The top of the upper projections on some of the letters, such as the "b", "d," etc., have tight turns but are rounded, meaning the pen is moving faster there than at the tops of the previously described upper projections.

Another observation that can be made at this point is, obviously, that this writer has a very strong preference for underhand or garland type writing movements. The letters "m" and "n" should have arches, but this writer writes the letter with a strong preference for garland or underhand movements. The downstroke forming the t-staff is not straight, nor does it show a preference for a garland movement. Rather, it is a compound curve, the pen moving to the right in a clockwise motion, then changing to a clockwise movement about halfway down the staff.

Having done this very brief analysis, are there some general signs or evidence within a writing to indicate if it is rapidly or slowly written, and indications of whether the writer is writing with a tendency to the right or left? Yes! Saudek developed what he called the "Primary Signs of the Speed of Execution" (Saudek 1978: 81). His work is shown in Table 8.1.

Before turning to the table, a few things need to be added to this discussion. A writer is able to write rapidly when there is no uncertainty with the language he is writing, the shapes and how to write letters and numerals, the writing instrument he is using, and the surface on which he is writing. Any of these factors can, and will, impact on the writer's relative speed of writing. For example, if a writer normally writes English but inserts a French word he is not familiar with in his text, the relative speed of his writing will decrease, as will his absolute speed, because of his uncertainty with the word, how it is spelled, or the shapes of certain letters within the word.

If he is writing with an unfamiliar writing instrument, say a fountain pen, when he always writes with a ballpoint pen, his relative speed of writing will also be affected. The same is true for the texture of the writing surface. If it is uneven or rough, he will slow his writing speed to compensate for the texture of the surface, and the line quality may be poor with evidence of tremor, not due to his writing habit but due to the writing surface.

SIGNS OF SPEED AND SLOWNESS IN WRITING

These signs (Table 8.1) are as applicable today as they were when Saudek first proposed them. They are based on the act of writing and are easily proven by both experiment and the careful examination of writing. While they are written in such a way that they seem to apply to extended bodies of writing, they are also true for signatures.

In addition to these primary signs, Saudek proposed some secondary signs as well. "Secondary signs increase or diminish the significance of the primary signs. They render possible a graduated estimate of the *tempo* and the spontaneity of the act of writing" (ibid: 107). Table 8.2 shows Saudek's secondary signs of the speed of execution.

Table 8.1

Primary signs of the speed of execution. (Adapted from Saudek 1978: 81.)

Primary Plus Signs (Speed)	Primary Minus Signs (Slowness)
1. Smooth and unbroken strokes and rounded forms.	1. Wavering forms and broken strokes.
2. Frequent signs of "tendency to the right" all through the manuscript, alternating with "tendency to the left" at the ends of lines . . .	2. Frequent signs of "tendency to the left."
3. Great uncertainty of aim after temporary interruptions of the act of writing – that is, after syllable or word impulses.	3. Conspicuous certainty of aim with scarcely perceptible deviations from the intended direction of motion.
4. Increased continuity of execution; for example, the connection of diacritical signs with the following letter, the joining together of words, numerals, etc.	4. Frequent pauses during execution, recognizable by meaningless blobs, blobs due to readjustment, angles, divided letters and unrhythmical separations within the word itself . . . "touching up" of letters.
5. Letters curtailed and degenerated almost to illegibility toward their end.	5. Careful execution of significant details of letter forms and amplification of strokes towards the ends of words.
6. "Primarily wide" script . . .	6. "Primarily narrow" script (especially in slanting handwriting).
7. Great difference of emphasis between upstrokes and downstrokes.	7. Hardly any difference in strength of upstrokes and downstrokes; writing produced with very little pressure, or "pasty" writing.
8. Widening of the left-hand margin as the writing proceeds.	8. Ornamental or flourishing connections.

Table 8.2

Secondary signs of the speed of execution. (Saudek 1978: 107.)

Secondary Plus Signs (Speed)	Secondary Minus Signs (Slowness)
1. (a) Increasing obliquity as compared with normal angle of school-copy. (b) Increasing tendency to reversed angle (over 90 per cent) when the school-copy was vertical and to a lateral grip of the pen.	1. Downstrokes parallel almost as in school copy.
2. "Secondarily wide" handwriting (especially if the script is at the same time "primarily narrow").	2. "Secondarily narrow" handwriting (especially if the script is at the same time "primarily wide").
3. Rising lines with paper and pen at normal angles.	3. Sinking of the lines (well marked from the beginning of the line, not only during the course of the line).
4. Infrequent changes of angle of writing.	4. Frequent change of angle of writing.

EXPLAINED WITH EXAMPLES

What do the primary and secondary signs of speed and slowness mean? Figure 8.9 shows three bodies of writing repeating the same material. (The author wishes to apologize to the reader for the quality of this illustration. I was not able to locate either the original documents from this experiment or the photograph from which this photocopy was made. However, the quality of the copy shown here is of sufficient quality that the points being discussed and illustrated will be understandable.)

These three paragraphs were written by the same writer using the following instructions.

- Write the material as rapidly as you can as if you were taking notes in a classroom while the instructor was lecturing.
- Write the material as you would normally write it if it were part of a letter to a friend or a message being left for someone.
- Write the material as if you wanted to conceal your handwriting habits; disguise your writing.
- An analysis of these three paragraphs will help to illustrate the influence of speed, and particularly relative speed, on writing. The analysis will refer back to Saudek's signs of speed and slowness.

Paragraph 1 was written rapidly. The writer had read the material several times and knew what she was writing. The second paragraph was written in what she referred to as her normal writing. In paragraph 3 she was trying to disguise her writing. At no time in the experiment did she see the paragraph she just wrote. After writing each paragraph, it was removed from her and she wrote the next one.

PARAGRAPH 1

The line quality is smooth with no wavering or broken strokes. Some of the indicators of the good line quality are the tapered beginning and ending strokes, t-crosses, slash marks for i-dots, light up and darker downstrokes, etc.

There is a mixture of tendencies to the right and left throughout the text. The writer is urging her pen on to the right in the normal contraction and relaxation of her muscles and consistent with her writing habits. The tent-shaped t-staff in the word "that" is one indicator of tendency to the right.

The uncertainty of aim in placing i-dots, t-crosses, and the period is evident by their location and shape. Most of these features are slash marks or long tapered marks.

Figure 8.9

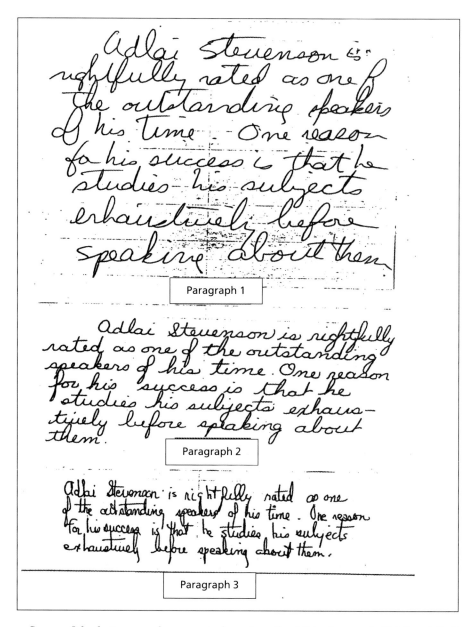

Paragraph 1

Paragraph 2

Paragraph 3

Some of the letters are degenerated, such as the "s" in the words "his" and "is," the "g" in "outstanding" the "m" in "them," etc.

The size of the writing is larger, and many of the letters are wider than in the other two paragraphs. A good example of the wider writing can be found in the spacing between the arches of the "n" in "Stevenson," and "outstanding," etc.

Although not as pronounced on the copy, there was a great difference in emphasis between up and downstrokes. An indication of this can be found on the upper projections of the "h," and "l" in "exhaustively" and the "k" in "speaking."

Another good indicator of the rapidness of this writing is found in the widening left margin. Because the writer is not paying attention to how she is writing but to the content of what she is writing, together with the desire to write the material rapidly, she did not notice that the left margin of the paper was actually becoming wider with each new sentence. In addition to the widening left margin, she paid very little attention to the pre-drawn baselines on the paper. As she moves across the paper from left to right, the baseline of the writing rises or, as in the case of the last line in paragraph 1, she curves the line in order to get the last bit of material on that line without having to start a new line of writing for just one word.

Notice the lack of consistency in the overall and relative slant of the writing. The overall slant tends to be more vertical, but with pronounced forward slanting long letters. Occasionally, some of the letters have a pronounced left slant; i.e., the "e" in "he."

PARAGRAPH 2

Paragraph 2 is also written rapidly, but not as rapidly as paragraph 1. Here the writer is not only concerned with the legibility of the writing, she is writing at a more normal relative speed of writing. The line quality of the writing is good, smooth, and there are numerous tapered beginning and ending strokes on letters. Some separation between the arches of the "m" in "them," the last word of the paragraph, indicates that she is increasing the relative speed of her writing. Further evidence of this can be found in the frequent use of rounded formations and connecting strokes.

The left margin is concave shaped to the right. As she is writing each line, the left margin becomes wider until she notices what is happening and starts to correct that by writing the bottom two lines farther to the left. In extended bodies of writing, the treatment of the left margin can be a gauge of the writer's relative speed and attention to the details of writing.

Note also the intermixing of counterclockwise and clockwise movements, particularly in the ending "g" on "outstanding" and "speaking." In the word "speaking," she writes this letter with a continuous counterclockwise movement while in the former she uses a capped oval formation. It takes more time to write the "g" in "outstanding" than it takes to write the same letter in "speaking."

Further, note the rightward overall slant of the writing. The overall slant is more consistent than that of the first paragraph, and the relative slant between individual letters is also more consistent.

PARAGRAPH 3

The line quality is wavering with some tremor, frequent pen stops, adjustments, etc. There is little if any real relative pressure habits between up and down-strokes, numerous blunt beginning and ending strokes, a mixing of printing and cursive letters, and a general inconsistency in the writing.

Some of the i-dots are placed directly above the staff and are dot shaped, indicating the pen was not moving when they were written. The t-crosses are more consistently placed both on the height of the staff, and the amount of the t-cross on either side of the staff is more consistent.

The overall slant of the writing is more vertical, with some features slanted to the left.

Notwithstanding the difference in absolute and relative speed of the writing of these three paragraphs and the effects caused by that difference in speed, are numerous writing habits this writer has that have remained constant:

- The relative spacing habits between words. Usually, this writer uses wide spacing between the words.
- The shapes of some of the letters within their context. For example, the "of" combination, the relative relationship between the components of the "f," the tent-shaped "r" in "reason" in paragraphs 1 and 3, the inconsistent use of terminal strokes on the letter "s," etc.
- The spacing between the lines of writing and the overlapping of those lines by the lower and upper projections.
- The attention to the left margin in paragraphs 2 and 3.

Relative speed of writing is important. While the absolute speed with which a person writes can vary significantly, the relative speed with which that writer writes remains uniform.

Because someone writes faster than another writer does not mean his writing is more natural than that of the slower writer. As Figure 8.9 has illustrated, writers can change the speed of their writing over very wide limits, and it is one of the easiest features of writing to change. It also can have a profound effect on the way people write each letter or other features, the shape and placement of diacritics, punctuation marks, etc. The slow writer's writing can be just as naturally written as the rapid writers, because the slow writer may not have the skill or ability to write rapidly for any length of time.

Circumstances and the importance of the document or the material in it can affect a writer's speed. If the writer is signing his name on a loan agreement to borrow a large sum of money to purchase a home, his writing may be more tremulous than when he signs a check to pay for food at the grocery store.

Other factors that can affect the speed of writing are the position of the writer when writing – standing, sitting, etc. – and the condition of the writing surface. If a rapid writer tries to write on a rough surface, the line quality will not be as good. The example in Figure 8.10 will help illustrate this point.

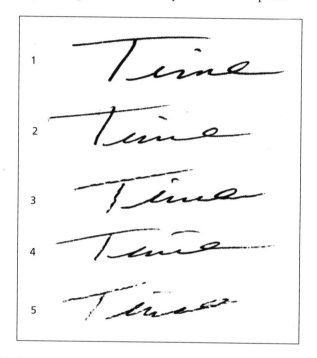

Figure 8.10

Figure 8.10 shows the writing of the word "Time" on five different surfaces:

1   On a desk with a piece of paper under the one being written on.
2   On the desk surface with no sheet of paper under the one being written on.
3   On the rough surface of a carrying case.
4   On an oak tabletop.
5   On a concrete slab.

In each instance, the writer tried to maintain the same overall speed of writing. Each of the writing surfaces had an effect on the writing. The first two show very little effect, except for the width and darkness of the line. Since the same ballpoint pen was used to write the five examples, the absence of a cushion sheet under the one being written affected the writing by providing a harder surface; and the size of the pen point, medium, is more obvious.

The tremor in the line, especially the "T" and terminal stroke of the "e" has a regularity about it caused by the texture of the surface. In numbers four and five, the regularity of the surface texture is less consistent, thus the consistency of the tremor is not as uniform.

Overall, speed of writing, relative speed of writing, the writing surface, and type of writing instrument used can all have an impact on each other. It is important that each be considered separately and collectively.

REFERENCES

Hilton, Ordway (1982) *Scientific Examination of Questioned Documents*, revised edn, New York, NY.

Huber, Roy A. and Headrick, A.M. (1999) *Handwriting Identification: Facts and Fundamentals*, New York: CRC Press.

Miller, Jr, Franklin (1977) *College Physics*, 4th edn, New York: Harcourt Brace Jovanovich, Inc.

Saudek, Robert (1978) *Experiments With Handwriting*, Sacramento, CA. First published in Great Britain by George Allen & Unwin.

CHAPTER 9

RATIOS –
RELATIVE RELATIONSHIPS

DEFINITION

Ratio is the relationship between two or more objects, in this case two or more components of handwriting. The components could be overall slant, spacing, and location of letters and words with respect to a pre-drawn or imaginary baseline, letter height, length of upper or lower projection, parts of the letter design, etc. In handwriting identification, another word frequently used for ratio is proportion.

> . . . it should be noted that it is not the *absolute* size of the basic letters which is of real importance.
>
> Much more important is the *proportion* in size between the various groups of letters. Still more important is the consistency with which a writer sticks to the table of proportions which he has sub-consciously selected for himself. (Quirke 1930: 33)

The writer goes on to say:

- Close adherence to normal size-proportions aids legibility.
- Consistent adherence to a fixed standard of size-proportions, even if the standard be not orthodox, also assists legibility.
- Exaggeration of the large letters does not affect legibility. (ibid.: 34)

He developed the following rule from his observations knowing that at the time it may not "be supported by experimental proofs of a summary nature" (ibid: 34) The rule states: "Each writer has a mean absolute size of handwriting, taking the basic letters as the index of size. This size varies within narrow limits for each writer. One and the same writer will have his absolute size of writing affected by the size of available writing space, presence or absence of ruling, width of ruling, degree of haste in execution, and temperament of the moment." (ibid.).

Since Quirke formulated the rule, many other FDEs have arrived at the same conclusion based on their observations and study of the handwriting of many different writers. One FDE, Harrison, states that: "Primarily, the ratio of a handwriting is a style characteristic, and it is the ratio in which there has been the greatest and most obvious change in those styles of handwriting which have been in vogue in the English-speaking world during the past two centuries." . . . "The relation between the heights of the short letters and the long is an important characteristic of a handwriting, as it tends to remain unaltered whether the writing be large or small, fast or slow and normal or disguised. . . . this is one of the features of copybook practice which is subjected to early and very considerable modification once the copybook fetters have been discarded" (Harrison 1966: 312). . . . "Once fixed, the ratio of a handwriting is very seldom altered, and experiment has shown that it is extremely difficult deliberately to effect a consistent change without a complete loss of fluency" (ibid: 313). " . . . the absolute size of a handwriting may vary according to the circumstances in which it is written, but this variability rarely extends to the *relative sizes* of the letters. This is a feature of handwriting which remains remarkably constant" (ibid: 313–314). Hilton observed that: "The proportional size of various letters and parts of compound letters, such as k and g, vary among writers . . . " (Hilton 1982: 157).

Ratios, proportions, whatever term is used, are very important. For any given writer, once established they are *relatively* constant as part of his handwriting habit(s), assuming he has reached graphic maturity. The reason for the use of the word relative is due to the fact that each of these features stands in relationship to another, i.e. a letter, word, line, etc. Realizing that ratios are important, exactly what ratios are being referred to? A few have been mentioned, but there are numerous others considered in some detail as follows:

RELATIVE SLANT

The *overall or average slant of the writing* is to be uniform for tall letters, small letters, and the components of individual letters. The degree of overall slant is dependent upon the copybook style of writing learned by the writer and, as a general rule, the angle should be the same as the slant of the legs of the small "m" and "n."

Because writers do not adhere to the copybook style of writing, but depart from it introducing into the writing their own individuality, the overall slant used is dependent upon each individual writer. One thing is certain: everyone's writing has a particular overall slant. The direction of that slant depends upon the preferences of the writer, the naturalness of his writing, and is influenced by the following:

- *The position of the writer's arm:* "If the elbow is held close against the side while writing, the degree of slant will be increased" (Quirke 1930: 47).

- *The way he holds his pen:* "If the pen be grasped at an unusually great distance from the point, . . . an increased slant will again be given to the writing" (ibid.).
- *The angle of the paper:* at what angle, relative to the center of his body, does the writer position the paper on the writing surface? One habit every writer has is to position the paper in front of him so that it is most comfortable to him when he writes. The place of the paper, primarily its angle, will affect the slope of the baseline (more about baseline later). Refer to the drawings below.

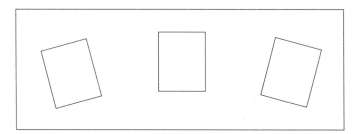

Figure 9.1

It is possible to view overall slant in three broad categories: right, vertical, and left (Figure 9.2). Some FDEs use terms like forward, straight up and down, or backward. Regardless of what name is given, the concept of overall slant is straightforward.

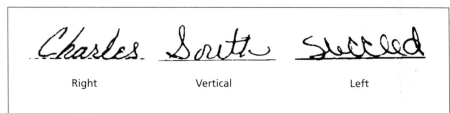

Figure 9.2
(Morris 1999: 7.)

Harrison determined that for all writers the normal range of overall slant, as shown in Figure 9.2, is within approximately 50 degrees (Harrison 1966: 329). Some handwriting examiners developed special handwriting protractors to measure the angle of slant. One of the main reasons for not using measuring devices of this type is the normal variation found in a person's writing. Normal variation is covered in Chapter 13. While such devices are not routinely used by the FDE today, they are useful for reference purposes when examining a traced signature or other occurrence where the writing is suspected of being duplicated from an original.

If the writer varies the overall slant of his writing beyond his normal limits, what effect would that action have on his writing?

- The symmetry of curved lines and letter size uniformity may be seriously affected.
- Significant changes in the qualities and features of the writing including letter design.

Because overall slant is one of the easiest things to change, most writers attempting to disguise their writing will usually change the overall slant because they know, or think, that by doing so the writing will be unidentifiable. Disguised writing is covered in Chapter 14.

There is another type of slant besides the overall slant of writing, it is the *relative slant between individual letters and the component parts of a letter.* Figure 9.3 shows the word "handwriting." The overall slant of the writing is to the right. The relative slant of the upper projections on the "h," "d," and "t" are not all the same. The slant of the upper projection on the "h," "d," and "t" are measurably different. Therefore, the relative slant of these upper projections is different. The relative slant between the upper projection of the "d" and the oval at its base is different. The slant of the oval is more to the right while the angle of the upper projection of the letter is vertical. This example illustrates the concept of relative slant between letters and between the component parts of letters.

Figure 9.3
(Morris 1999: 8.)

Also, note the difference in the angle of the "i" staff, following the "t," relative to the one preceding the "t." Their relative slants are also different. Another example is the difference in the angles of the legs of the "n" preceding the "g." It is this relative slant within and between individual letters that is hardest to duplicate when someone is trying to simulate another person's writing. Not only does the simulator have to duplicate these relative relationships of slant, they have to do it while writing at approximately the same relative speed as the writer of the model being simulated. This is virtually an impossible task and that is why relative slant is more significant than overall slant when the FDE is comparing writings for common authorship.

Figure 9.4

The writing of the name "George Babblemouth" by two different writers, taken from specimen handwriting forms used by the author as part of a class exercise on handwriting identification. The name and its relationship to any real person is purely coincidental (Morris 1999).

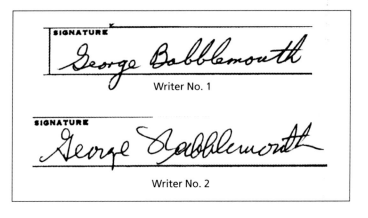

Figure 9.4 is another example of relative relationships. Two different writers have written the same name, "George Babblemouth." Besides differences in the shapes of letters, the use of connecting strokes, line quality, etc., there are differences in the relative slant between, and within, the components of common letters as written by each writer.

RELATIVE SPACING

Relative spacing is divided into four parts as follows:

1 Between words.
2 Between the name and initials in a signature.
3 Between letters within a word.
4 Between lines of writing in an extended body of writing.

Another relative spacing relationship that is important is the relative baseline relationship between individual letters within a word and the overall word with respect to the baseline, imaginary or pre-drawn. That topic will be discussed separately. First, a detailed discussion of the four topics listed above.

Between words

" . . . Narrow, normal, wide, or a mixture" (Morris 1999: 8). Word spacing in an extended body of writing; i.e., a sentence, paragraph, letter, etc., is not always uniform. Some writers leave little or no space between words while others space words farther apart using more normal spacing, or even larger spacing between words.

Using the width of the letter "o" as a reference, the spacing between words should be equal to the width of this letter. If the width of the spacing is less, it can be said that the relative spacing between words is narrow. If it is equal to the width of the letter, it is more normal; and if it is large enough that several "o's" could fit in the space, the relative spacing is large. It must be added here that the reason this topic is referred to as relative spacing is because writers do not always use uniform spacing between words. The topic of variation will be covered in detail in Chapter 13.

The example in Figure 9.5 can be referred to as typical of relatively normal spacing habits. Even though the spacing between each word is neither uniform or the exact size of the writer's letter "o," it is consistent enough and conforms to the average space expected for writing this size that it can be classified as a representation of normal spacing habit usage.

Figure 9.5

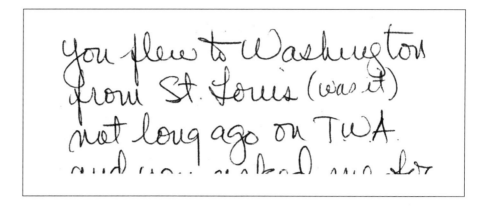

There are some writers who use such large spaces between words that it would be possible to fit five, six, or more "o's" in the space between the words. For example, in Figure 9.6 the spacing between the words "so" and "it" in the second line is much wider than between the other words in the example.

Figure 9.6

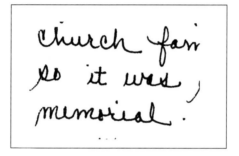

In both examples, the reader can easily see that the spacing between the words written by these two writers is not uniform. That is why the term "relative spacing" is used.

In some instances, writers use normal spacing habits between words but occasionally may connect the last letter of the word before the space with the first letter of the word following the space, for example, the "t"-cross and the "W" in the first line of Figure 9.5. Some writers leave little or no distance between the two words and, occasionally, even connect the letters with a lightly written pen drag. This writer lifts the pen briefly before placing it on the paper again to write the letter "W" in "Washington."

The importance of relative word spacing in handwriting identification cannot be overemphasized. Even if a writer is trying to disguise his writing by changing the slant and with the corresponding changes that occur in letter shapes, connecting strokes, etc., he frequently overlooks the relative spacing habits between words. So, what seems to determine how wide the relative spacing will be between words? Some of the things that can affect relative spacing between words are:

- The last letter of the word preceding the space and the first letter of the word following the space.
- The type and placement habits of punctuation marks.
- The relative speed of the writing and the direction of the pen after completing the last letter in the word preceding the space.

Between the name and initials in a signature

Some writers leave very little space between their given name and middle initial, or the middle initial and surname. The relative spacing between the name and initials is usually an important part of the signature. The writer may place the middle initial closer to the given name or surname thus offsetting it within the space between the two names. He may always place it in the center of the space between them, to the left of the punctuation mark usually located half way between the two, or the initial will be closer to the given name. Each writer is different and this writing feature must be based assessed on how each individual uses this space.

Between letters within a word

The relative spacing relationship between letters within a word is also very significant. The examples in Figure 9.7 help illustrate this point.

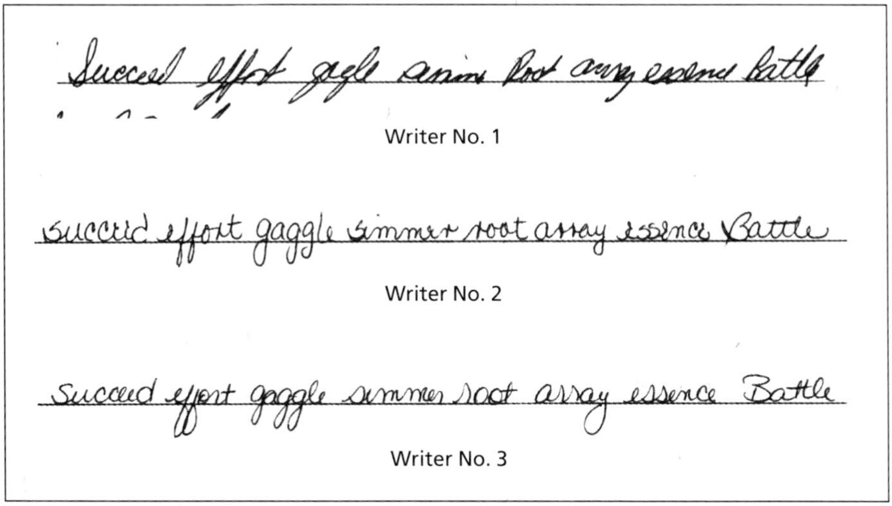

Writer No. 1

Writer No. 2

Writer No. 3

Figure 9.7

The writing of the same words by three different writers. Note the different relative spacing habits between letters.

Between lines of writing in an extended body of writing

When a person writes an extended body of writing, such as a letter or correspondence, possibly one or two pages long, they may use pre-lined or unlined paper. While the choice of paper can have an effect on some of the details of letter forms and other features of writing, it may have no effect on the relative spacing between lines. As illustrated in Figure 9.8, each of the four writers use different relative spacing habits between the lines of their extended writings, letters. Only the last writer used pre-lined paper. That is not to say the features found in his writing would only be exhibited when he writes on this paper and not pre-lined paper. In fact, the pre-drawn lines serve as a reference and possibly a strong reminder to him of how he should write the material.

Figure 9.8

Samples by four different writers.

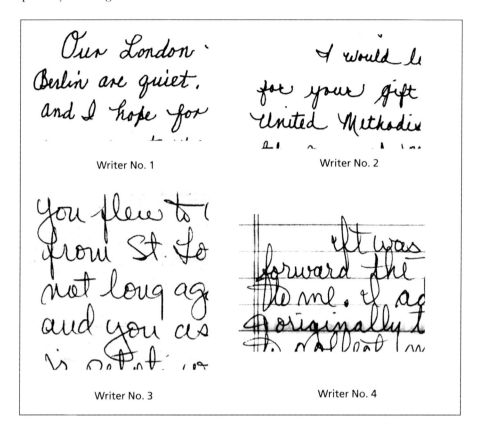

Writer No. 1

Writer No. 2

Writer No. 3

Writer No. 4

Writer No. 1 writes in such a way that the upper and lower projections of letters does not overlap the writing in the lines above or below them. The lines of writing are rather uniformly spaced, as are the words in each line.

Writer No. 2 writes long lower projections only on some of the letters such as the "f" and "y." On the letter, a part of which is shown in the figure, there were no occurrences of intersection, lower projections with tall letters, and upper projections of letters on the line below.

Writer No. 3 typically writes long lower projections so that they intersect with the tall and short letters in the line below. In the portion of writing shown in the figure, the writer does make long, wide lower projections on the letter "y" (and although not shown on the sample, the letters "f," "g," and "p,") such that they occasionally intersect the upper projections of some letters on the line above. In the sample shown in the figure, it appears this writer uses a uniform distance between the lines of writing. However, in the middle of the letter from which this sample was taken, the distance between the lines widens as the writer approaches the middle of the sheet of paper, and becomes narrower as the writing approaches the bottom of the sheet of paper. When this happens, the lower projections intersect the writing on the line below, more at the top and bottom of the sheet of paper and less frequently in the middle third of the sheet's length.

Writer No. 4 writes in such a way that the upper and lower projections of the letters intersect the writing on the line above; and occasionally the lower projections intersect the writing two lines below. For example, the lower case "f" in "forward" has such a long lower projection that it extends through the baseline of the writing below the line on which it is written.

Although the upper projections of letters are long, they are not as long as the height of the lower projection of the "f" in "forward." As a result, many of them cross the pre-drawn baseline immediately above, but they do not cross the baseline above the one just referred to.

Figure 9.9

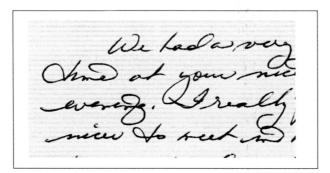

Figure 9.9 shows writing on a sheet of paper with wide pre-printed light gray horizontal lines as a background. They are not spaced or designed to be pre-drawn baselines for the writers use. However, for the writer, they can subconsciously serve as a reference line for the placement of the writing or have an affect on the writing the same way as a pre-drawn baseline.

RELATIVE PRESSURE HABITS

In the act of writing, there are essentially three types of pressure habits used by writers as follows:

- *Hand pressure* – the amount of pressure exerted on the writing surface by the palm of the hand during the act of writing. Not every writer writes this way. Some hold the palm of their hand above the writing surface, in which case their hand pressure is zero. Most writers though, place their palm on the writing surface and use it as a pivot point.

The amount of pressure exerted depends upon a number of factors, and for any given writer it can be very little or a lot of pressure depending upon the writer. For example, someone who has trouble controlling involuntary hand movements when writing, for example a person with a mild case of Parkinson's disease, may use more hand pressure than someone without the disease who just rests their palm on the writing surface, using it as a pivot point.

■ *Grip pressure* – this is the amount of pressure exerted on the pen by the fingers to hold it in the hand. How tightly does the writer grasp the pen with his fingers and hand when writing? The pen should be held comfortably in the fingers using just enough grip pressure to guide its movements in a rhythmical pattern determined by the contraction and relaxation of the writer's muscles. If the pen is clasped too tightly the writers hand tires rapidly, and the fingers and hand muscles will cramp. This is generally referred to as writer's cramp. If the grip pressure is too little, the pen can move in unwanted directions and leave a record of those random movements as extraneous marks on the paper.

During the act of writing, a writer at the letter impulse level or above usually uses varying amounts of grip pressure to hold the pen. As he pulls the pen toward his body, the grip pressure on the pen increases because the muscles in his hand and fingers contract. When the pen is pushed away from the body the grip pressure becomes less because those muscles that had contracted are now relaxing. This is true if the hand holding the pen holds it in such a way that the hand and finger muscles can contract and relax in a rhythmical pattern. If the writer grasps the pen in his hand, as he would a rope he is about to climb, then the combination of hand and finger muscle contraction necessary to write in a rhythmical fashion does not occur.

When the pen is held in the right or left hand, and the palm of that hand is placed above the line of writing, the wrist turned at a sharp angle so the point of the pen points in the direction of the writer, then the following relative pressure features will be found in the writing. When the wrist is held in this position, the manifestation of the relative pressure habits will be the opposite of those described above. The writer will write downstrokes as lighter lines and upstrokes as heavy or darker lines. This happens because as the muscles relax the writer pushes the pen point toward the writer and as they contract he pulls the pen away from his body.

■ *Writing pressure* – writing pressure is the amount of pressure exerted on the pen point during the act of writing, and is the result of a rhythmical interaction between grip and writing pressure. Relative pressure habits are usually manifested in the darkness of the written line that results from variations in writing pressure. This contrast in line darkness and lightness is also referred to as shading. Shading is seen as the variation in darkness of the written line (Figure 9.10). It results from the difference in the amount of ink applied to the paper by the pen from changes in pen point pressure on the paper during the act of writing and is caused by the contraction and relaxation of muscles as described above. Figure 9.10 helps illustrate this concept.

Uniform   Light up/heavy down   Heavy up/light down

Figure 9.10

Figure 9.10 shows the writing of three individuals. The first illustrates uniform relative pressure habits causing little or no relative variation in pen pressure on the paper, shading. The written lines are uniform in width, except for the tapered beginning and ending strokes of the "V" and two lowercase "I's."

The name "Nancy" was written by a writer whose relative pressure habits are more evident. Notice the light upstroke on the left arch of the "n" and the left side or upstroke of the lower projection of the "y." Although not as noticeable, the connecting stroke between the "nc" is also written with less writing pressure.

The "J" in "Johnson" shows the left side of the upper and lower loops of the projections on the "J" as heaver lines than the right side of the letter connecting them. The writer of this letter is left-handed and places his hand above the writing, turning the wrist so the finger muscles contract as he pulls the pen away from his body then relaxing as he pushes the pen toward him. Here the manifestation of relative pressure habits is opposite that of the other two writers who each hold their pen with the right hand placing the palm of their hand below the writing. This illustration does not mean that all left-handed writers write this way or have relative pressure habits opposite from those used by right-handed writers. Figure 9.11 shows an illustration of a left-handed writer who holds his hand and fingers below the baseline of the writing. The hand and finger muscles contract as the pen is brought toward the writer and relax as the pen is moved away from the writer.

Figure 9.11

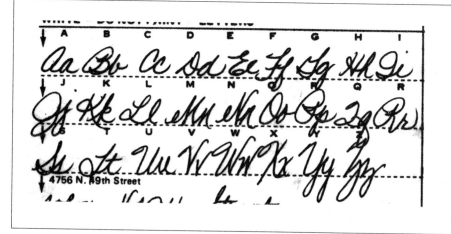

The key concept here is the placement of the hand, angle of the wrist (regardless of whether the writer is right- or left-handed), and the direction of the pen point during the rhythmical contraction and relaxation of the hand and finger muscles directing the pen point.

Figure 9.12

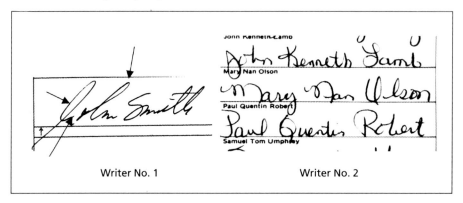

Writer No. 1   Writer No. 2

Figure 9.12 shows the writing of two different writers, each with their own unique application of relative pressure habits. For example, in writing the name "John Smith," writer No. 1 begins writing the upper loop of the "J" using enough writing pressure that the line is darker during the movement of the pen from the beginning of the letter to a point approximately one-fourth the way up the left side of the looped upper projection. Then the writing pressure is reduced and the line is lighter in color, indicating less writing pressure. Shortly before reaching the apex of the loop, the writer again starts to apply writing pressure to the pen and the line becomes darker. On the upper projection of the "h," the writer starts off using relatively more pressure on the connecting stroke; and at the point of its intersection with the downstroke, the writer begins using less pressure as evidenced by the lighter line. As he approaches the apex of the upper projection, he again applies pressure to the pen point creating a darker downstroke. However, the heavier writing pressure is not maintained for the length of the downstroke. Shortly after beginning the downstroke, pressure on the pen point gradually decreases and the width of the line narrows and becomes lighter through the turn of the connecting stroke to make the left side of the arch of the "h." The writing pressure becomes even less as the writer moves the pen away from the body until reaching a point near the arch of the "h."

Writer No. 2 also applies pressure to different parts of the letters. For example, the upper case "J" in "John," the upper case "L" in "Lamb," the arches of the "M" in "Mary," and "N" in "Nan," lower case letters such as the "l" in "Olson," and the connecting strokes between the lower case letters in "Paul," and "Robert." Relative pressure habits are not limited to just the making of letters as this example shows.

The rhythmical contraction and relaxation of muscles is individual to each writer and over time becomes a writing habit. Because this rhythmical activity is individualistic and becomes habit, it is a very important characteristic of hand-writing.

RELATIVE HEIGHT RELATIONSHIP BETWEEN LETTERS

In many of the examples already shown in this book, the reader has probably noticed that not all of the upper case and tall letters, as written by a single writer, have the same relative height relationship nor do all the lower case letters. As in the discussion on relative pressure habits, the relative height relationships between letters is a very important characteristic of writing. Relative height relationships between letters are described as follows:

- Between the heights of upper case letters.
- Between the heights of the upper projections of tall letters.
- Between the heights of upper case letters and upper projections of tall letters.
- Between the heights of lower case letters.
- Between the heights of component parts of lower case letters, such as the arch of the "h" and the tall and upper case letters.
- Between the heights of lower case and tall letters.
- Between the heights of lower and upper case letters.

In summary, this relationship exists between all the components of letters rising *above* the baseline of the writing. Without being repetitious, the same relationship extends to all components of a letter extending *below* the baseline.

THE RELATIVE RELATIONSHIP BETWEEN INDIVIDUAL LETTER HEIGHT AND WIDTH

Like the relative relationship between the overall heights of letters, each writer has his own way of treating the height to width relationship of each individual letter. Figure 9.13 shows examples of the words "Abbot," "Gaggle," and "Root" as written by four different writers.

Each letter in each word for each writer has a relative height/width relationship. In the word "Abbot," as written by Writer No. 1, the printed form of the letter "A" is approximately as wide as it is tall if the ornate approach stroke that resembles the letter "e" sitting to the left of the letter is included.

The measurement of these parameters is very easy to see with the aid of a grid (Figure 9.14). The height of the letter is measured by the distance from the baseline to the apex of the letter. The width is measured from the starting point

Figure 9.13

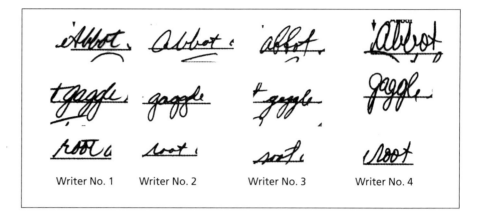

Writer No. 1   Writer No. 2   Writer No. 3   Writer No. 4

Figure 9.14

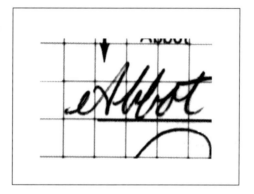

of the approach stroke to the foot of the right side of the letter where it makes contact with the baseline. If the width measurement is referenced between the starting point and the location of the apex of the letter, dropping an imaginary perpendicular line from the apex to the baseline at that point, then the width of the letter is approximately half again as wide as it is tall. Regardless of the chosen reference points, they must remain constant throughout an examination and comparison of the same letters, features, and other characteristics of the writing.

Turning to Figure 9.15, what is the height/width relationship between the component parts of the letter "b"? In this example, the upper projection of the first "b" is about twice the height of the bowl of the letter. The overall height of the upper projection of the letter compared to its width is approximately four times the width of the base of the letter. The same relationship, four-to-two, also applies to the second "b." In this situation the width of the letter is the distance between the two horizontal arrow heads pointing to the left and right side of the letter. The height is the distance between the bottom of the deep narrow bowl of the letter to the top of the upper projection of the letter.

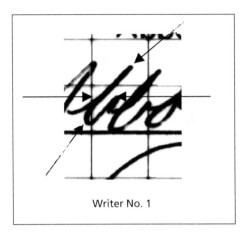

Writer No. 1

Figure 9.15

The word "gaggle," written by Writer No. 2, is enlarged and shown in Figure 9.16. Notice the variation in the size of the ovals written above the baseline and those written below the baseline. Also, notice the difference in the slant of each oval. This writing of the word shows the overall slant of the word, the relative slant relationship between each part of each letter in the word, the relative size relationship of the component parts of each letter, and the relative placement of each letter with respect to the baseline, which will be discussed in more detail later.

Figure 9.16

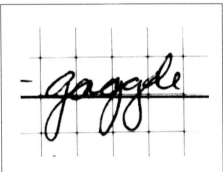

The reader is encouraged to obtain a transparent grid and samples of writing and place the grid over the writing to observe the relative relationship between individual letter height and width, and the other relative relationships between words. The grid will also serve as a useful tool for determining whether a signature or other writing has been traced.

RELATIVE RELATIONSHIP BETWEEN LETTER(S) AND BASELINE

When one learns to write, one of the lessons reinforced in the process is to write letters and words so that they sit on the pre-drawn baseline. Even when that baseline is imaginary, writers try to adhere to the rule. The concept behind this rule is rather simple: the base or foot of each letter is to rest on the baseline of the writing.

As writers mature, they depart from this training in the same way they departed from other training and again introduce into their writings their own individuality. In reviewing the examples of the same four words written by four different writers (Figure 9.13), we see how each one adheres to the baseline rule.

For Writer No. 1, the "Ab" and "ot" combinations in "Abbot" are written above the baseline. Only the bottom of the second "b" actually rests on the baseline. In "gaggle," the connecting stroke between the "le" and the "e" do not touch the baseline. The right side of the letter "r," the double "oo," and the ending stroke of the "t" in "root" do not sit on the baseline.

Writer No. 3 writes letters that intersect the baseline so that part of the letter is below and part above the baseline. Even though Writer No. 2 does the same thing in the word "Abbot," Writer No. 3 is more consistent in ignoring the baseline.

A review of Figure 9.12, Writer No. 2, shows how this writer treats the placement of letters with respect to the baseline. The process is easy if there is a pre-drawn baseline on the paper. But, what if there is no pre-drawn baseline?

When there is no pre-drawn baseline on the paper a number of factors must be considered. First, how does the writer place the unlined paper in front of him before writing? When he starts to write does the imaginary baseline rise as he proceeds from left to right, or does it fall?

Figure 9.17

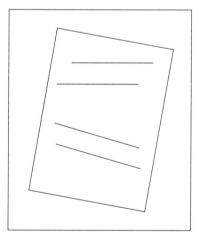

Figure 9.17 illustrates this idea of rising and falling baselines. As shown, it is assumed the writer is left-handed. It makes no difference whether the paper is angled, as in this illustration, or turned so it is angled to the right. The treatment of letters, letter combinations, words, phrases, and lines with respect to an imaginary baseline is individual to the writer.

The angle of the baseline may even change as he writes. The writer may begin by writing with an upward slanting baseline and then change to a more perpendicular baseline with respect to the edge of the paper. Whatever he does, it must be viewed as possibly a variation from copybook, individual to the writer, and that it has significance for identification purposes.

RELATIVE PLACEMENT HABITS

What are relative placement habits? The definition is best stated by asking the following question: where does the writer place the material he is writing? Placement of material on a form or a sheet of paper can be significant. As some of the illustrations in this book have shown, different writers start and stop their writing at different locations. Locations, such as sentence indentation, treatment and shape of margins, use of space, starting and stopping points, etc., all come under the general topic of relative placement habits. For example, Figure 9.18 illustrates the relative placement habits of the first word in a sentence as written by two different writers. Writer No. 1 usually indents the first word of a paragraph about one inch from the left margin. In this example, the left margin is set by a pre-drawn double red line. Writer No. 2 used a sheet of unlined paper and did not indent the first word of any of the paragraphs of the letter. The amount of indentation used by a writer can be a characteristic of an individual to its writer.

Figure 9.18

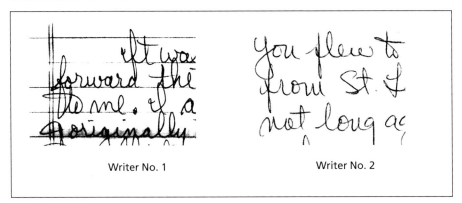

Writer No. 1   Writer No. 2

The relative margin habits of the writer are also important, particularly for extended bodies of writing, such as a letter. In Figure 9.18, Writer No. 1 places the written material against the pre-drawn left margin lines on the paper. Writer No. 2, having no pre-drawn lines on the paper, has a slightly bowed-shape left-hand margin. The slight bow is to the right, as illustrated in Figure 9.19. A more complete explanation of why this occurs is given in Chapter 8.

The relative length of parts of letters can also be determined by the presence or absence of a pre-drawn baseline and how it influences the writer. For example, a writer writes an upper-case cursive letter "L." When writing the terminal stroke of this letter, when there is a pre-drawn baseline present, the

Figure 9.19

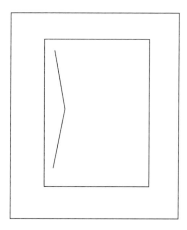

writer stops at a point on or very close to the pre-drawn baseline. When no pre-drawn baseline is present, the writer will write a longer ending stroke on the letter because he is not influenced by the pre-drawn baseline (Figure 9.20).

Figure 9.20

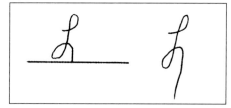

Not all writers do this; the point being made here is, if they do, it may be an individual characteristic and significant for identification purposes.

SUMMARY

Relative relationships are *very* important. An examination of handwriting for comparison purposes is not complete until all possible relative relationships of the writing(s) are determined and compared.

REFERENCES

Harrison, Wilson R. (1966) *Suspect Documents Their Scientific Examination*, 2nd impression with Supplement, London.

Hilton, Ordway (1982) *Scientific Examination of Questioned Documents*, revised edn, New York, NY.

Morris, Ronald N. (1999) "Handwriting and Hand Printing Identification for the Investigator," unpublished; a study guide written for use as a text when teaching the fundamentals of handwriting identification to investigators.

Quirke, Arthur Joseph (1930) *Forged, Anonymous, and Suspect Documents*, London.

CHAPTER 10

BEGINNING, CONNECTING AND ENDING STROKES

Beginning strokes are movements made by a writer either before or after placing the pen on the paper, even though they are typically referred to as those marks made on the paper before writing the body of a letter. Connecting strokes are pen movements used by a writer to connect letters, and sometimes even words, together. These connecting strokes may be recorded on the paper or take place in the air as the pen moves from one point to another. Ending strokes are movements made by a writer either on the paper or in the air after writing the last letter in a word before proceeding onto the first letter in the next word. As mentioned above, occasionally words are connected together by light pen marks left on the paper as the pen is moved from one word to another. Another name for these lightly written strokes is "feather strokes." This same name is applied to similar strokes occurring during the writing of individual components of a single letter.

The shape of beginning, connecting, and ending strokes is individual to the writer. Copybook standards show how the person is to write them, in accordance with a particular handwriting system. However, as with every other aspect of writing, as he develops in graphic maturity, he departs from the copybook style of writing and incorporates into his writing his own individuality. For beginning, connecting, and ending strokes these may be very plain or very embellished depending upon the writer.

Beginning strokes are also referred to as initial strokes (Harrison 1966: 315), a form of embellishment (Osborn 1929: 256), initial emphasis (Saudek 1978: 379), flying start (Roman 1968: 152), etc. Harrison, Osborn, and Saudek place emphasis on their presences or absences, but Harrison believes that their presence in one body of writing by a person and absence in another body of writing by the same person "does not mean that it cannot have been written by the author of . . . " (Harrison 1966: 315). The presences or absences of these strokes are part of the writer's normal variation. Figure 10.1 illustrates this point by showing upper case letters written by three different writers using and not using beginning strokes on the same letter. Their use or non-use can have a profound effect on the pictorial appearance of the letter. In the case of Writers

No. 2 and 3, they use two different beginning strokes, and in the case of Writer No. 3 he even changes the shape of the letter.

Figure 10.1

Writer No. 1   Writer No. 2   Writer No. 3

As mentioned above, beginning strokes are not always recorded on the writing surface, the paper. The following example will help illustrate this point. A writer sitting at a desk positions a piece of paper in front of him, picks up the pen, and moves his arm into position to write. Before the pen makes contact with the paper, his hand, fingers, and pen traverse a path in the air from where the pen was resting on the table to the starting point of his writing on the paper. The form and direction these air movements take can be directly related to the location of the beginning point of the writing as determined by the letter or figure to be written. An illustration of this is found in Figure 10.2.

Figure 10.2

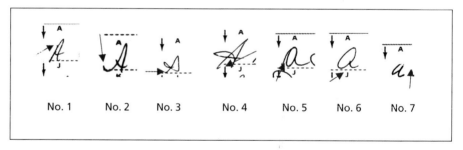

No. 1   No. 2   No. 3   No. 4   No. 5   No. 6   No. 7

Figure 10.2 shows two different styles of the letter "A" written by seven different writers. The direction of the pen and the point at which it made contact with the paper is pointed out by the large arrows. These same arrows show the direction of the hand movement before the pen point made contact with the paper. In addition to the different shapes of the letter forms, the way each writer wrote them, and the details of each letter, its components are also different and reflect the writing habits of its writer.

Some authors have referred to this motion of the fingers, hand, and arm above the writing surface as an air bridge. These air bridge movements can occur at any point in the writing, as shown in Figure 10.3.

Figure 10.3 shows the writing of different words by four writers. Writers No. 1 and 2 raise the pen off the paper between the upper and lower case letters within the word. Writer No. 3 drags his pen between the ending stroke of the

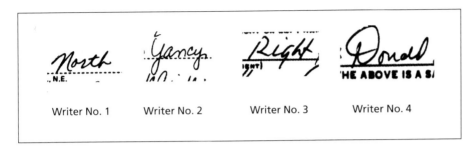

Figure 10.3

Writer No. 1   Writer No. 2   Writer No. 3   Writer No. 4

upper case "R" and lower case "i," leaving a feather stroke between them as well as between the "i" and "g." Writer No. 4 lifts the pen between the "D" and "o," but not between the "n" and "a." This writer drags his pen over the paper between the lower case "n" and "a," leaving a feather stroke between the end of the former and the beginning of the latter.

What is a feather stroke? Some FDEs refer to it as the light, non-continuous line between two letters, parts of a letter, words, etc.

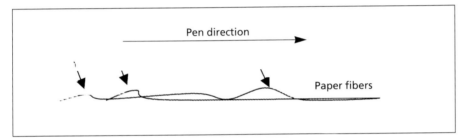

Figure 10.4

Figure 10.4 illustrates the movement of the pen over the paper surface. Paper is a porous substance made of fibers placed on top of each other in a random pattern. If a pen is raised from the surface enough so it skips along the top of the raised paper fibers, just touching them as it moves from left to right, a lightly written, non-continuous line would present. An example of a feather line is illustrated in Figure 10.5.

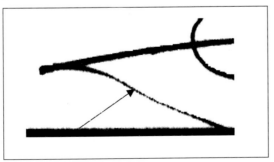

Figure 10.5

As mentioned previously, air bridges are not limited to pen motions at the beginning and ending of a letter, word, or any other part of the writing. They can, and frequently do, occur between letters within a word, punctuation mark, word, etc. and the point where the pen makes contact with the paper to begin the writing of the next letter or word.

Figure 10.6

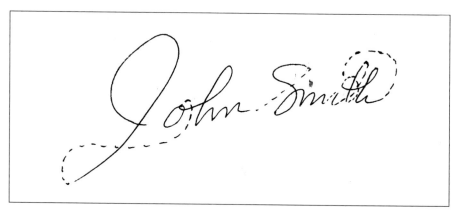

The dotted lines in Figure 10.6 show the movement of the pen between letters in the name "John Smith." The following is a description of the movements in the writing of beginning, connecting, and ending strokes, and the air bridges between the letters and words.

1   The pen was in motion at the time it made contact with the paper to begin the writing of the letter "J" in "John." Evidence of this pen movement is found in the tapered beginning stroke of the letter. Had the writer placed the pen on the paper before beginning the act of writing, there would be a well-defined pen point or spot of ink on the paper, as there is on the "R" in Figure 10.8. Microscopically, a small tapered point is present on the beginning stroke of the "J" in "John." The material in Figure 10.8 illustrates other examples of the pen being placed on the paper before the act of writing begins.

Further, the writing pressure at the beginning of the "J" is not heavy. It increases as the writer continues writing the letter, particularly the downstroke on the right side of the letter. The writer of the material in Figure 10.8 places the pen on the paper, starts the writing movement, and uses relatively uniform writing pressure throughout the material.

As the writer completes the letter "J," he starts raising the pen from the surface of the paper resulting in a long, tapered ending stroke. This gradual reduction of writing pressure as he nears the end of the letter is associated with the relative speed of his writing, graphic maturity, and the certainty he has about how the letter should be made.

The arrows point to the tapered beginning and ending stroke of the "J" in Figure 10.7, and the blunt beginning strokes on the "R," the numerals, and the "S" in Figure 10.8. The writer of the material in Figure 10.8 occasionally has tick marks at the beginning and ending of some letters, for example the foot of the downstroke on the number "7" and the cross bar and top of the staff on the number "4." Blunt beginning

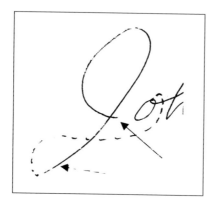

Figure 10.7

Figure 10.8

and ending strokes occur because the writer places the pen point on the paper before moving it. Tick marks are the result of the pen point being raised from the paper surface at a particular point and the small ink mark left on the fibers as it is removed.

2   The dotted line connecting the bottom of the "J" and the top of the "o" shows the movement of the pen between these two letters. The pen is placed on the paper in proximity with the loop at the top of the letter "o", which will be discussed shortly. After the writer reapplies the pen to the paper, he begins to make the downstroke, left side, of the "o." The downstroke is written with more writing pressure than the right side of the letter. This is the result of the writer's relative pressure habits, a topic discussed in Chapter 9.

3   After completing the writing of the oval of the letter "o," the writer makes a loop at the top of the letter using a counterclockwise stroke to form the small oval, see Figure 10.9, and then begins writing the connecting stroke between the "o" and the "h."

4   The connecting stroke between the "o" and "h" is made with a sweeping underhand movement between the end of the small oval on the "o" and the top of the upper projection of the "h." The relative pressure variation used when making this connecting stroke is seen in the density variation of the line. The pen rises slightly as the writer releases both his grip and writing pressure on the pen as he moves it away from his body. At the top of the upper projection of the "h," the grip and writing pressure increase as the pen is drawn toward the writer.

Figure 10.9

5   At the bottom of the left side of the upper projection of the "h," the writer comes to a complete stop. At this point, he changes the direction of the pen and makes the pointed arch of the "h," after which he again brings the pen to a complete stop at the foot of the right side of the arch. There is no "connecting stroke," as such, between the "h" and "n." The writer moves from the former into the latter at the stopping point, located on the foot of the right side of the arch.

6   After making the letter "n," he again brings the pen to a complete stop before starting the ending stroke, see Figure 10.10. The ending stroke is the short tapered, slightly curved line extending to the right from the foot of the down stroke on the right side of the second arch of the "n." It is relatively short and its tapered shape again illustrates the fact that the writer is gradually lifting the pen off the paper surface as the line is written.

Figure 10.10

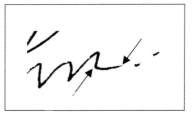

Figure 10.11

7   Figure 10.11 shows the movement of the hand, the air bridge, between the end of the ending stroke on the "n" in "John," and the beginning stroke of the capital "S" in "Smith." The beginning stroke of the "S" is not as tapered as the ending stroke of the preceding letter. It is more consistent with the way the writer writes the beginning

stroke of the "J" in "John." The writer does not actually stop his forward movement before starting to write the "S," nor does he bring the pen into contact with the paper over a longer period resulting in a long tapered beginning stroke. He applies writing pressure sooner on the beginning stroke without bringing the pen to a complete stop and there is no tick mark indicating contact with the paper surface at some point away from where he actually starts writing the letter. As he approaches the beginning point of the letter "S" his hand is still moving, just not as rapidly.

8   After completing the "Sm" combination, at the right foot of the "m," see Figure 10.12, he turns the pen slightly to the right and lifts it off the paper causing a small tick mark to be left on the paper. The air bridge connection between the "m" and "i" is made after which he again applies pressure to the pen making the downstroke or staff of the "i." The top of the "i" staff is tapered because the writer increases writing pressure as he moves the pen toward the foot of the letter. Another tick mark is found at the foot of the "i" staff even though the writer did not complete the turn at the foot of the "i" before lifting the pen. These two movements are virtually identical even though the angle of movements causing the ticks is slightly different.

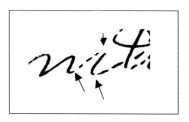

Figure 10.12

9   After making the staff of the "i," the writer again raises the pen from the paper and moves it away from him to the beginning of the downstroke or staff of the letter "t." The air bridge between the bottom of the "i" staff and the top of the "t" staff is a counterclockwise pen movement.

10   At the bottom of the "t" staff, the pen is again raised from the paper and another counterclockwise movement is made, through smaller in diameter, to the point where he begins to write the letter "h." This beginning stroke for the letter "h" is also the "t" cross. As the beginning stroke is made, the writer increases the writing pressure enough to have a dark line across the "t" staff and then begins to lessen the writing pressure as he pushes the pen away from him to make the looped upper projection of the "h."

11   In the name "John," the writer brought the pen to a complete stop at the foot of the staff of the "h" then began to make the arch of the letter. Here, he does not stop the writing act, but makes a curved line between the letter's staff and the left side of the arch of the letter.

12   After making the arch of the letter, he then makes the "i" dot placing it over the staff of the "i." He does this with a counterclockwise motion of the pen, after making the ending stroke on the arch of the "h" to a point above the "i" staff where he makes the

"i" dot. The "i" dot is actually a small slash mark because the pen was moving as it made contact with the paper and was shortly thereafter removed from the paper surface.

This analysis of the pen movements by this writer in the writing of "John Smith" is typical of the type of analysis that must be performed on all writings. Beginning, connecting, and ending strokes are not uniformly written by all writers. Even those written by the same writer contain some variation.

Figure 10.13 shows the beginning, connecting, and ending strokes of another writer with completely different writing habits. She frequently begins a letter when the pen is in motion; however, notice that at the end of most of the words she brings the pen to a complete stop, leaving a very blunt ending stroke denoted by the black dot at its end. Not all of the ending strokes have this blunt ending. Some of them are long tapered strokes, such as the one on the "s" in "thanks" and " . . . ness."

In addition to the different treatment of the ending strokes, also look at the beginning strokes on the letter "d." They are long, have taper ends, and show the writer coming up from under the imaginary baseline to the beginning point of the oval of the letter "d."

Figure 10.13

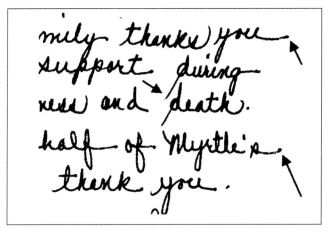

The length and direction of pen movements in making beginning, connecting, and ending strokes can be a unique feature of a person's writing, so too the embellishments added to letters by these strokes. Some writers use embellished beginning, connecting, and ending strokes. Their shape and the way they are made are important as they are a manifestation of how the writer moves the pen before and during the act of writing.

REFERENCES

Harrison, Wilson R. (1966) *Suspect Documents Their Scientific Examination*, 2nd edn, London.

Hilton, Ordway (1982) *Scientific Examination of Documents*, revised edn, New York.

Osborn, Albert S. (1929) *Questioned Documents*, 2nd edn, Albany, NY: Boyd Printing Company.

Roman, Klara G. (1968) *Encyclopedia of The Written Word*, New York.

Saudek, Robert (1978) *Experiments with Handwriting*, Sacramento, CA. First published in Great Britain by George Allen & Unwin.

CHAPTER 11

WRITING INSTRUMENTS AND THEIR INFLUENCE

THEIR INFLUENCE ON HOW A PERSON WRITES

The influence a particular type of writing instrument has on a writer today is a function of which type of instrument he uses on a daily basis. Today there are many different types of writing instruments; some of them are:

1 *The fountain pen.* A very old style of writing instrument, it uses either a refillable or disposable ink reservoir. Ink flows from the reservoir through a small opening to a feed bar consisting of an input capillary, fins to hold ink displaced by air in the reservoir, and a feeder capillary that is grooved which carries ink to, and supports the nib. Ink flows onto the paper through the slit in the nib that is aligned with the feeder capillary groove in the feed bar. There are many different types and sizes of nibs for these pens, and each one can have a significant impact on the writer's writing.

2 *The ballpoint pen.* The ballpoint pen is a relatively recent invention, 1954 in Argentina, compared to the fountain pen. It consists of a long, hollow ink column inside a cylinder attached to a ball housing. Inside the ball housing is a ball socket with ink flow channels that allows the thick pasty ink in the column to be transferred to the ball and onto the paper. The ink is made with oils and dyes, is very thick, and is actually printed on the paper as the ball turns in the ball socket. Ballpoint pens, like nib pens, come with different size points.

3 *The fiber tip or porous point pens.* These pens use capillaries to carry ink from the reservoir to the paper or other writing surface. The point consists of a stiff, cylindrically shaped rod of fiber material inserted into the end of the pen. They, too, can be purchased with many different point shapes and sizes ranging from ultra fine to broad markers used to mark on poster paper or special boards.

4 *The roller ball pen.* The roller ball pen is a more recent development and usually uses a combination of water-based, liquid ink with a ballpoint. Their operation is similar to the ballpoint pen. This writing instrument is usually marked to the writer who likes the feel of a nib pen with liquid ink but wants the convenience of a ballpoint pen. Like the ballpoint pen, the size of the ball and its contact with the paper will determine the thickness of the line.

5 *Gel ink pens.* This is the newest type of writing instrument. The ink is stored as a gel in

the reservoir until it is needed and is turned into a liquid by the movement of the ball.

6   *The pencil.* They come in both a wood case or in a mechanical housing that allows the lead to be replaced after it is used. Pencil lead is made using graphite for blackness, "China Clay" for hardness or polymer resin that gives it strength and smoothness when writing. Pencil lead is graded to describe its hardness. As a person writes with a pencil, the lead is worn away. It is also possible to erase pencil lines from a sheet of paper.

There are other types of writing instruments such as the crayon, etc., but they will not be discussed here.

The FDE should have a collection of different writing instruments at his disposal. Why? Because, there are many occasions when he will want to conduct an experiment to verify whether the effect he is observing on a document was made with a particular type of writing instrument. A few examples will help to explain why. Fountain pen and roller ball ink are liquid. Paper fibers will absorb this ink and there may even be some feathering of the ink in the fibers. Usually just looking at the line is not sufficient to determine whether the writing was done with a fountain pen or a roller ball. The written line must be studied under the microscope to see if there is an indentation in the paper caused by the ball.

Many times ballpoint pens will leave an impression of a ball in the paper. The difference between the ballpoint pen and the roller ball impression will be the optical appearance of the resulting line or mark on the paper.

The pencil will leave clumps of "lead" on the paper, an impression in the paper where it was used to write the line, and even black smudge marks where the "lead" has been wiped with a finger or another sheet of paper. Each writing instrument has its own individual characteristics and the FDE should be familiar with them.

SIGNS OF PEN MOVEMENT AND STROKE DIRECTION

Stroke direction is an important part of determining whether a particular writer wrote a questioned writing. Each of the writing instruments described above leave their own unique characteristics in the paper as they move across the papers surface.

Paper is a porous, fiber material. As a ballpoint pen, or pencil, moves across the surface sometimes a fiber will be encountered that will remove a chunk of the lead or blob of ink from the writing instrument's point and hold it under the edge of the fiber. This can be particularly true along the edges of the written line (see Figure 11.2).

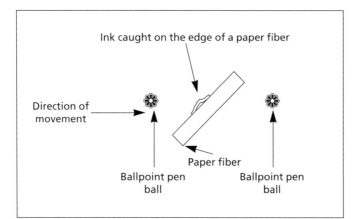

Figure 11.1

Ink caught on the edge of a paper fiber

Direction of movement

Paper fiber

Ballpoint pen ball

Ballpoint pen ball

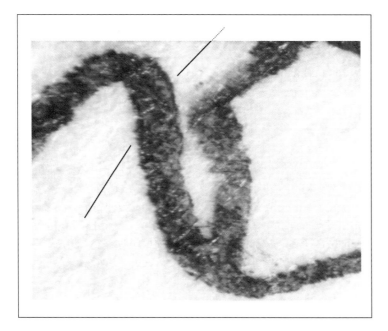

Figure 11.2

There are times when a ballpoint pen will have a defect on the ball socket and as the ball turns in the socket, ink will be picked up by the defect and deposited onto the socket housing. When this occurs, a line will usually be left in the ink line on the paper that contains little or no ink (see Figure 11.3).

In some situations, such as a traced signature, a pencil is used to make an outline of the writing. A ballpoint pen is then used to write over the pencil line as shown in Figure 11.4. Evidence of the use of a pencil is many times easier to see depending upon how much caution is used by the writer in covering the pencil line (see Figure 11.4).

When a pencil line or even a ballpoint ink line is written over with a fiber point writing instrument, the ballpoint ink line may be difficult to see. Extreme caution must be used when examining a possible tracing of any type.

Figure 11.3

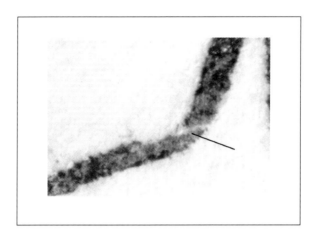

Figure 11.4

Ballpoint pens frequently produce an effect called gooping. It is caused by ink build-up on the socket housing, then breaking loose and being transferred to the paper surface as a mass of ink (see Figure 11.5).

Figure 11.5

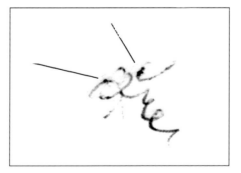

Gooping can occur when the pen is first used because the ink has dried and it is hard to get it moving, or it can occur as the writer is writing. In either instance, the effect is similar to those pointed out in Figure 11.5.

Writing instruments can have a profound effect on the way a person writes, what his writing will look like on the writing surface, its legibility, and the ability of the writer to accurately record his normal writing habits. The FDE, as has been said before, should keep a supply of different writing instruments on hand, experiment with them, examine their resulting markings on a writing surface, and when necessary, use them to duplicate an effect found in a writing that is being examined. Experiment, experiment, observe, observe, and record the results of the experiment. It is the only way to learn how a particular writing instrument works and what evidence it will leave on a writing surface.

CHAPTER 12

SOME GENERAL OBSERVATIONS ABOUT HANDWRITING IDENTIFICATION

ART OR SCIENCE?

Handwriting and hand printing identification is both art and science. This statement is not universally accepted by FDEs. Some believe that it is a science, and that there is nothing about it to suggest it is in any way an art or that it even contains elements that would lead anyone to think of it as an art. The degree of agreement with the statement, that it is both art and science, depends upon a number of factors, including the definitions of terms such as the following (Random 1992):

- ART
    1. the principles or methods governing any craft or branch of learning . . .
    2. the craft or trade using these principles or methods.
    3. skill in conducting any human activity . . . .
- SCIENCE
    1. a branch of knowledge or study dealing with a body of facts or truths systematically arranged and showing the operation of general laws.
    2. systematic knowledge of the physical or material world gained through observation and experimentation.
    3. any of the branches of natural or physical science.
    4. systematized knowledge in general.
    5. knowledge, as of facts or principles; . . . gained by systematic study.
    6. a particular branch of knowledge.
    7. any skill or technique that reflects a precise application of facts or principles.
- SCIENTIFIC
    1. of, pertaining to, or concerned with a science or the sciences.
    2. regulated by or conforming to the principles of exact science.
    3. systematic or accurate in the manner of an exact science.
- SCIENTIFIC METHOD
    1. a method of research in which a problem is identified, relevant data are gathered, a hypothesis is formulated, and the hypothesis is empirically tested.

- SKILL
  1. the ability to do something well arising from talent, training, or practice.
  2. special competence in performance; expertness; dexterity.
  3. a craft, trade, or job requiring manual dexterity or special training.
  4. Observation, discernment.
  5. Observation, reason; cause.

The following is the process of handwriting and hand printing identification.

- *Art,* because it uses "... principles or methods governing ..." a "branch of learning ...," (Random 1992) and like all professions, handwriting and hand printing identification is the application of those "principles or methods" by skilled practitioners using those well established "principles or methods" (ibid).
- *Science,* because the profession is "a branch of knowledge or study dealing with a body of facts or truths systematically arranged and showing the operation of general laws" (ibid). This statement is virtually identical to the idea that art is "the application of knowledge by skilled practitioners using well established 'principles or methods'" (ibid). The skilled practitioners of handwriting identification have, over many years, developed a "systematic knowledge of the physical or material world gained through observation and experimentation" (ibid).

  Learning the principles of handwriting identification is no different than learning and applying the principles and concepts of any science. As a chemist, physicist, engineer, or any other scientist must learn the principles, and their application, of his profession, each new generation of FDEs must systematically study and learn the principles of handwriting identification and their proper application. He must continuously conduct research and experiments designed to re-establish the validity of each element in the body of existing knowledge, and add to that body those concepts and observations derived from his work. Through research and experimentation, he continuously confirms his own understanding of the principles and how to apply them to known and new situations as "any skill or technique that reflects a precise application of facts or principles" (ibid).

  By using the *scientific method*, the FDE employs "a method of research in which a problem is identified, relevant data are gathered, a hypothesis is formulated, and the hypothesis is empirically tested" (ibid). What does the FDE do when he employs the scientific method? He is engaged in determining whether a writer(s) whose specimen(s) he is examining and comparing with a questioned writing(s) wrote the questioned material. He makes that determination by empirically applying principles he has learned, and his experience with similar situations; and by attaching proper significance to the evidence present within the document(s) he is examining, he should arrive at the correct conclusion based upon the available evidence. This procedure is no different than that engaged in by other scientists, such as chemists, physicists, mathematicians, etc.

Each handwriting identification case examined provides an opportunity for the FDE to re-establish the validity of the principles he has learned and previously applied. He collects relevant data – the amount of agreement or disagreement in the characteristics and features of the writing being examined – he tests the various hypotheses of possible authorship – by attaching significance to those various features – and empirically tests the hypotheses based on his knowledge and experience. In some situations, the FDE may be able to conduct experiments to test the hypotheses.

■ Like any scientist, the *skill* of the FDE is based on his " . . . ability to do something well arising from talent, training, or practice" (Random 1992). Part of his training requires him to demonstrate to the senior examiner(s) under whom he studies that he has a "special competence" (ibid) in the application of his knowledge. This is true for anyone engaged in any profession, "craft, trade, or job requiring . . . special training" (ibid). The work of the FDE is no different in this respect than that of any other scientist who demonstrates his skill based on his ability to reason and discern the significance that must be attached to *both* similarities and differences in the evidence he is evaluating as he conducts each examination.

It is for the reasons elucidated above that the author believes handwriting and hand printing identification is both art and science. A summary of those reasons will assist the reader in understanding why the FDE profession, more especially the identification of handwriting and hand printing, is performed by practitioners whose work is both art and science.

■ The practitioner learns an established set of principles derived from years of training and observation, and their accurate application, as established by many former and current skilled practitioners.

■ He re-confirms the validity of those principles by conducting research and experiments.

■ He continuously re-confirms the validity and reliability of those principles as he works cases, properly applying them to each traditional and new examination required by the circumstances of the case he is working.

Since the subject of this book is handwriting and hand printing identification, no discussion of the other knowledge, skills, and abilities, and their application, required by the FDE in the examination of other questioned document problems, will be included. There are many excellent text and technical papers available that focus on both handwriting and hand printing identification plus the broader subject of questioned document examination. Many of them have sections on handwriting identification that were used as resource materials for this work. The reader is encouraged to read, and study, those texts for insights into the many other areas of questioned document examination.

SUBJECTIVITY

Subjectivity can have an impact on the results of any scientific work. Subjective is defined as: "... existing in the mind; belonging to the thinking subject rather than to the object of thought (opposed to objective) ..., placing excessive emphasis on one's own moods, attitudes, opinions, etc." (Random 1992).

The process of comparing handwriting and hand printing, as we have seen, is like any other scientific field. It consists of a multiplicity of factors, including a subjective element brought to the examination process by the scientist. A major goal of every scientist, including the FDE, is to keep his subjective element in check, objectively evaluate the evidence he finds – both for and against an identification – and record the results of his work in a clear, concise, and easily understood report. All scientists, whether they are willing to admit it or not, have the same challenge, the control of the subjective element they bring to their work, relying instead only on the significance of the evidence in the study. This is one reason why the training period for any professional scientist, including the FDE, is so long.

Probably the best example of how the subjective element can influence science is found in history. Aristotle concluded that the earth was at the center of the universe and all the planets, including the sun, revolved around it. During the Age of Enlightenment, Galileo discovered in the course of new studies he performed with equipment unavailable to Aristotle that Aristotle was wrong. Many "scientists" in Galileo's time took issue with his conclusions which were contrary to the prevailing knowledge of the time based on the intertwining of religion and "science." Many of the "scientists" of his time did everything they could to discredit his work and suppress his conclusion. The reason he and his work were discredited was because the supporting data results conflicted with the body of "accepted knowledge" at that time.

Those who accepted the original explanation, Aristotle's view, would not accept Galileo's conclusion based on the new evidence because subjectively, the new conclusion did not place the earth at the center of the universe. Eventually, Galileo's new data and conclusions were accepted because his data could be verified by the observations of many different scientists and the application of principles developed by Galileo to explain the results of his work. The principles developed by Galileo were eventually accepted and expanded, and are collectively applied by many scientists today. Now it is a "scientific fact" that the sun is the center of our small part of the universe, and that the earth and other planets revolve around it, not they around the earth. Exactly where the true center of the universe is located, no one knows.

TERMS – QUESTIONED AND SAMPLE

Before proceeding further, the reader should be introduced to two very important terms in handwriting and hand printing identification. They describe the two broad categories into which handwriting and hand printing can generally be placed: questioned writing, and sample or specimen writing. These terms are covered more completely in Chapter 15. However, they are introduced here and a generally accepted definition is given because of their use in this chapter.

First, questioned writing: in other words, writing the authorship of which is unknown. A questioned writing can consist of any quantity of writing, from a signature, handwritten letter, entries on a form, etc. or even graffiti on a wall.

Second, sample or specimen writing: this category is sub-divided into two groups. The general definition of specimen writing is that writing the authorship of which *must be known* if it is to be used by the FDE for comparison purposes. There are two sub-groups of specimen writing: request and non-request or collected writings.

Request writings are those the authorship of which is known because their preparation is confirmed by a witness who solicited them from a known individual or who can attest to the *fact* that he witnessed preparation.

The second group is *non-request* writings. Non-request writings are typically those writings by an individual during the normal course of business and living, the writer not knowing or realizing that they may later be used for handwriting comparison purposes.

MAJOR PRINCIPLES OF HANDWRITING AND HAND PRINTING IDENTIFICATION

To expand on these concepts, there are certain universal principles governing the writing of individuals. What is a principle? It is:

- an accepted or professed rule of action or conduct.
- a fundamental law, axiom, or doctrine.
- a determining characteristic of something; essential quality (Random 1992).

Using this definition, the following principles have been confirmed by observation, experimentation, and by the experiences of FDEs throughout the history of the profession. They are recorded in major works by FDEs such as Saudek, Quirke, Osborn, Hilton, Harrison, Conway, to name a few. These principles are being reconfirmed and stated anew by their application and confirmation by FDEs today.

Since the first recorded record of these principles, some minor changes have occurred; however, the truly significant changes are in the development of new writing instruments and their effect on handwriting (Briem 1979), and the decreasing emphasis placed on penmanship in the educational system. Even with these changes, the principles have been, and are continually being, reconfirmed today because they deal with the act of writing regardless of the copybook system or the writing instrument used.

Interspersed with the major works of the individuals listed above are hundreds, even thousands, of excellent and significant technical papers written on the subject of handwriting identification. Most of them have been presented at training seminars sponsored by organizations such as the American Academy of Forensic Sciences, the American Society of Questioned Document Examiners, the Canadian Society of Forensic Sciences, and other equally prestigious and recognized organizations or they have been printed in recognized scientific journals.

From the earliest practitioners, and their subsequent verification by more contemporary FDEs, the following major principles of handwriting and hand printing identification have been established:

1   No two people write exactly alike.

2   No one person writes, exactly, the same way twice.

3   The significance of any feature, as evidence of identity or non-identity, and the problem of comparison, becomes one of considering a features rarity, the relative speed and naturalness with which it is written, and its agreement or disagreement with the feature(s) to which it can be compared.

4   A writer is not able to imitate *all* the features of another person's handwriting or hand printing while simultaneously writing at the same relative speed and skill level as the writer he is seeking to imitate. This is especially true the greater the relative speed the model writer uses. Further, in simulating another's writing, the simulator will try to imitate those features that are most striking to his eye. He frequently either disregards those features that are less conspicuous to him or, if noted, fails to imitate them successfully.

5   For those writings where the writer successfully disguises his normal handwriting habits or where he imitates – traces – the writing habits of another writer while leaving no trace of his own, it is virtually impossible to identify the imitator.

These are the more significant principles. There are numerous other principles governing relative relationships, relative speed, spacing habits, letter formation, etc. that will not be covered here. However, they are covered as topics in this text in the discussions on individuality, variation, etc. These five will now be looked at individually.

PRINCIPLE NO. 1

No two people write exactly alike

It is an accepted matter of fact, among FDEs, that no two people write exactly alike. *No* FDE could ever examine the writing of all the people who ever wrote, or now write; nor could he examine the writings of all those who learned to write a particular style or copybook system. In reality it is not necessary for him to have examined all of these writers because as has been shown, any person who learns to write any given style or system of handwriting will depart from it and incorporate into their writing their own individuality. They use "master patterns" of letters and features developed over time as they have learned to write and approach graphic maturity. As we have seen, these "master patterns" stay with a writer until circumstances cause them to change. For limited amounts of writing, the FDE may not be able to absolutely determine which was written by a particular writer (Crane 1999: 39–45).

Just as it would be an impossible task for a FDE to examine the writing of everyone who learned to write a given style or copybook system, it is just as impossible to obtain fingerprints of every person who ever lived, study and classify them to categorically establish that no two people have exactly the same fingerprints. However, not withstanding the impossibility of these tasks, FDE's have concluded, based on their own experience and that of their peers that no two people write exactly alike; just as fingerprint specialists have concluded that there are no two people with exactly the same fingerprint patterns. This concept of identicality is not just limited to handwriting and hand printing, and fingerprint identification, it also exists in other physical sciences.

What this statement says is, based on the collective experience of all the competent, qualified and ethical FDEs who have examined and studied writings of different people, there have never been found two people who write identically. Had there ever been such an occurrence, that observation would have been the topic of numerous research projects to verify the observation. The same would be true if a fingerprint specialist found two identical fingerprints.

Figure 12.1 shows how two different writers make the letters "M" and a terminal "s." The two letters are not *identical* either in the way each writer makes them or in the way each writer writes the letter multiple times. Each writer has his own "master pattern" around which he habitually writes each letter and its features. That "master pattern" is different for each of these two writers. However, when the same letter, for example the "M," is written by the same writer and analyzed there are found the following differences around the pictorial "master pattern."

Figure 12.1

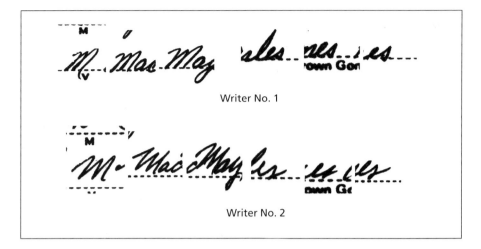

Writer No. 1

Writer No. 2

- Writer No. 1: *The upper case "M."* The following differences in the letter "M" are the result of normal variation: the absolute size of the letters; the length and angle of their approach strokes, the absolute height and width of the arches and the spacing between them, the length of the ending stroke on the right side or downstroke of each letter, and the placement of each letter with respect to the baseline.

  The lower case "s." The following differences in the letter "s" are the result of the writer's normal variation: the slope of the back of the letter; the absolute height of the letters, the straightness of the downstroke on the right side of the letters, and the placement of the letter with respect to its own baseline.

- Writer No. 2: *The upper case "M."* The following differences in the letter "M" are the result of the writer's normal variation: the length of the re-trace on the approach stroke of each "M;" the spacing between the arches, the angularity of the tops of the arches, and the placement of the letter with respect to the baseline is different.

  The lower case "s." The following differences in the letter "s" are the result of the writer's normal variation: the height of each letter; the spacing between the upstroke on the left and downstroke on the right side of the letter, and the length and angle of the ending stroke on each letter.

PRINCIPLE NO. 2

No one person writes exactly the same way twice

In the same way, based on the observations and studies by FDEs throughout the ages, there has never been found a single writer who writes exactly alike every time he sets pen to paper, or any other writing surface for that matter, when he writes the same letter, letter combinations, or words. Figure 12.2 shows the writing of the letters "a" through "d" by five different writers. Although some of the letters are pictorially similar, there are numerous differences present. Note how each of these letters as written by each writer has its own "master pattern."

Figure 12.2

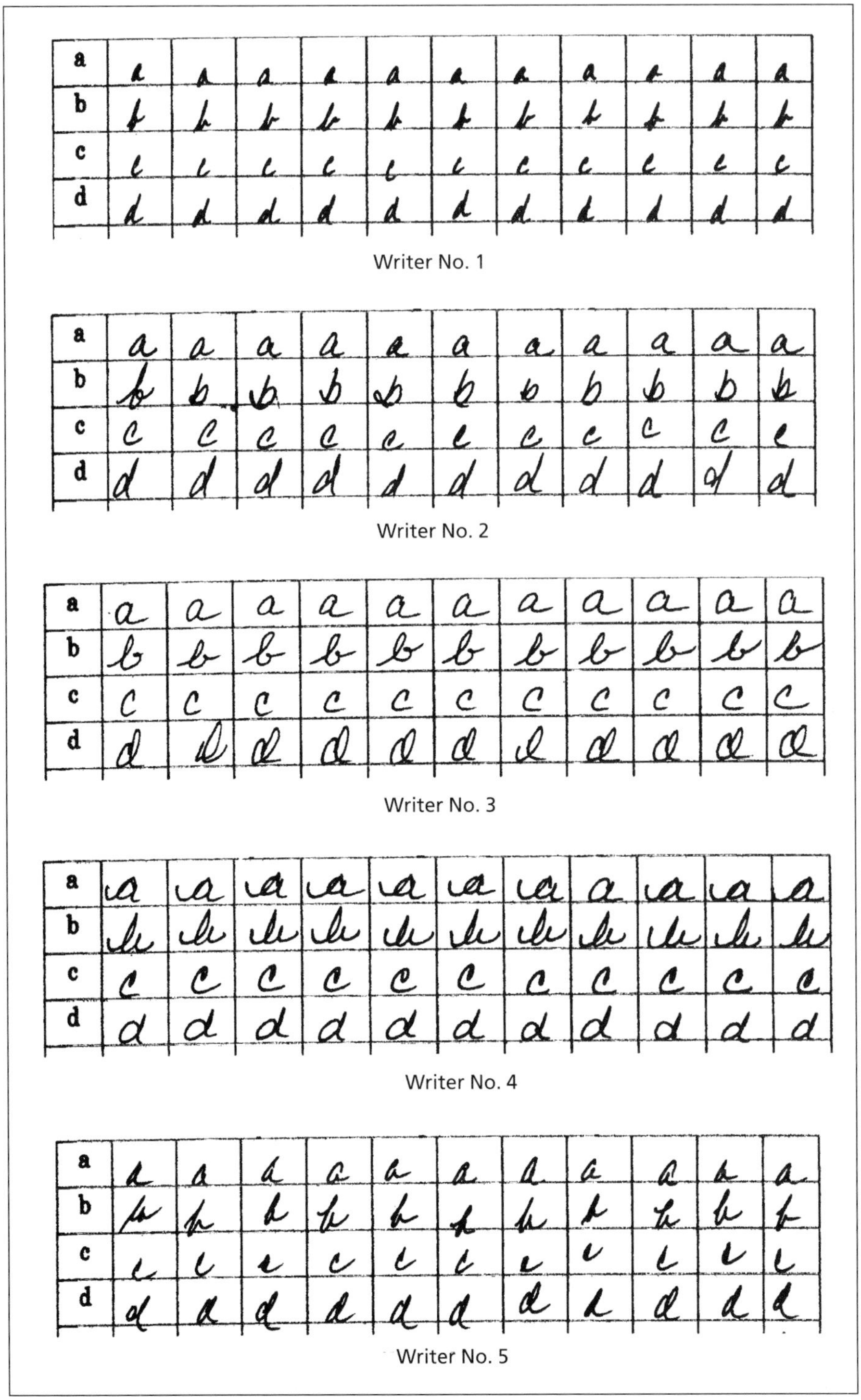

Writer No. 1

Writer No. 2

Writer No. 3

Writer No. 4

Writer No. 5

To illustrate the point that the concept of variation applies to all writers regardless of where they learned to write, refer to Figure 12.3 which shows the same group of letters as written by someone who learned to write in Cameroon.

Figure 12.3

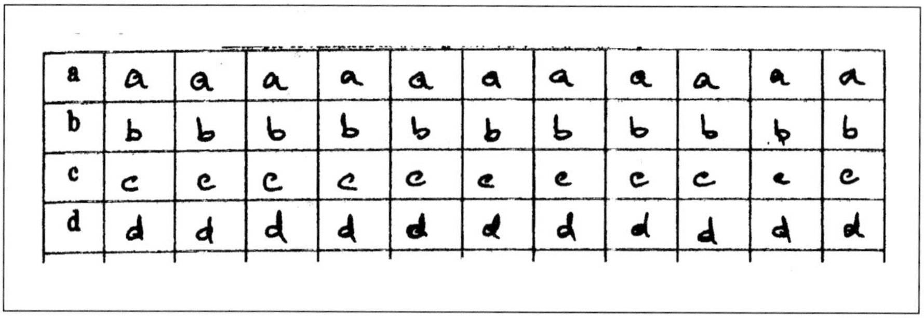

There is no way to tell where the writer learned to write based just on the pictorial appearance of these letters. It is doubtful that anyone could tell exactly where she learned to write, even if they were to examine writing by her which repeats all of the letters in the alphabet.

Principles 1 and 2 introduce the concept of variation in writing. What is meant by variation in writing? Variation is " . . . a deviation in structure or character from others of the same species." (Random 1992). Handwriting and hand printing are dynamic activities resulting in a product that reflects that dynamism. Variation in writing occurs because the human body is not a machine of such precision that it makes repetitive movements exactly alike over and over again. Every writer is expected to have some normal variation or deviation in the way they write features such as letters, connecting strokes, words, etc. As we have seen, Harrison refers to these variations in features as existing around a writer's "master pattern" (Harrison 1966: 298–307).

How important is the concept of variation? " . . . a handwriting may be characterized, not only by the form of its master patterns but also by the nature and extent of the variation around the master patterns exhibited by each of the individual letter designs. . . . In some handwriting, it may prove advisable to regard some of the letters as conforming to three different master patterns, according to whether they are initial, medial or terminal letters" (ibid: 301). " . . . irrespective of the general appearance of the different specimens, all the handwriting of any individual will be characterized by the same master patterns for the letter designs which remain essentially unaltered. This will be the case whether the handwriting has been carefully or carelessly written, whether the writer is alert or fatigued and whatever the nature of the writing instrument which has been used" (ibid: 303). Harrison chose his words carefully when he said, " . . . remain essentially unaltered" (ibid: 303).

Hilton goes further: "No repeated act is always accomplished with identically the same results regardless of whether it is produced by a machine or human effort. An individual's handwriting is made up of a complexity of habitual patterns that are repeated within a typical range of variation around the model patterns . . . Regardless of the class of problem, variation is ever present and must be accurately evaluated. It is as much a basic part of the identification as each identifying characteristic itself" (Hilton 1982: 10–11).

Normal and natural variation is just that, normal and natural, and is due to the inability of a writer to reproduce repetitive movements with machine-like precision. When conducting an examination, it is important for the FDE to have sufficient questioned and/or specimen writings to accurately determine the range in variation of a person's writing. The range of variation is in large part governed by the "master pattern" of all the writing features. Accidental features outside of the range of variation around the "master pattern" is possible; but before a feature is classified as an accidental, the FDE needs to satisfy himself that the writer is capable of writing such a feature. The "master pattern" provides the reference point around which the FDE begins his evaluation.

PRINCIPLE NO. 3

> The significance of any feature, as evidence of identity or non-identity, and the problem of comparison becomes one of considering its rarity, the relative speed and naturalness with which it is written, and its agreement or disagreement with comparable features.

This principle encompasses three significant ideas: a features rarity, the relative speed and naturalness with which it is written, and its agreement or disagreement with comparable features.

Rarity

It is not possible to devise a scale or consistently assign values to each feature that, adequately and accurately, represent its rarity. There are a number of reasons for this: the experience of the FDE, the relative placement of a feature within a unit of writing, and the variation in the "master pattern" of that feature because of its placement. For example, is the feature, letter, etc. printed or cursive?

- Does it stand alone?
- Is it located at the beginning of a word?

- Is it located within the word?
- If it is located within a word, what letter(s) precedes and follow(s) it?
- If it is located at the end of a word, what letter precedes it and what letter begins the next word?
- If it is located at the end of a word, is there a feather connection between it and the following letter or feature?

The same series of questions should be asked if the feature is part of a numeral or a series of numerals. Letters or numerals, it makes no difference, because the process of establishing rarity, "master pattern," the significance of features in combination, etc. for comparison purposes is essentially the same. To disregard the above when comparing letter forms and numerals is to invite error.

How does the FDE determine a features rarity? Returning to the beginning of this chapter where a number of terms were defined, the common thread that runs throughout the discussion and that is applicable for all arts and sciences as well is experience. In this case, the FDE determines a features rarity based on his years of experience critically examining handwriting. There is *no* substitution for experience! Not only is his experience an important factor, so is the experience of all FDEs with whom he associates, exchanges information ideas, or consults with when examining the writing under examination.

The relative speed and naturalness with which it is written

In establishing the significance of a features rarity, the FDE must establish that the feature has the following criteria. It is:

- made rapidly,
- hard or difficult to make,
- not readily noticeable and not likely to be imitated,
- seldom found in writing taken at random,
- not taught in any writing system,
- part of a complex or pattern,
- seldom if ever found in company with certain other features, and
- part of an unusual pattern.

Every handwriting examined by the FDE should be examined with consideration given to the factors listed above, or to as many of them as are applicable, when determining the significance of a feature. The FDE does not assign a number or percentage value to each feature to show the significance he is attaching to it resulting from his study and examination. The reason, because of the commonality of some features found in copybook systems, or features learned by a writer's observation, practice, and incorporation of non-copybook features into their writing. Also, because of changes that naturally take place in one's writing as they mature graphically and due to the aging process, physical problems, disguise, etc.

The naturalness of a person's writing is determined not by the writing's legibility – that can be affected by relative speed and subsequent attention to detail – relative writing pressure habits, etc., but by his level of skill based on the impulse level at which his writing is most natural to him. When rapidly written, writing appears to be more natural and spontaneous than when it is slowly written, having poorer line quality and frequent pen stops. When a person writes too rapidly, regardless of his level of graphic maturity, his writing frequently becomes illegible. The relative speed of a person's writing is a feature that can be easily changed by the writer, just as he can change overall slant, letter form and design, etc.

Since relative speed is covered in Chapter 8, another in-depth discussion is not necessary here. However, as a refresher, when a writer is writing naturally and rapidly, he uses the natural contraction and relaxation of his muscles to move the pen which is controlled by his mind's eye because it visually understands what each feature, letter, combination of letters, etc. should look like after it is written. His ability to write each feature rapidly, coupled with the frequency of its occurrence in random writings – rarity – is what gives each feature its significance. If the writer writing rapidly dramatically reduces his relative speed of writing, he usually writes more legibly, with poorer line quality due to the significant reduction in writing speed, and rests his hand more frequently because of cramping muscles that are not working rhythmically.

Its agreement or disagreement with comparable features

The non-FDE (layman) who is not aware of the principles of handwriting and hand printing identification believes variation poses an almost insurmountable obstacle to identifying a person by their handwriting. He does not know that even within normal variation there are those constant features such as "master pattern," etc., the significance of which must be appraised when trying to compare handwriting. Typically, he arbitrarily selects features, regardless of whether they are easy or difficult to produce, their rarity, conspicuousness, etc., and makes a decision based on the pictorial appearance of the writing rather than on the application of established principles.

The extent of the agreement and/or disagreement between comparable features can be significant. Going back to the concept of "master pattern," the features, letters, letter combinations, etc. being compared *must fit within the writer's range of variation as determined by the "master pattern."* The identity or non-identity of the writer is based on the cumulative agreement or non-agreement of comparable features, letters, letter-combinations, etc. around the "master pattern" of each feature. The following is the requirement for concluding that two or more writings are of common authorship: if two naturally written writings, having sufficient individuality, are in complete agreement with no significant differences other than those resulting from normal variation, then it can safely be concluded that the writings are of common authorship. If the writings lack sufficient individuality or contain features that are not in complete agreement, then reaching a definite conclusion concerning common authorship is not possible. What is possible in such situations is to arrive at some qualified statement concerning common authorship, a topic covered extensively in Chapter 18.

PRINCIPLE NO. 4

No one is able to imitate all the features of another person's handwriting and simultaneously write at the same relative speed and skill level as the writer he is seeking to imitate. This is especially true the greater the relative speed the model writer uses. Further, in simulating another's writing, the simulator will try to imitate those features that strike his eye most forcibly. He will tend either to disregard those features that are inconspicuous or else fail to imitate them successfully.

The probability of two people writing in such a way that every feature of their writings is in complete agreement is so remote that its occurrence is, for all practical purposes, impossible. As stated above, when the FDE is conducting his examination and comparison, he attaches significance to each feature of writing based on the relative speed and naturalness with which it is written, and its frequency of occurrence within random writing.

It is expected that a simulator will fail to accurately imitate the same relative writing speed and fluency of a writer unless he is imitating the writing of a very slow writer or the writing of a person having a very low level of skill. In that case, he could still fail to accurately imitate the writer's relative speed and other details of the writing even though the model is slowly written. Further, even if he imitated the exact relative speed of a slow writing, he still would not be expected to imitate all the inconspicuous features of the writing.

If a simulator does not notice all the features of a writing, which ones, or how many, will he observe and write simultaneously? Can the relative degree of difficulty necessary to produce various features be assigned a value? If the answer to either of these is yes, then the importance of those features, for identification purposes, can be scaled.

Features such as letter size, slant, and form are three of the easiest for a writer to alter. They are also the ones that the layman is prone to attach greatest significance to for identification purposes. If there were a scale to record the relative conspicuousness of various features of writing, and there is not, then there must be another scale to appraise the value of those features. As we have seen, no such scale exists.

If the FDE is dealing with a limited amount of writing, as Crane did in his study of the name "L. Lee," it is unlikely that the FDE will ever be able to identify the writer of a particular repetition of this name. The slight reservation here is due to the fact that any given writer may incorporate a sufficient amount of individuality into their writing this name that it might be possible to make a strong statement concerning the probability of its authorship. "The criteria vary according to the number of letters available for comparison combined with the degree of individuality noted in the letters. However, in all instances, the Document Examiner must rely on his training and experience to evaluate when a questioned text is a 'reasonable amount'" (Crane 1999: 44).

If the name is "George Babblemouth," there is a much greater probability that the FDE will be able to identify the writer of a signature in that name. One reason is that it has a greater number of features, different letters and letter combinations, giving the writer more opportunity to demonstrate individuality based on the rarity of the collective features, the relative speed, and the naturalness with which they are written.

PRINCIPLE NO. 5

For those writings where the writer successfully disguises his normal handwriting habits or where he imitates – traces – the writing habits of another writer while leaving no trace of his own, it is virtually impossible to identify the imitator.

If the questioned writing is slowly written, with many stopping and starting points and directional changes of the pen, the FDE must exercise extreme caution when attaching significance to every feature of this writing. Why? Because the examined writing could be a tracing, simulation, or the result of some other meticulous method of writing to copy another writer's writing habits. This is especially true if the person who purportedly wrote the material usually writes rapidly.

Figure 12.4 shows a specimen written by a writer having average writing skill, relative pressure habits, etc. To the left of the specimen is questioned writing number one and to the right is questioned writing number two. The question is,

Figure 12.4

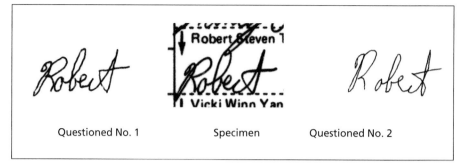

Questioned No. 1	Specimen	Questioned No. 2

did the person who wrote the specimen also write either or both of the questioned writing? The answer is, no.

Questioned No. 1 is a tracing of the specimen, and Questioned No. 2 is a freehand simulation of the specimen. Notice the poor line quality, lack of relative pressure habits, frequent pen adjustments and stopping points, etc. in the questioned writings. Both questioned writings contain features consistent with slow writing, tracing, and simulation. Because some features, in this instance the relative speed of the writing, can have more than one cause, it is important to evaluate all of the writing features, considering them as a whole and not in isolation – a perfect example of why experience is so important to the FDE.

The tracing, Questioned No. 1, was done by placing a plain sheet of paper over the original writing, putting the two on a window to backlight the writing, and copying the name written on the bottom sheet onto the top sheet. Could the writer of the specimen trace his writing of the name "Robert" and produce Questioned No. 1? Absolutely, but not likely.

The simulation, Questioned No. 2, was done by placing a sheet of paper in proximity to the one bearing the specimen; then the writer attempted to "draw," freehand, a pictorial representation of the specimen. The writer of the simulation did not pay close attention to many of the original writer's details of writing; however, he did produce a writing that could be mistaken for a genuine signature by someone without the proper training to recognize the possible indications of a simulation.

How successful was the writer of the two questioned writings? Figure 12.5 shows how this specimen writer would normally write the name "Robert" and both questioned writings of the name from Figure 12.4. Although there are some pictorial similarities between the specimen writing and the two questioned writings, there are sufficient significant differences such that he could never be identified as the writer of either questioned writing. Why? Because he is *copying* the handwriting habits of another writer while at the same time *not* incorporating his own in either of the questioned writings.

Figure 12.5

Questioned No. 1   Specimen writer   Questioned No. 2

In Figure 12.5, the specimen writer writes rapidly, as demonstrated by the good relative pressure habits, tapered beginning and ending strokes, and the rarity of the combined features of the writing that are different from both the specimen writing of the name "Robert" in Figure 12.4 and both questioned writings.

The examination of this questioned writing would be no different than the process used to examine any questioned or known writing. The actual process of comparison is discussed in Chapter 13.

In a simulation, the writer is generally not identifiable, partly because he is attempting to draw the handwriting habits of another writer while concealing his own. However, there have been instances when a writer (drawer) did not adhere to the model before him and a sufficient amount of his own handwriting features and habits were incorporated into the simulated writing so that their significance for or against identification could be assessed. In such a situation, it would be possible to make some probability statement about the writer's attempt to simulate the questioned signature. In a very few instances the author has been able to reach some positive probability of the drawer's involvement.

As the above example demonstrates, the greater success the writer has in disguising his writing habits, the less likely it is that he will be identified through handwriting identification. The same can be said if he writes competently using more than one writing style. The greater the differences in the details of the writing features and letters of the two styles of writing, the less likely it is that he will be identified.

In addition to these very broad statements, there are additional concepts dealing with the details of writing that are also important for the identification of handwriting. In some instances, they are derived from the general statements above and observations over many years of examining handwriting.

The next question is, when is handwriting compared correctly? It is compared correctly when:

1   All features of the writing are carefully examined.
2   All features of the writing are assigned their correct level of significance based on their rarity and the relative speed and naturalness with which they are written.

3   The evidence for and against common authorship is predicated upon the correct interpretation of the significance attached to those features.

4   The conclusion reached by the FDE is based only on evidence contained within the writings being examined. One exception, when some transitory factor (for example, a physical problem, illness, or condition affecting the writer's motor function(s) such as the use of drugs or some other transitory factor(s), etc.) could have an effect on the writer. The FDE should then be made aware of those conditions that were present, insofar as possible, at the time the questioned writing is written and the sample writing is provided.

One short example will help to clarify the importance of an FDE having this information. Many years ago when the author worked in a police laboratory, one of his fellow FDEs was asked to go to the Check and Fraud Squad and help take specimen writing from a suspect who was "disguising his writing." When the FDE arrived, he saw the suspect sitting in a chair, writing handcuffed at the wrist with a long chain running from the cuff down to the bottom of one of the table legs where he was sitting. In addition, the writer was experiencing withdrawals from an overdose of drugs and was very ill and barely lucid. This writer, at that point in time, would never be able to provide naturally written specimens because of the cumulative effect of all these transitory factors. The FDE explained this to those present, left the room, and returned to the laboratory.

SUMMARY

The purpose of this chapter has been to show that like other sciences, handwriting and hand printing identification is a combination of art, science, the application of the scientific method, and some of the major principles on which it is based. There is no substitute for time, skill, experience, and working with competent, qualified, and ethical FDEs to learn the theory and principles and their practical application to handwriting and hand printing identification.

This chapter does not contain all of the principles of the science. Many are found in other chapters of this book dealing with select topics. They are equally important and in most cases are derived from those presented in this chapter. It is a brief summary of some of the principles governing the process, and the reader is encouraged to study the other works referred to in this chapter. Unfortunately, several of them, including those by Saudek and Quirke, are now out of print.

REFERENCES

Briem, Gunnlaugur S.E. (1979) "Wanted: Handwriting that Fits Modern Pens," *Visible Language*, 13(1), 49–62.

Crane, A. (1999) "Does the amount of handwriting on a cheque constitute a reasonable amount of sample?" *Canadian Society of Forensic Science Journal*, 32(1).

Harrison, Wilson R. (1966) *Suspect Documents Their Scientific Examination*, 2nd edn, London.

Hilton, Ordway (1982) *Scientific Examination of Questioned Documents*, revised edn, New York, NY.

Kam, Moshe, et al. (1994) "Proficiency of Professional Document Examiners in Writer Identification," *Journal of Forensic Science*, 39(5).

Random (1992 and 1999) *Random House Webster's Electronic Dictionary and Thesaurus* College Edition, Reference Software International.

CHAPTER 13

THE PROCESS OF COMPARISON

The process of comparison, what is it? Compare is the root word and comparison is the process. Two or more items can be compared pictorially, as patterns, or in extensive detail. The FDE compares handwriting and hand printing: pictorially, based on its patterns; and in detail, based on the characteristic writing habits of the writer.

While it is possible to compare an apple and an orange to determine if they are similar or different, the observer could immediately conclude that they are different pictorially; and when examined in extensive detail, numerous additional differences in their minute details would be found. In this example, the observer making the comparison could have stopped the examination when he observed that the apple and orange were different pictorially, their having different patterns.

The comparison of normal, naturally written handwriting is similar to the above of the apple and orange. In this case, however, the FDE seeks to determine whether two or more writings are by the same or different writers. The process of comparison can be thought of as consisting of three very broad levels, as follows:

- First, the FDE conducts an examination to determine if the writings are pictorially similar.
- Second, and if pictorially similar, he conducts a more in-depth examination to determine if all the letters and other features have the same pattern(s).
- Third, and if they have similar patterns, he conducts an examination and comparison in extensive detail to determine if they were written by the same person.

The examination and comparison process consist of established procedures that may vary from FDE to FDE; but regardless of the process used, they generally conform in the depth with which the writings should be studied and the qualities and features considered. The principles discussed in this book are applied to each handwriting and hand printing comparison conducted by its author, and they have been found to be reliable and accurate over many years of experience.

If a level one examination reveals that the writings are not pictorially alike, and the result of a level two examination determines that the writings have no similar patterns, it is generally not necessary for the FDE to go any further with the examination. This is not to say that it can be concluded at this point that the writings being examined are absolutely by different writers. It only means that they have neither pictorial or pattern similarities sufficient to make them suitable for comparing their details. For example, try comparing the block printed "A" with the cursive "a" in Figure 13.1.

Figure 13.1

Comparing these two letters is like comparing apples and oranges. They are different pictorially and have different patterns, yet they could have been written by the same writer, and they were.

After completing level one and level two examinations, determining that two or more writings are pictorially similar and have numerous common patterns and characteristics; the examiner then conducts a level three, or an in-depth examination and comparison of the writings to determine whether they were written by the same writer.

DEFINING TERMS

Before proceeding further, it is necessary to define a couple of terms. A questioned writing is one the authorship of which is unknown. The objective of a handwriting examination and comparison is to try to determine the authorship of a questioned writing by comparing it with known writing samples or specimens these two terms are used interchangeably; and occasionally, the term "known" is also used.

Sample writing is subdivided into two categories: requested samples and non-request or collected samples. First, requested samples are those written by a known individual under the direct supervision or direction of the requester. For example, an investigator develops a suspect in a document case. He interviews the suspect and as part of the interview asks him to provide a writing sample for comparison purposes. The requested sample is usually written on standard handwriting forms with writings that do not repeat the questioned material and some that repeat it numerous times. When providing requested specimens, the writer is given instructions on what to write and, if necessary, the writer is requested to vary his style of writing, etc. The requestor observes every phase of the process.

The second type of sample is known as non-request or collected sample. These are writings written by a person during the normal course of his life. Let's assume that before requesting specimens from a writer the investigator asks him to produce a driver's license or other identification card he has signed during his normal conduct of business. The driver's license produced for the investigator is a collected or normal course of business writing. Before interviewing the suspect, the investigator finds writings purportedly written by his suspect that he believes can also be used for comparison purposes. Not having a witness to the writing of this material the investigator must be very cautious in using them as sample writings of his suspect.

It is imperative that the authorship of any non-request samples be established before they are used for comparison purposes. If not, any opinion rendered by the FDE that relies on characteristics and features found in the non-request writings could be negated at the time of trial. The reason is, if they are not admissible in a court of law because their authorship has not been established, then any opinion rendered based on their use is inadmissible as part of the evidence. Further, unless the examiner has performed a common authorship examination among all of the specimen writing, request and non-request, to determine whether they were written by the same writer, he may rely on handwriting characteristics that in fact do not belong to the suspect and the resulting opinion would be in error. If those non-request writings are very limited or are on a document containing the writings of more than one writer, both the investigator and FDE are at risk when such writings are used for comparison purposes.

SUITABILITY OF THE WRITING FOR COMPARISON PURPOSES

There are two types of writings that are not suitable at any time for a meaningful comparison. They are an *excellent* simulation or tracing of another person's writing. The reason they are not suitable is because of the way they were written. By definition, neither one provides a basis for a meaningful examination and comparison because they are neither naturally written nor do they contain the handwriting habits of their writer. Rather, they are drawings and not the result of someone writing in a natural and spontaneous manner.

WHAT PROCEDURE DO I FOLLOW?

A suggested procedure is recommended to the reader; but it must be said that no single procedure, when fully implemented, will always insure reaching the correct conclusion. The establishment of a procedure serves no other purpose than to attempt to insure that all the required items are covered. In handwriting comparison, it may be possible to adjust the procedures depending upon the strength of the evidence contained within the writing(s).

A level three examination involves a detailed analysis of the qualities and features of the writing, and attaching the proper amount of significance to each; whether that significance is sufficient to conclude that they are of common authorship, or that they were written by different writers, is irrelevant. Regardless of which way the opinion may go, at no time is the FDE relieved of his responsibility to conduct a complete examination and to report the results of his examination. One of his primary responsibilities is to perform his work competently in conformity with the highest possible ethical standards of the profession.

The following are typical items that must be considered before comparing two or more writings for common authorship:

- All the writing(s) *must be* suitable for comparison purposes.

  What does this mean? We have already seen that they must consist of common letters and letter combinations, be of the same style and, ideally, they should be used within the same context, standing alone, or in combinations. They must be of the same style – cursive with cursive, printed with printed, numerals with numerals, etc. – and they must have been written with the same relative speed.

  The process of comparing two or more writings requires that they be suitable for comparison purposes, as shown above. This does not mean that a naturally written sample cannot be compared with a disguised or unnaturally written questioned writing. They can be compared, insofar as is possible, given their suitability and the significance of the qualities and features.

  If at all possible, they should be original writings and not photocopies. If the questioned or specimen documents are photocopies of documents bearing writings, there is always the possibility that the original of the photocopy is a fabricated document. What does this mean? The following is one process for creating a fabricated document using the photocopying process:

  1 Take an original document (document 1) and make a photocopy of it (document 2).

  2 Cut out the writing on the photocopy (document 2) that is to become a part of another document (document 3).

  3 Place the cutout on the new document (document 3) at the desired location. Lets assume we have cut out a signature from document 2 and have now placed in on document 3.

  4 Photocopy the altered or modified document (document 3) described in "3" to produce the new document (document 4). This new photocopy now becomes our

questioned document. The writing (from document 1) may be genuine, but the document on which it is placed (document 4) is not.

- They should be contemporary.

    The questioned and specimen writings should be written around the same time frame. A vital part of this depends upon a number of factors, the major one being has the writer(s) reached graphic maturity? If the writer is young and has not reached graphic maturity, then the writing(s) to be examined should be written as closely together in time as possible. If the writer has reached graphic maturity, then the time differential between the writing(s) does not have to be as closely spaced, but they should still be contemporary in time. There are variations to this requirement, depending upon such things as the effect of transitory factors on the writer between, or during, the time of the writings.

- They must have been written naturally, at approximately the same relative speed, and represent the writer's normal writing habits.

    The significance of any feature, as evidence of identity or non-identity, and the problem of comparison become one of considering a features rarity, the relative speed and naturalness with which it is written, and its agreement or disagreement with the feature(s) to which it can be compared. Again, this does not mean that a naturally written specimen cannot be compared to an unnaturally written or disguised writing.

- They should be written with comparable materials: pen, paper, etc.

    If one of the writings is written with a broad fiber marker and the other with a fine ballpoint pen, then it may not be possible to meaningfully compare the two writings. If both are done with similar writing instruments on similar paper, then a more meaningful comparison can be conducted.

After completing the above preliminary items, the FDE is ready to begin a detailed analysis of the writing to determine whether they are of common authorship or not. The procedure used by the author is as follows:

1   An examination of the questioned writing is conducted to determine whether it is suitable for comparison purposes, if it is written by one writer, and if it reflects the normal, natural writing habits of that writer.

    Even if the writing is a signature endorsement on a check, the FDE should examine it and try to determine whether the given name, middle initial, and surname are of common authorship. In one case the author examined, the given name and surname of the endorsement were written by one writer, and the middle initial by a second writer.

    When the questioned writing is either an extended body of writing or consists of numerous entries in a journal, there is always the possibility that the writings could be by more than one writer. It is vital to eliminate this possibility before beginning the comparison process with a known writer.

2   An examination of the specimen writing is conducted to determine whether or not it is suitable for comparison purposes; written by one writer; or reflects the normal, natural, writing habits of that writer.

Why is it necessary to conduct a common authorship examination of the specimen writing? It is absolutely essential if the writings are collected or are non-request specimens, or if some portion of the specimens to be used are collected. If a common authorship examination is not performed, the FDE runs the risk of relying on writings that will be either excluded from use in court or that were actually written by someone other than the person who purportedly wrote them. It can never be assumed that when collected writings are provided to the FDE that they are in fact the writings of a particular person who purportedly wrote them.

3   An examination of the specimen writing is then conducted to determine which qualities and features of that naturally written writing reflect the writing habits of the author and, when taken collectively, comprise the individuality of his writing.

4   As a part of the examination described in 3 above, a determination of the writers normal range of variation is made so if qualities and features found in the questioned writing are outside of that normal range, they can be noted and the appropriate significance attached to them. If they are within the specimen writer's normal and natural range of variation, this too can be noted and the proper amount of significance attached to them for identification purposes.

5   The next step is to conduct a side-by-side comparison of the questioned and specimen writings to try and determine if they are by the same writer.

The similarities and differences are evaluated, their significance for or against common authorship is considered, and a determination is made concerning the probability of common authorship.

DESCRIPTIVE TERMINOLOGY

Before proceeding further, a list of descriptive terms needs to be developed to describe the features of writing being examined. This list should consist of simple descriptors that can be related to everyday movements or objects. Take, for example, the two letter "A's" shown in Figure 13.2.

Figure 13.2

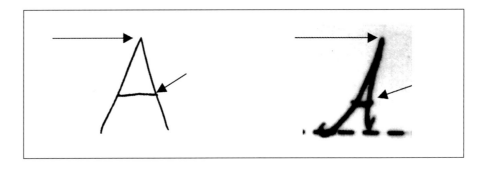

The one on the left is a block printed letter form having two angle lines extending from the baseline to a point where they meet at the top of the letter. This part of the letter could be compared to an Indian tepee. The use of the tepee illustration may not have meaning to someone who has never seen one, so another way of describing this part of the letter is just simply to say it consists of two angular lines connecting at a point above the base of the letter. The use of lookalike illustration is acceptable so long as it does not become the primary focus of the description.

There is also a horizontal line connecting the two angular lines. It is located near the halfway point between the letter base and its top. Its length is such that it makes contact with, but does not extend beyond, the two angular lines.

The "A" on the right was written by its author starting with a counterclockwise pen motion near the baseline and then making a small hook before moving the pen away to make the left leg of the letter. The pen is again stopped at a point above the baseline, the letters apex, where it is stopped, the direction is changed, and the pen then pulled toward the writer. There is a small hook formation at the foot of the right leg of the letter. This hook is a continuation of the writing act in making the right side of the letter. The letter slants to the right, so the length of the left leg is longer than that of the right leg. The bulk of the top of the letter, located just above the cross bar, is retraced. The cross bar extends just to the left of the left side of the letter and just to the right of the right side of the letter.

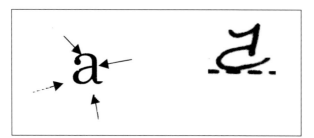

Figure 13.3

The lower-case letter "a" on the left in Figure 13.3 can be described as having a cane-shaped formation with an arcade top covering an elongated oval connected to and extending to the left of the vertical staff of the cane. Although the author used a type font to illustrate the "a" on the left, there are people who make the letter as it is shown above. The cane portion is made using a clockwise pen motion. The oval is made with a spiral counterclockwise motion, it is open on the right where it connects to the staff of the cane; it has a flat top, and the bottom of the oval is made with a continuation of the counterclockwise motion back to the staff of the letter. The handwritten lower case letter "a" on the right appears to be the number "7" with a spiral counterclockwise bottom that resembles the letter "C."

Below is a list of general words and terms that can be used to describe the parts of letters, connecting strokes, beginning and endings, baseline direction, etc. They are as follows:

1   Arcade, clockwise, or overhand motions.
2   Garland, counterclockwise, or underhand motions.
3   Smoothly written uniform lines.
4   Tremulous lines – random pen movements.
5   Compound or serpentine motions.
6   Uniform or misshaped circles and ovals.
7   Feather strokes – lightly written recorded lines on the paper.
8   Tick marks – short pointed marks.
9   Needle-shaped beginning and ending strokes.
10 Indentations, dimples, etc.
11 Rising or ascending baseline from left to right.
12 Arcade, garland, or serpentine baseline.
13 Straight, vertical, left and right margin.
14 Concave left and right margin.
15 Convex left and right margin.
16 Angular left and right margin.
17 Narrow, average, or wide left margin.
18 Narrow, average, or wide right margin.
19 Narrow, average, or wide top margin.
20 Narrow, average, or wide bottom margin

Two writings may look pictorially alike, have similar patterns, and yet it is determined that they may not be by the same writer. It must be remembered that just because two features or writings "look alike," it does not mean that they are of common authorship. Looking at Figure 13.4, one of the writings could be a tracing – Questioned No. 1 – of another writer's signature (the specimen), a freehand simulation – drawing, Questioned No. 2 – or a machine copy of a signature. If it were a machine copy, it would be identical to the original with the possible exception of its absolute size and color.

Figure 13.4

Questioned No. 1   Model   Questioned No. 2

Another example is found in two writings that are very limited in nature, for example the name "L. Lee." A study by Crane of a number of writers writing this name helps illustrate the reason why limited writing such as this name is not necessarily suitable for identification purposes. His conclusion is "The criteria vary according to the number of letters available for comparison combined with the degree of individuality noted in the letters. However, in all instances, the Document Examiner must rely on his training and experience to evaluate when a questioned text is a 'reasonable amount'" (Crane 1999: 44).

Before beginning the process of comparing handwriting, the assumption made here is that the FDE has access to adequate lighting, sufficient magnification equipment, and other technical aids and references necessary to conduct a complete and comprehensive examination. What technical aids are necessary depends upon the type of examination(s) necessary for the documents being studied. Some examples of the basic equipment necessary are shown below.

- *Light sources:* different types of sources to illuminate the document, or portions of it, with white, ultraviolet, infrared, etc.
- *Magnifiers:* suitable magnifiers, such as a microscope, handheld magnifiers, etc., as required to assist the examiner in his examination of minute details of the writing.
- *Grids:* generally speaking, the FDE does not use handwriting protractors, or similar devices when comparing handwriting. One reason he does not is due to the lack of machine-like consistent agreement in the writing features. Many years ago, such instruments were used, in part because of the emphasis placed on handwriting and the required adherence to good penmanship. Today, the emphasis placed on handwriting by teachers, schools, parents, etc. is almost non-existent compared to the past; thus writing is more individualistic and contains more variation. However, the FDE does have an assortment of grids that he uses when comparing two signatures to determine if one may be a tracing of another, whether a letter or letters sits on an imaginary baseline, etc.
- *Specialized equipment:* the FDE usually has a series of different color filters, special narrow and wide band filters, etc., viewing devices such as video cameras with spectral sensitive photo cathodes, etc., as required for non-destructive testing. If the FDE, who is in private practice, or the organization he works for, can afford to purchase some of the commercially available specialized equipment, he will also have at his disposal equipment such as an electron microscope, and spectral photometers for the analysis of inks, etc. Typically, only FDEs who work in government laboratories have access to these types of equipment. Explanations of all of the possible equipment commercially available to the FDE is beyond the scope of this text and are covered in other more general text and technical papers on questioned document examination written by numerous FDEs.
- *Cameras:* generally, the FDE has either an assortment of specialized cameras, or a high quality single lenses reflex 35 mm camera with interchangeable lenses, that can be

used in conjunction with special magnifiers and microscopes. Some new digital cameras offer the FDE an opportunity to expand his capabilities even further. In conjunction with these cameras, he needs a range of special filters and photographic films. The type of equipment the FDE has in his laboratory in large measure determines the extent to which he can conduct certain types of examinations.

THE PROCESS OF COMPARISON

The process of comparing handwriting is more than just *looking* at a letter, combination of letters, feature(s), etc. in a writing and then *looking* at their counterpart(s) in another writing to see if they *look* pictorially alike or different. Assuming they *look* pictorially alike, that alone is not sufficient for comparison purposes, nor is it sufficient to say that they are by the same writer. Taking the example above in Figure 13.4, if the simulated and traced writing is done with extreme care and attention to detail, they should be pictorially similar to their true owner's signature – the specimen. In this case, if someone examined these two questioned writings only for pictorial similarity, they could conclude that the writings were done by the writer of the specimens, with some degree of certainty. This conclusion would be based, though, only on the pictorial similarities present and not on the significance of the features of the writings. By any standard, a wrong conclusion would have been reached.

It is possible for two letters, etc. to look pictorially alike and yet be by different writers. This does not mean that two writers will write every letter form and feature exactly alike! Two letters must have some similarities in appearance if they are to be understood as representing a copybook letter form or a specific word if they are in a particular combination; and if they were not, then it would be impossible for two people using the same alphabet and letter combinations to be able to communicate with each other in writing. They may be able to write pictorially alike but not fundamentally alike.

These two fundamental principles of handwriting identification are extremely important.

- First, *no two people write every letter and/or feature exactly alike*. The latest research in handwriting supports this fundamental principle (Crane 1999). This principle was established because, based on the experience of FDEs over many years, there have not been any reported instances of two writings, by different writers, being *exactly* alike. This process is no different than any other scientific field. Can it be stated categorically that no two people write exactly alike? No; but what can be said is that based on the collective experience of all the examiners who have ever practiced, there have been no confirmed reports of the writings of two individuals being exactly alike in every respect. As Crane pointed out in his study, the amount of writing and the choice of letter forms, etc. used by the writers will certainly impact on this statement. The same fundamental concept is used in fingerprint identification; and it has even been said that no two snowflakes are identical, but who has conducted the studies necessary to prove conclusively that these statements can be relied upon as absolutes?

■ Second, *no one writer writes the same way twice*. In every person's writing, the FDE expects to find some normal variation that must be accounted for when doing a side-by-side comparison. Again, the same logic applies as above. Based on the collective experience of FDEs, no case has been reported of one writer writing exactly the same way twice. Again, Crane's study has shown that this statement is correct, but it is a function of the extent of the material written by the writer.

Assuming we have sample writings from two different writers, when comparing them, the FDE expects to find differences having sufficient weight that he is led to the conclusion that they are by different writers. Whether the evidence present is sufficient to reach a completely negative opinion is not the issue. What is important is that the two writings have differences that cannot be reconciled based only on their content.

VARIATION

One of the first basic concepts that must be learned before attempting to compare two writings is "variation." Variation as a concept has been discussed previously. Harrison referred to it as a "master pattern." What is important here is for the FDE to make a determination of the range of the writer's variation. The extent of the writer's variation can only be based on the examination of the specimen writing before the FDE. If a feature is not in that writing, it cannot be assumed that because the writer writes this way in another instance, he should be expected to recreate that writing in this instance. The FDE cannot add to the writing being studied. To do so is to hazard making an error.

When comparing writing(s), it is important to understand how each letter, letter combination, etc. is written, what was the direction of the pen when the feature was written, etc. Understanding variation and its limits is important to every examination. Why? Lets assume that an FDE is examining a questioned writing. During his examination of the specimens he determines the range of variation of a feature having some significance for identification purposes. In his examination of the questioned writing he finds that the same letter with its features are present in the questioned writing. The question he must ask himself, and establish by observation and by weighing the evidence, is are they the same in both sets of writing? If the answer is no, then the possibility exists that more than one writer could be involved, the one who wrote the questioned writing and the one who wrote the specimens.

Figure 13.5

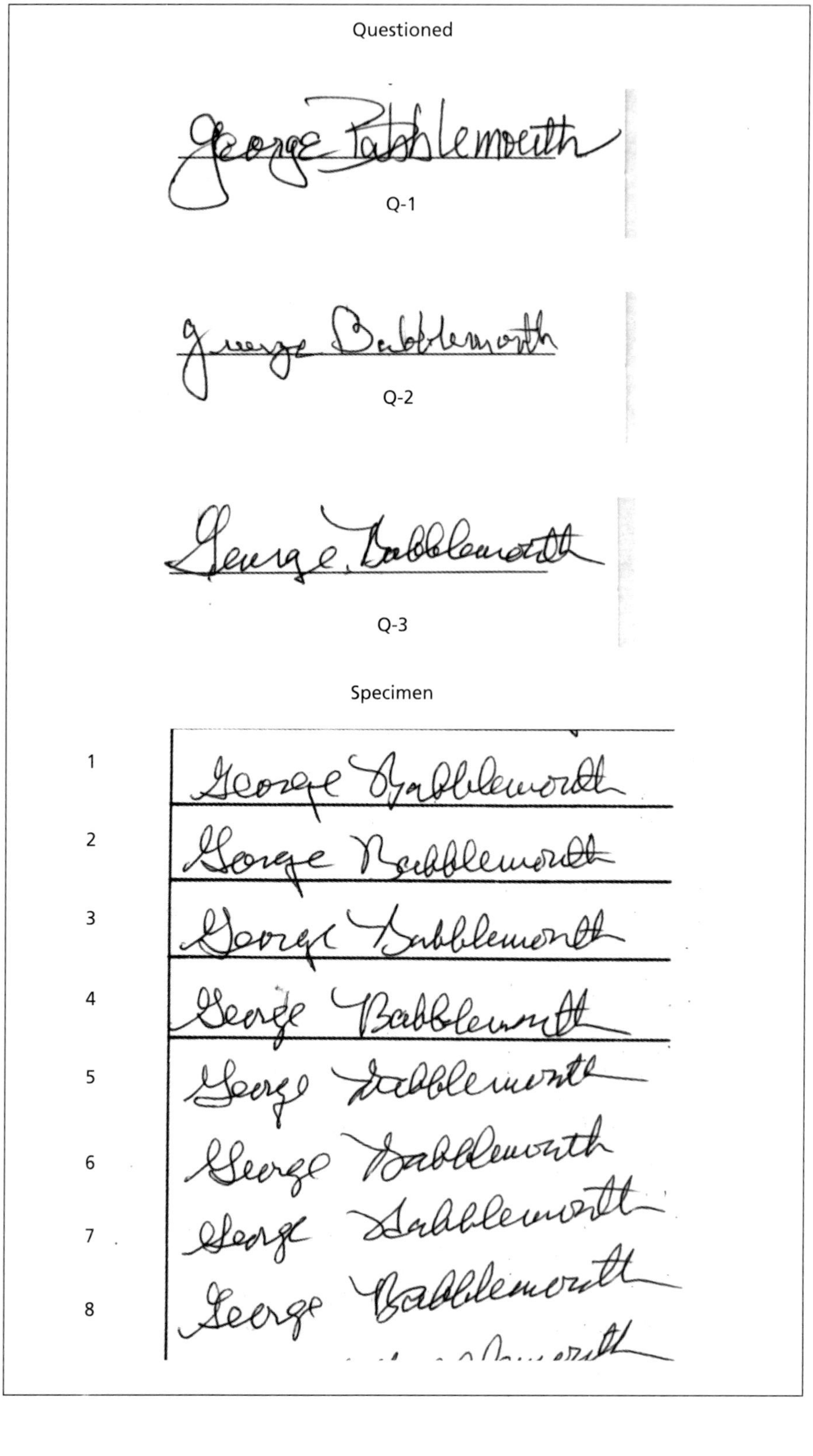

Figure 13.5 is an illustration chart showing three questioned signatures in the name George Babblemouth, and eight sample signatures from a handwriting specimen form. The name was selected by the author and, as far as he knows, no one by that name exists. If there is a person with that name, the selection of that name for use here is purely coincidental. This name is used by the different writers who assisted the author in creating work problems for classroom instruction on handwriting and hand printing identification.

For the purposes of this discussion, the assumption is made that the eight specimen signatures are all the writing available for comparison purposes. In actuality, the author had approximately 30 signatures repeating this name plus two sheets of additional handwriting written on a general handwriting specimen form similar to the one in the chapter on "Obtaining Handwriting Samples."

The question is. Did the writer of the specimen write the questioned signatures Q-1, Q-2, and Q-3? To try and answer this question, each question signature will be considered at a time. A complete discussion of every quality and feature of the writing will not be discussed in this explanation, it will be left up to the reader to apply the principles given in this text and from his own experiments perform a complete analysis of the writing.

DISCUSSION OF Q-1 AND THE SPECIMEN WRITING

The following is a description of the Q-1 "George Babblemouth" signature. Q-1 has the following qualities:

- It is naturally written, as evidenced by the tapered beginning and ending strokes and tick marks; variation in writing pressure – relative pressure habits – and the rhythm of the writing; the roundness of portions of most of the letters, such as the "g's," ending "e," in "George," the upper case "B," in "Babblemouth;" and the eyelet formations such as in the "e" and on the left side of the "u," etc.
- The writing is legible. Even though legibility is a quality of writing, a writing can be illegible, and still be of good quality.
- Some of the other qualities of the writing that denote it is naturally written are the relative speed of the writing as evidenced by the light upstrokes and heavy downstrokes, which are a manifestation of the rhythmical contraction and relaxation of the writer's muscles, and the smoothness of the line quality.
- The writing is not awkward.
- The embellishment of the initial letters in both names, etc.

Q-1 has some of the following features important for identification.

In the name "George":

- The enlarged lower case "g" used as an upper case letter in the name "George."
- The relative size relationship between the upper and lower parts of each of the "G's."
- The hooked terminal stroke of the first "G" and the relative slant of the "e" following the "G."
- The relative relationship (ratio) between the components (top and bottom) of the lower case "g" following the "r" is approximately the same as that of the larger "G" at the beginning of the name. This does not mean that the size of the top and bottom are the same.
- The triangular shape of the letter "o" with the two eyelets, one on the left side and one horizontally across the top of the letter.
- The differences in the relative height relationship between the lower case letters, i.e. the first "e" in "George" is shorter than the "o" following it, the "r" following the "o" is approximately the same size as the "o," the oval of the "g" is smaller than the height and width of the preceding "or" combination and the "E" following it, etc.
- The use of what is frequently called the "Greek E" by FDEs or upper case "E" as the last letter in the given name.

In the name "Babblemouth":

- The large printed form of the letter "B," its shape, the location of the back or left vertical stroke of the letter, and the extremely large "3" formation that makes up the right side of the letter. In addition, the difference in the size of the upper and lower portions of the right side of the letter, the lower portion being larger and extending further to the right than the upper part of the letter.
- The differences in the relative size relationship between the upper case letters in the beginning of the two names, i.e. "g" and "B."
- The differences in the relative height relationship between the lower case letters.
- The relative slant of each individual letter compared to the overall slant of the writing.
- The manuscript style of writing, the mixing of printed and cursive writing styles.
- The shape of the ovals in the "a", "b's," and "o."
- The triangular shape of the ovals of the "b's."
- The angular connecting stroke between the "le" combination.
- The triangular shape of the "o" following the "m," and the relative slant of the eyelet loop at the top of the letter before the connecting stroke to the "u" following the "o."

■ The two eyelet formations on either side of the "u", the angular bottom of the "u" on the left.

■ The angular formation of the connecting strokes between the "u," "t," and "h."

■ The relative placement of the letters with respect to the pre-drawn baseline – some of the letters being written over or extending below the baseline – i.e. the "eo" combination in "George," the double "b" combination and the "uth" combination in "Babblemouth."

■ The variations in the heights between the lower case letters in the name "George," the large printed "B" formation in the name "Babblemouth."

In summary, in and of itself, there are no indicators in Q-1 that the writing is anything other than the normal, natural writing of a writer. All of the qualities and features of the writing are what the FDE would expect to find in natural writing.

When the questioned writing, Q-1, is compared to the specimen writing S-1 shown in Figure 13.5, the following similarities/differences between these writings are noted:

■ The enlarged lower case "g" formation used for the first letter of the name in Q-1 has no counterpart in the specimen writing. In fact, the writer of the specimens consistently uses the cursive form of the "G." This is a significant difference between the two writings.

■ There is a pen lift between the "g" and the "e" in "George" in Q-1, and no pen lift is used between these two letters in the specimen signatures.

■ The writer of the specimens, signatures Nos. 4 and 5, occasionally writes the "e" very close to or touching the preceding letter, "G."

■ The spacing between the "eo" combination in the questioned writing is larger than that in the specimens.

■ The shape of the "o" and the angle of the eyelet formation above it in line 1 of the specimen is similar to that in the questioned, Q-1. The "o" in lines 3 through 8 of the specimens is similar in shape to that of the questioned letter "o," but it does not have the same eyelet formation over the letter that connects to the "r."

■ Neither the shape of the oval of the "g," nor the shape of the lower projection of the letter in the specimen, is similar to that used in the questioned.

■ The ending "e" is also different, as previously discussed.

■ There is no printed form of the letter "B" in the specimen with which to compare it to the one in the questioned signature, Q-1. In the specimen signatures on lines 2 and 3, the lower part of the letter extends beyond the top part of the letter. However, there is *no* basis for saying that because the specimen writer does that with the cursive form of the letter that he will do it with the printed form. Printing must be compared with printing and cursive with cursive. In this situation they must be considered as different letter forms.

- The "a" following the "B" has a different slant, starting point, shape, etc. in the questioned signature than that in the specimens. The closest one in shape is the "a" in the fourth specimen signature. However, the differences in how the letters are made, their placement with respect to the baseline, etc. are significant differences that must be weighted.

- The double "b" combination in the questioned signature has no counterparts in the specimen signatures.

- The same is true for the "le" combination.

- The "M" in the questioned signature is similar in shape to an upper case formation of this letter. In Q-1, this upper case formation is being used where a lower case letter should be used. Further, it is printed while those of the specimens are cursive. The writer of the specimens has a preference for counterclockwise movements when making the letter "m" in the specimens, and the resulting letter formation pictorially resembles a "w."

- The relative size relationship between the "ou" letter combination in the questioned signature is very different from those in the specimens. Typically, the "o" is significantly larger than the "u" in the specimens. Also, the shape of the "u" is very different.

- The "th" combination in the questioned signature is very legible, the t-cross is near the top of the staffs of the letters, the arch of the "h" is well defined, and the terminal stroke is long on approximately a 30° angle and has a tick mark at its end that shows the pen was moving away from the writer. The t-cross is off balanced on the left side of the upper projection of the "t." In the specimen writing these letters are not as legible, the arch of the "h" is not as well defined, the terminal stroke of the "h" typically is long and points downward. The t-cross is similar to that in the questioned signatures except that the one in the specimens is more needle-shaped than the one in the questioned signature.

Having gone through this analysis, pointing out both similarities and differences, in summary it can be said that the *differences* outweigh the similarities. Therefore, it could safely be concluded that the author of the specimen writing may not have written the questioned signature. The author would not eliminate the specimen writer; but if this were all that was available for comparison purposes, it could be concluded that "Based on the available material, there is some evidence to suggest the writer of the specimens may not have written the questioned signature, Q-1."

The qualification is due in large part to the fact that there was a very limited amount of specimen writing available, plus there were some similarities present, such as the "o" in "George," the overall relative height relationship between the upper and lower case letters, some of the relative pressure habits, such as those in the "o," etc.

Turning now to Q-2, the same type of analysis can be done on this signature and the specimen writing. In this instance, there are more differences present between this questioned signature and the specimens than when it is compared to Q-1. To summarize this analysis, even though the same letter form "g" is used as the first letter in the given name, it is different from that in Q-1 in every respect: relative size relationship between its components, direction of its ending stroke, etc. Further, the writing of the lower case letters in the given name is generally a series of counterclockwise movements – except where the "r" connects to the letter "g." The style of the upper case "B" is more of a cursive form, the bulk of the letters written in the surname contain pen stops – i.e. the "bl" combination, the angularity of the "m" that in some respects resembles the "m" in signature 8 of the specimens, the "ou" combination that has some similarities with its counterpart letters in lines 4, 5, 7, and 8 of the specimens. A big difference between questioned and specimens is in the t-cross. The taper of the t-cross in the questioned goes from right to left while the taper of the t-cross in the specimens is from left to right.

With respect to the writer of the specimens having written the Q-2 signature, based on the available specimen writing it would have to be concluded, "There is no evidence to suggest the writer of the specimens wrote the Q-2 signature." However, if this were a case before me for examination purposes, the report would also contain a request for specimen writing written by the writer of the current specimens, but written with his unaccustomed hand.

The Q-3 signature was written by the writer of the specimens. All of the qualities and features important for identification found in the questioned signature, Q-1, are also present within the specimens.

The *fact* is that the writer of the specimens also wrote the three questioned signatures. The author witnessed their writing and provided the writer with the following instructions:

- Q-1. Write the name "George Babblemouth" in such a way that your handwriting habits will not be present in the writing. The writer knew nothing about what is important for identification purposes before writing this signature.
- Q-2. Write the name "George Babblemouth" with your unaccustomed hand. In other words, write the name with your left hand. In this case the writer normally writes with his right hand.
- Q-3. Write the name "George Babblemouth" in your normal natural writing. Do not attempt to change your writing in any way.

The three questioned signatures were written *after* the specimens.

The next example involves an extended body of writing, a note, shown in Figure 13.6. In Figure 13.6 two bodies of writing are shown. The first body is the questioned material and the second is the known. They repeat the same material and are written on lined paper. There are numerous pictorial differences between the qualities and features of these writings, such as line quality,

Figure 13.6

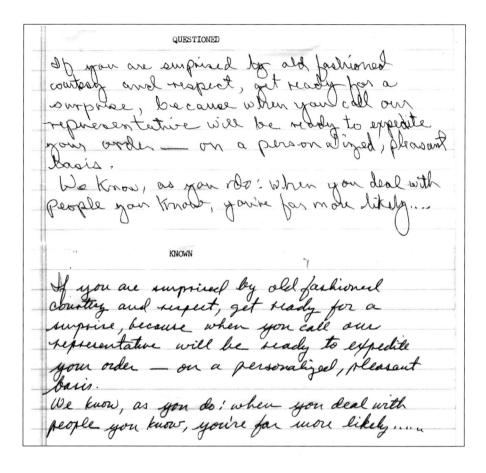

rhythm, connectedness of the letters, average slant of the writing, relative slant of letters within the writing, etc. Figure 13.7 shows a few examples of both writings.

These are some of the similarities between the questioned and specimen writings:

- The scissor shaped "I" in the questioned, and specimen, are not identical, but there is a slight pictorial similarity between them – box 1. The "f's" are very different; however, there is a good deal of pictorial similarity between the "f" in the questioned writing here and the similar style of "f" found in the specimen writing.
- The use of two different styles of "r" in "surprised" – box 2: The tent shape "r" after the "u," and the speed "r" after the "p." The fact that both styles of "r" are used and in exactly the same location has some significance for identification.
- The wider spacing between "by" and "old" than between "old" and "fashioned" in box 3. Further, the use of the same style of "f" as the first letter in the word "fashioned," and the relative placement of the i-dot with respect to the staff of the letter.
- The use, again, of a speed "r" as the first letter in the word "respect" – box 4.

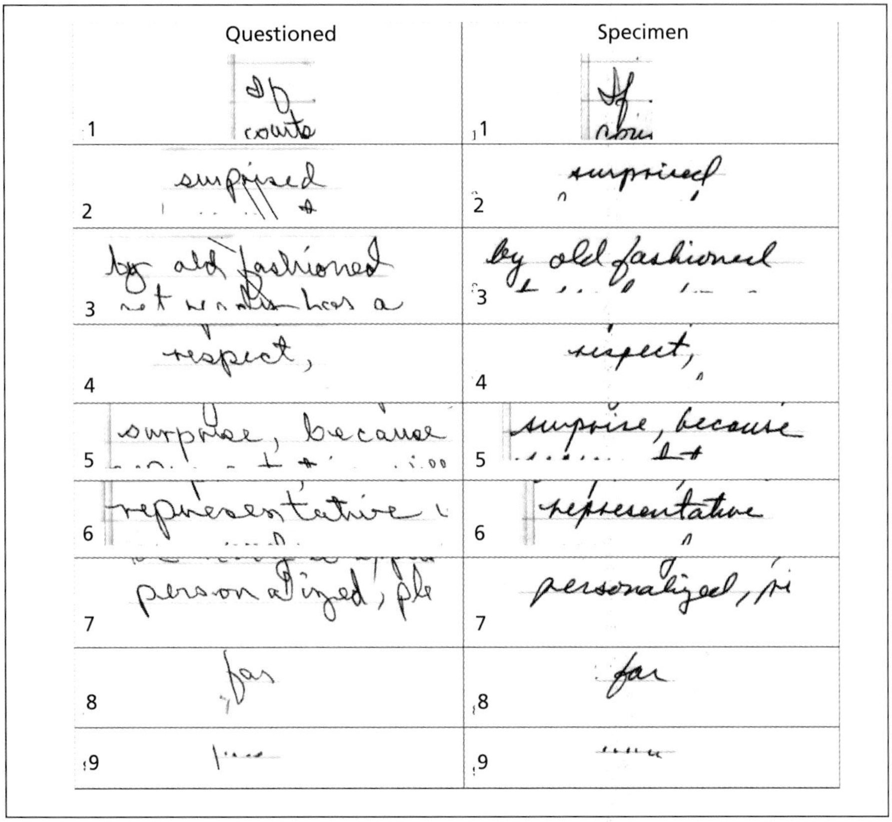

Figure 13.7

- The placement of the comma at a location approximately half the distance between the two words – box 5.
- The use of the speed "r" at the beginning and as the fourth letter from the left – interior – letter in the name "representative" – box 6.
- The use of a different style of "r" in "personalized," together with the placement of the comma approximately halfway between the two words, and the wider spacing between the "z" and "e" than between the "e" and "d" – box 7.
- The use of the same style "f," again – box 8.
- The pattern of placing two dots close together, then using a slightly wider space between the first pair and second pair, etc. – box 9.

There are other similarities between these two writings as well. There are also many, many differences. What might be the cause of those differences? In this instance, the writer wrote the questioned material with his left hand and the specimen with his right hand. As was explained to me, as a child he would practice writing with both hands, even though he was discouraged from writing with his left hand.

If all that was available for examination and comparison purposes was the questioned writing, an FDE would conclude that the material was written by someone having a low level of writing skill, and it would be correct. This writer had not written very much with his left hand as an adult, so his level of skill is significantly different, depending upon which hand he uses.

One of the features that is very evident is the relative spacing habits between words, between the end of a word and a punctuation mark. This attention to relative spacing is one of the more important features of this writing for identification purposes.

Again, in this instance, the FDE would recognize some of the signs in materials written with the unaccustomed hand and would request that the specimen writer provide a sample repeating the questioned material but written with the left hand.

SUMMARY

The process of comparison consists of examining both the questioned and specimen writings for their pictorial impression and the use of similar forms and patterns, and then in detail noting all of the similarities and differences between the writings. Due notice being taken of the two, significance is attached to each quality and feature of the writing, important for identification purposes, and then evaluated to determine which has the greater weight. The level of the opinion rendered, many times, depends upon the FDE's level of experience. As a trainee, he would probably be more inclined to reduce the significance that should be attached to a feature indicating that another writer could be involved – understating the importance of differences and overstating the importance of similarities.

When describing a writing's quality or its features, the FDE should use easy to understand words – counterclockwise, clockwise, staff, oval or circle, retraced, etc. – to describe what he sees. The use of complicated descriptors benefits no one, especially the reader of a report. The author remembers his training and the senior examiners under whom he studied being able to take the description of a letter or a series of letters in every detail report he had submitted and draw a good "likeness" of the letter using only his written description. I challenge the reader to try that as an experiment at some time. Put in writing how a letter is made, give that description to someone else, and have them draw what you have described. Is what they draw the letter you described? It should be very similar.

REFERENCES

Crane, A. (1999) "Does the amount of handwriting on a cheque constitute a 'Reasonable Amount Of Sample?' *Canadian Society of Forensic Science Journal*, 32(1).

Harrison, Wilson R. (1966) *Suspect Documents Their Scientific Examination*, London: Sweet & Maxwell Limited.

CHAPTER 14

ABNORMAL/DISGUISED WRITING

THE DIFFERENT TYPES AND THEIR CAUSES

The definition of disguise:

1 to change the appearance of so as to conceal identity or mislead, as with deceptive garb.
2 to conceal the truth or actual character of by a counterfeit form or appearance; . . .
3 something that serves or is intended for disguising identity, character, or quality; . . .
   (Random 1992)

Huber and Headrick (1999: 399) define disguised writing as: "The consequence of any deliberate attempt to alter the elements of one's own writing . . ." Hilton said, "A writer may deliberately try to alter his usual writing habits in hopes of hiding his identity. The results, regardless of their effectiveness, are termed disguised writing" (Hilton 1982: 19).

In each of the above definitions, the operative word is "deliberate." The FDE must properly evaluate the writing he is examining and even then proceed with great caution lest he makes a mistake and concludes that the writing is disguised when it is not. There are situations when the writing can be unnaturally written and disguised. The difference between the two is that the former is an intentional act on the part of the writer to avoid detection and the latter is not necessarily the result of an intentional act; rather it is something possibly beyond the writer's control which has affected his ability to write.

Typically, unnatural writing occurs when the writer is affected by some transitory factor, such as his writing hand is cold, the effect of medication or even illegal drugs, an awkward writing position, a defect in the writing surface, a malfunctioning writing instrument, etc. The writer does not necessarily intend to alter his writing to avoid detection; the writing is altered because of the effect of the transitory factor at the time.

In addition to disguise and unnatural writing, there are times when a writer will produce a letter or other feature that is an accidental. Accidental features occur rarely and when they do, they may never occur again in exactly that same form. In small amounts of writing, their occurrence could take on characteristics found in another writer's writing for whom that feature is a normal part of his writing habit.

Harrison observed that,

> A deliberate departure from normal handwriting habits, generally referred to as "disguise," can be expected whenever:
>
> 1 the handwriting is that of an anonymous letter which the writer has no desire to have traced back to him by recognition of the handwriting;
> 2 the signature of a fictitious person is fabricated on a receipt or other similar document;
> 3 the signature of a real person is carefully copied from a genuine signature;
> 4 the handwriting, or more often the figuring, of another person is copied in an endeavour (endeavor) to place the blame elsewhere (Harrison 1966: 349).

Suspicion of disguise alone is not sufficient cause to say that writing is disguised. The very concept of disguise involves deliberation – 'careful consideration before decision . . . " (Random) – and intent – ' . . . something that is intended; purpose; design; intention: . . . Law. the state of a person's mind that directs his or her actions toward an objective . . . ." (Random) on the part of the writer before he writes.

The evidence necessary to say that writing is disguised must be so persuasive that there is no other explanation for why that particular combination of features occurred in the writing. When the FDE concludes that the writing is disguised he is at the same time saying that the writer intentionally altered his writing to avoid detection. Some would infer from that statement that the writer is possibly guilty of a crime or his intentions are certainly questionable. The burden of proof necessary to reach the conclusion that a writer is disguising his writing is formidable, especially when some of the signs of disguised writing are also signs of slowness or that of a writer with a low level of writing skill.

The FDE must constantly be on guard that he is properly evaluating all the evidence within the writing, applying the proper significance to each feature, and reaching a conclusion consistent with the evidence in the writing. He cannot dismiss any consistent differences that might actually be the result of a different handwriting habit, as disguise. To do so is to increase the probability of an error.

Let's assume that the FDE is examining a case consisting of a questioned writing of some length, more writing than just a signature, and comparing it to specimens by a known writer, for example paragraphs 2 and 3 from Figure 8.9, shown below in Figure 14.1. The writing of paragraph 3 was done after the writer was instructed to deliberately disguise her writing. Paragraph 2 is shown here because it is a correct representation of the normal, natural writing of the writer.

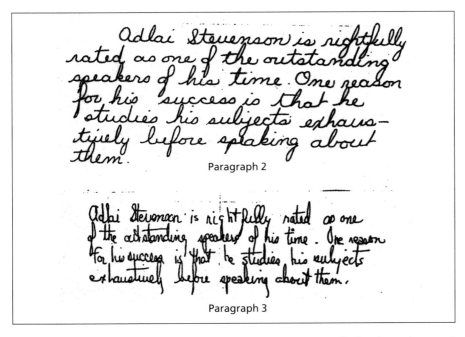

Figure 14.1

Two further examples of this paragraph, written naturally by the writer and then with instruction to disguise their writing, are shown in Figures 14.2 and 14.3. They will be referred to as writers No. 1 and No. 2.

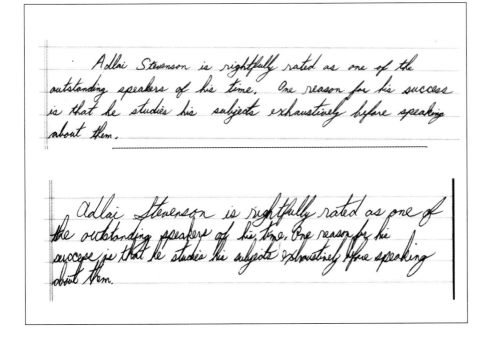

Figure 14.2

At the top is the writing of writer no. 1. It is his normal, natural writing. Below is his "disguised" writing; note that it is the same material. Based on the evidence present in the writing below, it could not be concluded that it is disguised.

How did he disguise his writing? He wrote the words larger, used a couple of alternative letter forms (a printed "A" in "Adlai" and "S" in "Stevenson"), constricted the writing by narrowing the spacing between words in lines 2 through 4, and not much else. While a few other features are different, if asked the question, "did he disguise his writing?" The author's answer would be no! Certainly, if he "intended" to disguise his writing because he was asked to, his attempt was unsuccessful. In this instance, the argument could be made that his writing may not be naturally written, but there is insufficient evidence to say that he disguised his writing.

Figure 14.3

At the top is the writing of writer no. 2. It is her normal, natural writing. Below is her "disguised" writing; note that it is the same material. Based on the evidence present in the writing below, there is more evidence to suggest that she attempted to disguise her writing than writer no. 1.

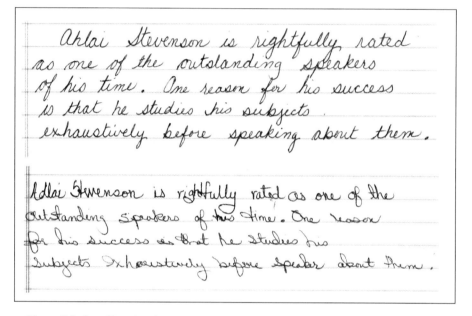

How did she disguise her writing? She too started off by using alternative letter forms (a printed "A," "S," and "r"), and for a short time she reduced her writing speed, as evidenced by the uniform line quality, increased pressure, and lack of relative pressure habits. The "reduction in speed" attempt lasted almost through the first sentence, after which she increased her writing speed, again incorporating relative pressure habits, improved line quality, etc. What was her major attempt to disguise her writing? She changed the angle of slant from rightward to vertical, and then to a backward slant. She started by using a vertical writing with increased writing pressure, then gradually increased the backward slant of the writing while increasing speed. The combination caused some changes in letter formation or parts of letters, i.e. the lower projection, the beginning stroke on the "o" in "of" etc.

What are the basic elements to look for in determining that writing is possibly disguised? What constitutes disguised writing? These are two distinctly different questions, even though they overlap.

What are the basic elements to look for in determining that writing is possibly disguised? There are four basic elements involved in disguising one's writing: slant, speed, style, and size.

- *Slant* – there are two types of slant that must be considered: overall and relative slant. If a writer deliberately alters the overall slant of his writing from, say, his normal forward to a backward, or left leaning slant, his writing will change depending upon the degree of change he makes in the slant and his level of graphic maturity. The changes can be minor or dramatic and are a function of the angle of the writing and his ability to write at that angle.

  When slant changes, the pictorial appearance of the writing changes, as does the writer's relative speed and pressure habits, letter styles and their construction, connecting strokes, the rhythm with which he writes, etc. No single characteristic of writing can be changed without also affecting other characteristics. When the writer changes the slant of the writing, the following features of writing are also affected: the writing speed, the style and features of the letters, as well as the size of the writing (both absolute and to some extent the relative relationships between the letters written.)
- *Speed* – when a writer changes his speed of writing, he either writes faster or slower than normal with a corresponding change in relative speed of writing caused by the change in the interaction of contracting and relaxing muscles, etc. A more detailed discussion of writing speed is found in Chapter 8.
- *Style* – changes in slant and speed can have a profound effect on the style of the writing and the shapes of letters, connecting strokes, placement of i-dots, t-crosses, etc. Refer to Figure 14.3. If a writer changes the style of the letters and writes letter forms he is not accustomed to, his speed of writing is also affected because he is uncertain of what he is writing and how it is supposed to look.
- *Size* – the size of the writing is as easily changed as slant and speed. If the writer writes larger letter forms naturally, the relative speed of his writing will remain close to normal (refer to Figure 14.2). If he writes smaller, constricting letters and other features, his relative pressure habits can change dramatically (refer to Figure 14.1).

The types of movements used by different writers can be categorized into the following broad groups: (1) finger movements; (2) finger, hand movements; (3) finger, hand, forearm movements; and (4) compound movements incorporating the former three. At this point, it would be a good idea for the reader to pick up a pen and perform the following exercise.

First, write the paragraph shown in Figure 14.1 in your normal, natural writing. Then write the paragraph several times each as follows:

1   Write the paragraph rapidly, as fast as you can, as if you were taking notes in class.
2   Write the paragraph slowly, as if you were paying attention to every detail of the

writing, making sure they are written perfectly.

3   Write the paragraph several times and each time change the slant to a more forward slant.

4   Write the paragraph using a vertical slant or straight up and down.

5   Write the paragraph several times each with a backhand slant at an angle of approximately 135°, and then 150°.

6   Write the paragraph using only finger movements, by placing the palm of the hand firmly on the writing surface, as if it were a pivot point, using only finger movements to write each word – move the hand to the right after completing each word, placing it on the writing surface in preparation for writing the next word.

7   Raise the palm off the writing surface and use a combination of finger, hand, and arm movements; write the paragraph.

8   Write the paragraph using your unaccustomed hand – the one you do not normally use when writing.

What this experiment demonstrates is the interaction of all of the factors discussed in the book and their effect on writing. A dramatic change in slant can affect speed, the shapes of letters and connecting strokes, attention to baseline, writing consistency, etc. As has been said, disguised writing is someone making a conscious decision to change their writing to avoid detection by using a combination of these different ways.

When dealing with a small amount of writing, such as a very limited signature, say, in the name "John Doe," the FDE may not be able to determine, from that one signature, that it was written with deliberation, and thus disguised. Sometimes it is not possible to make that determination even with a more complicated name.

Figure 14.4

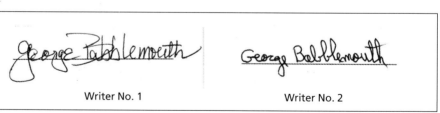

Writer No. 1   Writer No. 2

Figure 14.4 shows the name "George Babblemouth" written by two different writers. Based solely on each writing of the name, is there sufficient evidence to say that either or both of these signatures is the disguised writing of their author? No! Both writings appear to be naturally written by writers having very different levels of skill.

If the writer uses his unaccustomed hand to write the name, occasionally there is sufficient evidence of a writer's normal writing habits in the writing for the FDE to request that he provide specimens written with the unaccustomed hand for comparison purposes.

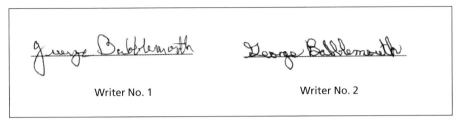

Figure 14.5

Writer No. 1   Writer No. 2

Figure 14.5 shows the writings of the name "George Babblemouth" done with the unaccustomed hand of their writers. Writers No. 1 and 2 wrote the signatures attributed to them in both Figures 14.4 and 14.5.

Figure 14.6

Writer No. 1   Writer No. 2

Figure 14.6 shows the natural writing of the name "George Babblemouth" by both writers. In this case, writer No. 1 has accomplished his disguise with greater success than did writer No. 2.

HOW TO RECOGNIZE DISGUISED WRITING

The methods used to disguise one's writing are relatively simple. We have already covered most of the mechanical means. If a writer is trying to disguise his writing only for the writing of a short time, say the signature in the name "John Doe," or even longer signatures like "George Babblemouth" in Figure 14.4, he may be able to successfully accomplish his task and go undetected. If, on the other hand, he is trying to disguise his writing for a longer time, say to write the paragraph in Figure 14.1, he may not be as successful. It is almost impossible for a writer to maintain the level of concentration necessary to disguise his writing for a long time. Of course, part of this depends upon whether he is simply trying to avoid detection, based on his writing habits, or whether he is trying to simulate the writing habits of another's writing, suppress his own, and avoid detection. How is disguised writing recognized?

CHANGES IN WRITING SKILL

Usually, disguised handwriting is not as fluent and rhythmically written as natural handwriting. There are exceptions like the one shown in Figure 14.4 by writer No. 1. Of course the assumption made here is that the writer is relatively skillful with a pen, rather than someone with a low level of skill. If the writer has a low level of writing skill, many of the features in his normal writing will also be present in his disguised writing, i.e. tremor, frequent pen stops, awkward letter forms, etc. That is not to say that a person with a low skill level cannot successfully disguise their writing.

CHANGES IN THE SLANT OF WRITING

Normal, natural writing usually has a uniform overall slant characteristic, even though the relative slants between letters may vary depending upon the letter and/or letter combinations written. One of the most frequently chosen methods of disguising writing is by changing its slant – overall. An exception to this is found in the disguised writing of writer No. 1 shown in Figure 14.4. Because the writer is not able to maintain speed, rhythm, etc. for any length of time at this new slant, the FDE expects to find an inconsistency in writing slant over the length of the body of writing (refer to Figure 14.3). Therefore, inconsistencies in slant, beyond that found in normal, natural writing, is an indication that the writing could be disguised.

CHANGES IN LETTER DESIGN OR STYLE

If the writer recognizes he writes some letters or letter combinations in what he would consider an "unusual way," then when he deliberately disguises his writing he will attempt to change the design or style of those letter(s). When he makes the change in letter design or style, he usually writes slower, with more uniform pressure, and other signs of deliberation.

Some writers substitute printed and/or block letters for cursive ones. In extended bodies of writing such substitutions will occasionally look out of place in the context of the writing, plus the substituted letter(s) may not be consistently used, and would be obviously outside of the writer's "master pattern" of writing that particular letter form. The great caution here is to not misinterpret an accidental for a disguised feature, or vice versa, particularly in small amounts of writing, such as a signature or a single word.

CONSISTENCY, THE KEY

Normal, natural writing is usually consistent, and the writer has certain "master patterns" of letter forms and other features around which there is the expected normal range of variation. This consistency is present until either some transitory factor adversely affects the writer's ability to write, or the writer intentionally alters his writing to avoid detection – disguise.

Consistency is not limited to cursive writing. Block letters, hand printing, numerals, diacritics, punctuation marks, etc. are all written consistently around a "master pattern" in natural writing. When that consistency is interrupted intentionally, the FDE can suspect that the cause could be a deliberate attempt by the writer to alter his normal writing habits.

In disguised writing, inconsistency is a primary component. When a letter or letter combination is written naturally, the "master pattern" around which variation takes place is rather limited because the same basic movements are reproduced each time they are written. In disguised writing, the range of variation around a "master pattern" may be non-existent or wider than in normal, natural writing because the writer is not able to repeat the same basic movements each and every time he writes to avoid detection.

If the reader has taken time to perform the experiments outlined above, an examination and comparison of those writings will show that in those writings where the writer deliberately altered their writing, they were not able to repetitively reproduce the same movements. A review of Figure 14.1 will help to illustrate this point.

In paragraph 3 of Figure 14.1, the writer did the following to try to disguise her writing: the attempt is rather simple as she slowed her writing speed, chose some alternative letter forms, and made some minor adjustments to the slant of her normal writing.

In this particular case, the attempted disguise is not very good. In spite of the pictorial differences between the writings in paragraphs 2 and 3, an FDE would be able to say with a significant degree of certainty that the author of paragraphs 2 and 3 are one and the same. The same is true for the writer shown in Figure 14.2. Other writers are able to disguise their writing better and for a significantly longer time than the writers of this material.

SUGGESTIONS ON WHAT TO DO IF THE WRITER IS DISGUISING HIS WRITING

If the writer has disguised his writing in the questioned material and not in the specimens, identifying him as the writer of the questioned writing depends upon his successfulness in disguising his writing and the amount of writing involved. There are some occasions when the writer of a disguised writing would in all probability never be identified based on his handwriting, and the disguised writing of writer No. 1 in Figure 14.4 would have to be placed in that group.

The greater the amount of disguised writing, the greater the likelihood that its author will not maintain the disguise, and could be identified. The smaller the amount of disguised writing, the more likely it is that its writer will maintain the disguise, and will not be identified as the writer (see Figure 14.4, writer

No. 1). The assumption being made in this statement is that for the latter situation, the writer was successful in not incorporating any or very few of his habits into the writing.

When the disguise attempt is made in the preparation of the specimen writing, if it is detected or even suspected, the FDE can ask for additional request and non-request – i.e. normal course of business – writings to assist him in determining whether the questioned writing is truly disguised. This is done frequently in criminal cases when a suspect attempts to disguise his writing in preparing the specimen writing forms. The material in chapters on obtaining handwriting specimens gives a list of possible sources from which to obtain specimen writing. The reader is referred to that chapter for further instruction.

REFERENCES

Harrison, Wilson R. (1966) *Suspect Documents Their Scientific Examination*, 2nd Impression with Supplement, London.

Hilton, Ordway (1982) *Scientific Examination of Questioned Documents*, revised edn, New York, NY.

Huber, Roy A. and Headrick, A.M. (1999) *Handwriting Identification: Facts and Fundamentals*, New York: CRC Press.

Random (1992) *Random House Webster's Electronic Dictionary and Thesaurus*. College Edition, Reference Software International.

CHAPTER 15

OBTAINING HANDWRITING SAMPLES

DEFINING TERMS

In Chapter 12, the following terms were defined: questioned writing, sample or specimen writing. Samples or specimens are interchangeable terms used to describe writing(s) obtained and used for comparison purposes. It was important to define these terms in Chapter 12 because of the discussion on the background of handwriting and hand printing identification. The definitions are restated and expanded here.

QUESTIONED WRITING

First, questioned writing is defined as writing, the authorship of which is unknown. Its authorship will remain unknown until determined by the proper application of established handwriting identification techniques, comparing it with known writing(s) of the person who wrote it or by the admission of its writer that he in fact wrote the material. Any document containing handwritten or hand printed material can become the subject of an investigation and forensic examination.

What is a document? For the FDE, the definition of a document is as follows: anything movable or immovable under the canopy of heaven that contains written material or for which there is a question concerning its source, alteration, identification of a writer, etc. This may seem like too broad a definition and includes everything in the world; but, in reality, a document could fit within this broad definition. FDEs have been asked to examine and render opinions about the authorship of writing on building walls; recover engraved or obliterated writings on different types of surfaces, such as metal, plastic, paper, determine the identity of typewriters, printers, embossers, inks, printing processes; and link documents based on their fabrication and component parts, etc. Typically, though, the questioned document is a check, threatening letter, hold-up note, credit application or receipt, will, investment record, tax form, medical record, plastic identification or credit and debit cards, etc. The most frequently asked questions are: who wrote a questioned writing on the document? How was the information on the document altered? What business machine was used to create the document, or emboss the information in it?

Determining the authorship of writing(s) on such documents is generally the critical part of a criminal investigation or civil matter, and many times the outcome of the case hinges on the FDE identifying the writer of the questioned material. The questioned writing may consist of a signature(s), all the writing on the document, initials, etc. The larger the quantity of questioned writings or the more individuality the writing has, the greater the probability that its writer(s) will be identified (Crane 1999). Occasionally, the FDE is asked to examine only a couple of initials, numerals, or a word. Although examination of a limited amount of material is possible, it is not always possible to arrive at any definitive statements or any relatively strong degree of probability concerning the identity of its writer. Occasionally, the limited amount of writing in question is on a document having a substantial amount of writing that may not be in question because it appears to be irrelevant. In fact, sometimes, the FDE determines that the examination of just that small amount of material is not sufficient and that it would be best to consider all of the writing as a collective whole. This does not mean that the FDE is trying to do the job of the investigator. Most of the time when this occurs it means the FDE has determined from his preliminary examination that other portions of the writing should also be questioned.

One such case the author worked on serves as a good example. An attorney called on the author to examine a payer signature on several checks. The questioned documents were photocopies of checks and the questioned material was the payer signature on the front of the checks and some of the endorsements on the back of a few of the checks. There was no way of knowing what generation photocopies were the subject of the exam; and while the writings in question were not very good, a few were borderline suitable for examination purposes. The bulk of the checks' face material was suitable for examination purposes. My client did not want an examination of that material because of the amount of time that would be involved in performing the examination. However, when comparing *all* of the writing collectively that should have been questioned with the specimen writing, it would have been possible to arrive at a stronger degree of belief – opinion – concerning the identity of the writer than would be rendered by examining only what my client thought should be the questioned writing.

SAMPLE OR SPECIMEN WRITING

Sample or specimen writing is subdivided into two groups. The general definition of specimen writing is that writing the authorship of which *must* be known, if it is to be used by the FDE for comparison purposes. Specimen writing can be broken down into these two sub-groups, request and non-request or collected writings.

Request writings are those the authorship of which is known because their preparation is witnessed, usually by the individual soliciting the writing. The solicitor may be an investigator, lawyer, FDE, or someone else who will attest to the authenticity of the writing as being written by a particular writer. The purpose for the solicitation is to use the requested writing for handwriting comparison. The only requirement is that whatever sample writings are provided by the writer must be witnessed by someone at the time of their preparation. Therefore, the witness attests to the fact that they observed the writing of the sample offered as "requested writings." Another name sometimes used to describe these writings is "known writings."

Known writings are usually obtained using pre-printed handwriting sample forms. There are many different types of forms, and no one form is better or worse than any other specimen writing forms. Each has its specific purpose and is generally designed by an FDE who believes that it will provide him with those features of the writer's writing that are most useful in conducting a handwriting examination. Examples of several handwriting sample forms developed and used by the author are shown in Appendix 15.1 through 15.5 of this chapter.

The second group is known as non-request writings. These are writings typically written by an individual during the normal course of business, not knowing that later they could be used for handwriting comparison purposes. Non-request writings are also referred to as collected writings. There are many sources of non-request writings. A list of possible sources is provided in Chapter 15, Table 15.1 (page 185).

REQUESTED SAMPLES – PROCEDURES, FORMS, LONDON LETTER, ETC.

There is no single correct way to obtain requested samples. There are definitely some ways *not* to take samples which, taken in those ways, will in all probability seriously jeopardize the investigator's case, if not have it thrown out of court.

Requested samples are usually obtained from a specimen writer using standard handwriting sample forms. There is no standard handwriting sample form that is better than any other; each one has its own good and bad features. Even though there are a large number of standard forms in existence, frequently a special form is jointly designed by the FDE and investigator(s) to meet the needs of a particular situation. Usually the FDE is the one who designs the form for the investigator; however, there are times when both must become involved in this activity.

Certainly, investigators and FDEs have preferences about which form they would like to use because each has found a certain form(s) to be more success-ful than another. What is meant by "successful?" For the investigator, when he uses a certain form, he usually receives better opinions from the FDE. The FDE is more comfortable working with a particular handwriting form because he believes it will provide him with the characteristics and features of the writing he needs in order to make a complete and comprehensive examination. This does not mean that the use of a particular handwriting form increases the identifica-tion ratio of his work. What it says is that the design of the form, the material the specimen writer is asked to write, and the greater the number of useful repeti-tion of letters and letter combinations are of more assistance to the FDE. Over the years, the author has worked with a number of different handwriting sample forms and has found each one to have some advantages over others.

Using a particular handwriting sample form is not the only reason an investi-gator receives a "positive opinion" from the FDE. In fact, the main reason(s) he receives a positive opinion is the result of a combination of factors such as the following:

- The questioned and specimen writing are naturally written and individualistic enough to support that opinion.
- The writings obtained accurately reflect their writer's natural handwriting habits. This is particularly true when the specimen writer is both repeating and not repeating the questioned material.
- The samples are sufficient in quantity, not just quality, for comparison purposes with the questioned writing.

Some examples of handwriting forms that can be used are found in Appendix 15.1 through 15.5. Starting with the first, the following is an explanation of how and why each one is used.

THE LONDON LETTER

The London letter is a standard text of extended writing composed in such a way that each letter of the alphabet is used in both its upper and lower case form, and all of the numerals are used in different combinations. By being an extended body of writing, features such as how the writer indents, treats the margins, spaces his words and lines, etc. will be found in the writing of this letter.

A lot has been written about the London letter. It is not recommended for use in all handwriting cases, nor is it recommended by every FDE. For extended bodies of writing, such as correspondence, it does provide a sample of the writer's habits when writing an extended body of material that does not repeat the extended questioned writing.

The text of the London letter reads:

Our London business is good, but Vienna and Berlin are quiet. Mr. D. Lloyd has gone to Switzerland and I hope for good news. He will be there for a week at 1496 Zermott St. and then goes to Turin and Rome and will join Col. Parry and arrive at Athens, Greece, Nov. 27th or Dec. 2nd. Letters there should be addressed: King James Blvd. 3580. We expect Chas. E. Fuller Tuesday. Dr. L. McQuaid and Robt. Unger, Esq., left on the 'Y.X.' Express tonight. (Authorship of letter unknown)

An example of a London letter handwriting sample form is found in Appendix 15.1. This form contains pre-drawn lines on which the writer can write the text; however there are occasions when no pre-drawn lines should be used. In those instances, the text found here can be typed on a sheet of paper and presented to the specimen writer along with several sheets of unlined paper. If the questioned material is written on paper having a pre-drawn baseline, the specimen writing should be written on paper having a pre-drawn baseline. It is also desirable to use paper having the same spacing between the pre-drawn lines when obtaining specimens from a writer. If the questioned writing is written on paper having no pre-drawn baselines, then unlined paper should be provided to the specimen writer. The key element here is consistency.

GENERAL HANDWRITING AND HAND PRINTING FORMS

There are other standard handwriting and hand printing forms used to obtain handwriting samples. Appendix 15.2 and 15.3 show two general handwriting forms designed and used by the author. The form shown in Appendix 15.2 is for cursive writing, and Appendix 15.3 is for hand printing.

These forms are designed to obtain a representative sample of the writer's normal writing habits when writing letters and letter combinations, not when repeating the questioned material. While the words, names, numeral combinations, etc. on these forms are not the ones actually in the questioned writing, they are letters and letter combinations and numerals and numeral combinations frequently found in text and numerical material. By having these combinations repeated in non-emotive words, names, and numeral combinations not found in the questioned writing, the specimen writer is more likely to write them in his normal, natural style of writing than if he were repeating the questioned material, especially if *he* wrote the questioned material.

SPECIAL FORMS

The check form, Appendix 15.4, is used when the questioned material is written on the face of a check. The format shown here is typical of most checks, as is the space provided for writing.

When the writer is asked to write any material that is in question, he is *never* to be shown the questioned writing before writing *all* of the sample. If he is shown the questioned writing after completion of the entire sample, he should only be shown a copy of the document on which the writing appears. More about this topic later in the chapter.

The signature form, Appendix 15.5, can be used for signatures written with or without a pre-drawn baseline. When no baseline is used in the questioned document, the specimen writer is instructed to write inside each area shown on the form, as in Figure 15.1.

Figure 15.1

When the questioned writing is written on a baseline, the writer can be instructed to write on the line at the bottom of the box, as in Figure 15.2.

Figure 15.2

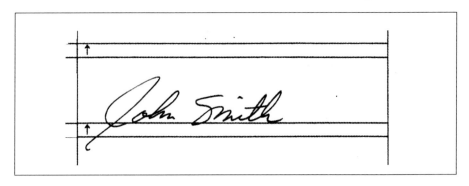

While one form will not meet every need, this form may be useful for these two situations. However, it may also be necessary to provide the writer with a plain sheet of paper or with a sheet of ruled paper, and request that he write a series of signatures.

THE EFFECT OF SPACE LIMITATIONS ON WRITING

Regardless of whether or not a form is used, it must be remembered that any time the writer sees boundaries, his writing is probably going to be affected. For example, try this experiment. Take a sheet of paper and tear it into smaller sheets, approximately 2" × 3" in size. Draw a different size box on each sheet. Write your signature in each box trying to stay within each boundary line. This exercise is similar to a child coloring in a picture coloring book. What happens to the writing?

As you try this experiment, you will notice changes taking place in your hand-writing. The smaller the box, the smaller the writing and the less rapidly you will write using more constant writing pressure with less relative pressure variations in order to stay inside the boundaries of the box. Your writing may even become a little more legible as you spend more time concentrating on the physical characteristics of writing, and the relative spacing habits between letters will be less noticeable.

The larger the box the faster you will be able to write, and less attention will be paid to the details of each letter; also the relative pressure habits between up and downstrokes will be greater. Further, when you write faster you pay less attention to the relative placement of the base of each letter with respect to the baseline, imaginary or pre-drawn. In summary, the more limitations imposed by the physical space provided the more the writing will be affected. The effects on the writing will vary, depending on the writer's level of skill. Figure 15.3 will help to illustrate this point.

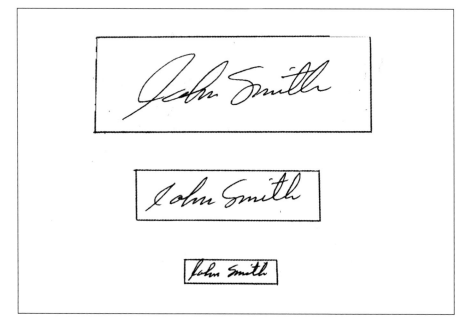

Figure 15.3

OBTAINING REQUESTED HANDWRITING SPECIMENS

The handwriting comparison process starts with the investigator! Preparation by him is essential. The following are some things he must do before, during, and after interviewing the person providing the requested specimens.

BEFORE THE INTERVIEW

1   *Know the questioned material!!* Study it! Duplicate, if possible, the type of paper or form on which the material is written and the writing implement – pen, pencil, etc. – used to write the questioned material. If possible, determine whether the questioned writing is naturally written or disguised.

2   Collect all items – paper and writing implements – necessary to obtain the specimens before the interview; there will be less confusion during the interview and the writing session. The investigator has a dual mission in this interview: to conduct his interview and to obtain suitable handwriting specimens for submission to the laboratory.

3   If possible, obtain a sample of the writer's normal, natural writing as written during the normal course of business before the interview. This writing, properly vouched for and authenticated, will help determine whether the requested specimen writing submitted is the writer's normal, natural writing or if it is un-naturally written or possibly disguised.

SUGGESTED PROCEDURE FOR OBTAINING HANDWRITING SPECIMENS

1   *Do not* allow the writer to see the questioned material!!!! The writer should *never* be allowed to view the questioned material before or during the writing of the requested specimens. It is acceptable to show the writer a *copy* of the questioned document after he completes the sample only if the investigator is satisfied with the performance of the writer and the naturalness of the sample, and, based on his experience as an investigator, if the writer has not tried to be deceptive.

2   *Duplicate the writing materials.* Even though this was discussed in paragraph 1 above, it is expanded here. Have the writer use the same size paper, type of form – check, prescription slip, sales draft, etc. – writing instrument – pen, pencil, etc. – the same size writing space on the paper, and if possible obtain some specimens written in the same or similar position as the questioned material was written. As stated above, general handwriting specimen forms can and should be used when obtaining requested specimens, however they should be supplemented with documents similar in type and format to the questioned document(s).

3   *Dictate the questioned material or provide the specimen writing with a typed copy of the questioned material.* The investigator must *never* write/print any of the questioned material to give to the writer as a model. Why not? Because the person writing the requested

specimens will frequently draw or simulate the writing or written character(s) placed before him rather than write in his normal, natural writing style.

4 *Watch* the writer as he writes the requested specimens. Is he writing larger or smaller than his normal style of writing? Is he writing faster or slower? Is he writing using an extreme slant, either forward or back? If the answer to any of these is yes, then the writer may be attempting to write unnaturally or is disguising his writing. The investigator can compare the specimen writing submitted with the sample of authenticated, collected writing obtained before the session began to see if the writings are the same. Any differences between the two can be brought to the attention of the writer, if necessary, to encourage him to write the specimen naturally.

5 *Remove* completed specimens from the writer's view as soon as he finishes them, and turn them face down on the table out of his reach. It is important that he does not see, or have access to, what he has just written. This is particularly important if the writer is writing unnaturally, using a different writing style, or is simply disguising his writing. Occasionally, a writer will try to see how he wrote a previous letter or combination of letters, especially if he believes they are critical.

6 If the investigator suspects the questioned material is written with the unaccustomed hand, then he should obtain some specimens from the writer that are written in a similar manner. Occasionally, a person providing requested specimens will write them with his unaccustomed hand. It has been my experience that persons who write questioned materials with their normal writing hand try to disguise their writing by using their unaccustomed hand in the specimen writings. At least he will start to do this, unless the investigator observes him laboring over his writing and tells him to write with his normal writing hand. This is one reason why the investigator should be prepared when he meets with the writer by having a sample of the person's normal course of business writing before the requested writing session begins. It is also a reason why the investigator should watch the person as he writes and not leave him sitting alone during this part of the interview.

7 If the writer is given any instructions before or during the writing session, the instruction should be noted on the specimen form being used at the time the instructions are given. What does this mean? Let's assume that the writer is requested to write the name "Joseph" using all of the different styles of "J" that he can write. This instruction should be written on the form or sheet of paper bearing the specimen. Another example; suppose the interviewer requests that the writer always write the name using a printed form of the letter "J," this instruction should also be written on the form the writer is using to provide the specimen.

8 *Each* sheet of requested writing should be sequentially numbered as it is written by the writer. The investigator or interviewer *must* sign and date each sheet or form after it has been completed by the writer. *No* sheet or form should go un-numbered, un-signed, or un-dated. The writer *should* sign every handwriting specimen sheet or form, acknowledging that the writing he has provided is a sample of his normal, natural writing.

SUBMISSION OF THE WRITING TO THE LABORATORY

The investigator should submit *all* specimen writing, together with the questioned material, to the laboratory. *Never* hold back any of the specimen writing doing so can influence the result of the handwriting examination. Too often investigators will cull the writing and send in only that portion of the writing they believe the FDE will need. When they do so, they run the risk of withholding samples containing features that could have helped the FDE reach an identification rather than the probable opinion he rendered because he did not have sufficient specimen writing. Unfortunately, this occurs all too often.

If non-request or collected specimens are obtained, the investigator should submit *all* of them to the FDE along with the requested specimens. The same reasoning applies; however, there is another consideration. If some of the requested writing is not written by the same writer as the requested specimens, the FDE will be able to determine that as part of his examination and possibly save everyone a great deal of embarrassment.

If the examiner asks that additional requested specimen writing be submitted, after the additional specimen writing is obtained the investigator should submit to the FDE all of the writing he previously submitted together with the new specimen writing. The FDE must have all of the writing when he makes his new examination.

In summary

1 Be prepared!
2 Be observant!
3 Be thinking!

COLLECTED SAMPLES – SOURCES, CAUTIONS, ETC.

There are numerous sources of collected specimens. The number is limited only by the lack of imagination on the part of the investigator and the FDE. One list of possible sources of collected writing has been in existence for many years and has been duplicated and given out to many investigators and FDEs. As far as this author knows, the authorship of the list is unknown. Therefore, it is not possible to give the individual the full credit deserved. It can only be said, thank you, whoever you are, because you have made what I believe is a significant contribution to investigators. The list, consisting of 101 possible sources of collected specimens, is shown in Table 15.1.

Item No.	Sources	Item No.	Sources
1	Account books	52	Leases, real property
2	Affidavits	53	Letters
3	Assignments	54	Library card applications
4	Autographs	55	Light company applications
5	Automobile insurance applications	56	Life insurance applications
6	Automobile license applications	57	Loan applications
7	Automobile title certificates	58	Mail orders
8	Bank deposit slips	59	Manuscripts
9	Bank safe deposit entry records	60	Marriage records
10	Bank savings withdrawal slips	61	Membership cards
11	Bank signature cards	62	Memoranda of all kinds
12	Bank statements, receipts for	63	Military papers
13	Bible entries	64	Mortgages
14	Bills of sale	65	Newspaper advertisement copy
15	Bonds	66	Occupational writings
16	Books, signatures of owners on covers	67	Package receipts
17	Building "after hours" registers	68	Parent's signatures on report cards
18	Business license applications	69	Partnership papers
19	Charity pledges	70	Pawn tickets
20	Checkbook stubs or record book	71	Passports
21	Checks, including endorsements	72	Payroll receipts
22	Church pledges	73	Pension applications
23	Convention registration books	74	Permit applications
24	Contracts	75	Petitions, referendum, etc.
25	Cooking recipes	76	Photograph albums
26	Corporation papers	77	Pleadings
27	Criminal records	78	Postal cards
28	Credit applications	79	Probate court papers
29	Credit cards	80	Promissory notes
30	Deeds	81	Property damage reports
31	Deeds of trust	82	Receipts for rent, etc.
32	Depositions	83	Registered mail return receipts
33	Diaries	84	Releases of mortgages
34	Dog license applications	85	Rental contracts for equipment
35	Drafts	86	Reports
36	Drive-it-yourself applications	87	Retail store sales slips
37	Drivers licenses and applications	88	School and college papers
38	Druggists' poison registers	89	Social security cards and papers
39	Employment applications	90	Sport and game score cards
40	Envelopes	91	Stock certificates, endorsements on
41	Fishing licenses	92	Surety bond applications
42	Funeral attendance registers	93	Tax estimates and returns
43	Gas service applications	94	Telegram copy
44	Gasoline mileage records	95	Telephone service applications
45	Gate records at defense plants	96	Time sheets
46	Greeting and Christmas cards, etc.	97	Traffic tickets
47	Hospital entry applications, etc.	98	Voting registration records
48	Hotel and motel guest registers	99	Water company service applications
49	Hunting licenses	100	Wills
50	Identification cards	101	Workmen's Compensation papers
51	Inventories		

Table 15.1

101 possible sources of collected specimens

Even though this list is somewhat dated, it does provide the investigator with a number of very useful places to search for collected writing. However, there is a caution in using non-request – collected – writings for comparison purposes. Their authorship *must* be verified before they are used for examination purposes. There are two reasons for this. First, if there are a number of documents each containing written material, the possibility exists that not all of the writing on each document is written by the suspect writer. Therefore, it is vital that the suspect's writing be unequivocally established before any examination and comparison is done. Second, if after the examination has been conducted, the report written, and the lawyer says, "I cannot get all of those collected writings into evidence . . . ," it will be necessary for the FDE to re-examine the case and render a new opinion that might be different from that stated in the first report. If this happens at the time of trial, those who really get hurt in the process are the lawyer trying the case who wants to submit these documents into evidence and his client.

Not enough can be said about verifying the authorship of collected writing. All too often mistakes occur when the FDE is told that the collected signatures or writings are in fact the writing of a particular person, when in fact they are not. Whenever collected writings are presented to the FDE as part of the writings he will use for examination and comparison purposes, they should *always* be described as "purported writings of" the person. Further, when using such writings it is a good idea for the FDE to say in his report that the opinion is based on the specimen writings, submitted for examination. Further, that he reserves the right to change that opinion should the authorship of any of the collected writings he used as "purported writings of" either be removed from consideration at the time of trial or it is established that the writing's authorship may not be by the person who purportedly wrote it.

WHAT ARE THE INVESTIGATOR'S RESPONSIBILITIES?

In a forensic handwriting case, one of the most important functions of the investigator is the collection and preservation of evidence. The questioned document(s) and handwriting samples obtained from individuals for comparison purposes constitute the evidence examined by an FDE. If that writing is in any way compromised or tainted, it loses its value as evidence. The procedures followed by the investigator when collecting evidence are as important as the evidence itself. If proper procedures are not followed, the evidence obtained may be removed as evidence by the court because it would be tainted.

The primary role of the investigator or solicitor of handwriting samples is to properly obtain requested specimen writing, insure the validity of all collected writings, and submit them all to the laboratory in accordance with established procedures. The best procedures to follow are those established by the American Society of Crime Lab Directors (ASCLAD).

LEGAL ASPECTS OF OBTAINING HANDWRITING SAMPLES

There are a number of court cases establishing the fact that the taking and providing of a handwriting sample for comparison purposes is not a violation of an individual's right against self-incrimination. Probably one of the most frequently referred-to cases is the case of Gilbert v. California 388 US 263. This case was decided by the Supreme Court on 12 June 1967. In the decision, the court held that even though the defendant's attorney objected to the admission of requested handwriting specimens provided by his client on the grounds that they violated his Fifth Amendment right against self-incrimination and Sixth Amendment right to counsel, the court upheld the lower court's decision that the specimens provided had not violated his client's rights. The court cited Schmerber v. California where the court held that the Fifth Amendment offers no protection against compulsion to submit to fingerprinting, photographing, or measurements, to write or to speak for identification, to appear in court, to stand, to assume a stance, or to make a particular gesture.

Samuel B. Lewis v. the United States was decided by the Supreme Court in 1967. Here the defendant was asked to give, and provided, a requested handwriting sample before his counsel was present and he was taken to a committing magistrate. The court ruled that his Fifth Amendment rights had not been violated because written words used as a handwriting sample and not for their meaning does not automatically mean that the defendant had knowledge of a particular crime. The sample is relevant only for the shape of the letters and for the direction of some lines and marks, which may identify the writer in the same way a fingerprint or photograph does.

The United States v. Richard Mara was decided by the Supreme Court in 1967. In this case a grand jury subpoenaed a witness and directed him to provide a sample of his handwriting and hand printing to be used for identification purposes. The witness, Mr Mara, refused, citing that compelling him to produce such a sample would constitute an unreasonable search and seizure. He continued to refuse and was held in civil contempt and remanded to the custody of the Marshals. The court ruled that the grand jury directive to provide a handwriting sample did not violate his Fourth Amendment rights because it was not a "seizure" his writing was constantly exposed to the public every time he wrote.

The United States v. Antonio Dionisio was decided by the Supreme Court on 22 January 1973. In this case the sample sought was a recording of Mr Dionisio's voice. The court upheld the grand jury subpoena for the same basic reason as in the Mara case.

The decision in the United States v. Nix case was based on a judge's instruction to the jury that the defendant's refusal to provide a court-ordered handwriting sample could be inferred by the jury as a sign of guilt by the defendant.

State v. Carr, decided in 1973, held that a suspect may be compelled to copy the exact wording of a questioned writing without violating his Fifth Amendment rights.

Today in the United States, it is well established that it is not a violation of a person's rights to provide a requested sample of their writing for comparison purposes. What has been disputed of late is the accuracy of handwriting identification, its methodology, and whether the opinions of FDEs should be admitted into courts as evidence. The litigation with respect to this issue is referred to as "Daubert Cases." This topic is too large to be covered here and the reader is referred to organizations like the American Society of Questioned Document Examiners (ASQDE) for information on this issue. If the reader wants a short summary of this issue, they could do no better than to read "Handwriting Identification Evidence in the Post-Daubert World" by Andre A. Moenssens. It contains an excellent discussion of the issues.

REFERENCES

Crane, A. (1999) "Does the Amount of Handwriting on a Cheque Constitute a Reasonable Amount of Sample?" *Canadian Society of Forensic Science Journal*, 32(1).

Moenssens, A.A. (1997) "Handwriting Identification Evidence in the Post-Daubert World," *UMKC Law Review*, 66(2).

APPENDIX 15.1
THE LONDON LETTER HANDWRITING SAMPLE FORM

This form appears as an example only. You may download, free of charge, all the evidence collection forms shown in this book at www.academicpress.com/apforensics.

Handwriting Specimen Form
"THE LONDON LETTER"

"Our London business is good, but Vienna and Berlin are quiet. Mr. D. Lloyd has gone to Switzerland and I hope for good news. He will be there for a week at 1496 Zermott St. and then goes to Turin and Rome and will join Col. Parry and arrive at Athens, Greece, Nov. 27th or Dec. 2nd. Letters there should be addressed: King James Blvd. 3580. We expect Charles. E. Fuller Tuesday. Dr. L. McQuaid and Robert. Unger, Esq., left on the 'Y.X.' Express tonight." (Authorship of letter unknown)

Signature   Date

Witness   Date

The above is a sample of my normal handwriting

Writing hand: Right ( ) Left ( )

RNM Form HSF No. 4 © 1999 RNM&AI   Ronald N. Morris & Associates, Inc.
Rev. 1/5/2000

APPENDIX 15.2
HANDWRITING SAMPLE FORM (CURSIVE)

This form appears as an example only. You may download, free of charge, all the evidence collection forms shown in this book at www.academicpress.com/apforensics.

Handwriting Specimen Form

CURSIVE
_____

_____   _____/_____/_____
↑ Name   ↑ Arthur   Bob   Charles

_____   _____/_____/_____
↑ Street address   ↑ Don   Edward   Frank

_____/_____   _____/_____/_____
↑ City   State   ↑ George   Henry   Johnson

_____   _____/_____/_____
↑ Place of birth   ↑ Ken   Ivan   McMay

_____/_____/_____   _____/_____/_____
↑ Date of birth Sex   Age   ↑ Nancy   Olson   Paul

_____   _____/_____/_____
↑ Occupation or trade   ↑ Robert   Steven   Tom

____/_____/_____/_____/_____   _____/_____/_____
↑ A   B   C   D   E   ↑ Vicki   Winn   Yancy

____/_____/_____/_____/_____   _____/_____/_____
↑ F   G   H   I   J   ↑ Lloyd   T.   MacGriff

____/_____/_____/_____/_____   _____/_____/_____
↑ K   L   M   N   O   ↑ James   H.   McQueen

____/_____/_____/_____/_____   _____/_____/_____
↑ P   Q   R   S   T   ↑ Larry   Brown   Gonzales

____/_____/_____/_____/_____   _____/_____/_____
↑ U   V   W   X   Y   ↑ Wilson   Earl   Jones

Writing hand: Right ( ) Left ( )

The above is a sample of my normal handwriting

Signature _____   Date _____

Witness _____   Date _____

RNM Form HSF No. 1 © 1999 RNM&AI   Ronald N. Morris & Associates, Inc.
Rev. 1/5/2000

Handwriting Specimen Form

CURSIVE

_____/_____/_____/_____/_____/
↑ Z   a   b   c   d

_____/_____/_____/_____/_____/
↑ e   f   g   h   i

_____/_____/_____/_____/_____/
↑ j   k   l   m   n

_____/_____/_____/_____/_____/
↑ o   p   q   r   s

_____/_____/_____/_____/_____/
↑ t   u   v   w   x

_____/_____/_____/_____/_____/
↑ y   z   #   &   @

_____/_____/_____/_____/_____/
↑ 0   1   2   3   4

_____/_____/_____/_____/_____/
↑ 5   6   7   8   9

_____/_____/_____/
↑ $10.00 $21.32 $32.50

_____
↑ Five hundred dollars

↑ 2736 East Place, South West

↑ Route 6, Box 358, Apt. 842

↑ 4468 Boxer Circle Dr., N.W.

↑ 4756 N. 49th Street 12345-6789

↑ 1928 North 300 Ave. 01357-9246

↑ 3745 West Blvd., N.E. 23456-7890

↑ 819 E. South Terrace, S.E.

_____/_____/
↑ Abbot   succeed   effort

_____/_____/
↑ gaggle   simmer   root

_____/_____/
↑ array   essence   battle

↑ Two hundred dollars and fifty-three cents

↑ Six hundred and forty-five dollars and twenty-six cents

The above is a sample of my normal handwriting

Signature _____ Date _____

Witness _____ Date _____

RNM Form HSF No. 1 © 1999 RNM&AI   Ronald N. Morris & Associates, Inc.
Rev. 1/5/2000

APPENDIX 15.3
HANDWRITING SAMPLE FORM (PRINTING)

This form appears as an example only. You may download, free of charge, all the evidence collection forms shown in this book at www.academicpress.com/apforensics.

Handwriting Specimen Form

PRINTING

_____

↑ Name

_____

↑ Street address

_____ / _____

↑ City   State

_____

↑ Place of birth

_____ / _____ / _____

↑ Date of birth   Sex   Age

_____

↑ Occupation or trade

____ / _____ / _____ / _____ / _____

↑ A   B   C   D   E

____ / _____ / _____ / _____ / _____

↑ F   G   H   I   J

____ / _____ / _____ / _____ / _____

↑ K   L   M   N   O

____ / _____ / _____ / _____ / _____

↑ P   Q   R   S   T

____ / _____ / _____ / _____ / _____

↑ U   V   W   X   Y

_____ / _____ / _____

↑ Arthur   Bob   Charles

_____ / _____ / _____

↑ Don   Edward   Frank

_____ / _____ / _____

↑ George   Henry   Johnson

_____ / _____ / _____

↑ Ken   Ivan   McMay

_____ / _____ / _____

↑ Nancy   Olson   Paul

_____ / _____ / _____

↑ Robert   Steven   Tom

_____ / _____ / _____

↑ Vicki   Winn   Yancy

_____ / _____ / _____

↑ Lloyd   T.   MacGriff

_____ / _____ / _____

↑ James   H.   McQueen

_____ / _____ / _____

↑ Larry   Brown   Gonzales

_____ / _____ / _____

↑ Wilson   Earl   Jones

Writing hand: Right ( ) Left ( )

_____

The above is a sample of my normal handwriting

Signature _____   Date _____

Witness _____   Date _____

RNM Form HSF No. 2 © 1999 RNM&AI   Ronald N. Morris & Associates, Inc.
Rev. 1/5/2000

Handwriting Specimen Form

PRINTING

_____/_____/_____/_____/_____/
↑Z   a   b   c   d

_____/_____/_____/_____/_____/
↑e   f   g   h   i

_____/_____/_____/_____/_____/
↑j   k   l   m   n

_____/_____/_____/_____/_____/
↑o   p   q   r   s

_____/_____/_____/_____/_____/
↑t   u   v   w   x

_____/_____/_____/_____/_____/
↑y   z   #   &   @

_____/_____/_____/_____/_____/
↑0   1   2   3   4

_____/_____/_____/_____/_____/
↑5   6   7   8   9

_____/_____/_____/
↑$10.00 $21.32 $32.50

_____
↑ Five hundred dollars

↑ 2736 East Place, South West

↑ Route 6, Box 358, Apt. 842

↑ 4468 Boxer Circle Dr., N.W.

↑ 4756 N. 49th Street 12345-6789

↑ 1928 North 300 Ave. 01357-9246

↑ 3745 West Blvd., N.E. 23456-7890

↑ 819 E. South Terrace, S.E.

_____/_____/_____
↑ Abbot   succeed   effort

_____/_____/_____
↑ gaggle   simmer   root

_____/_____/_____
↑ array   essence   battle

↑ Two hundred dollars and fifty-three cents

↑ Six hundred and forty-five dollars and twenty-six cents

The above is a sample of my normal handwriting

Signature _____   Date _____

Witness _____   Date _____

RNM   Form HSF No. 2 © 1999 RNM&AI   Ronald N. Morris & Associates, Inc.
Rev. 1/5/2000

APPENDIX 15.4
HANDWRITING SAMPLE FORM (CHECK FORMAT)

This form appears as an example only. You may download, free of charge, all the evidence collection forms shown in this book at www.academicpress.com/apforensics.

Handwriting Specimen Form

CHECK FORMAT _____

Date _____

Pay to the $
order of _____

_____

_____   _____

Date _____

Pay to the $
order of _____

_____

_____   _____

Writing hand: Right (   )   Left (   )

_____

The above is a sample of my normal handwriting

Signature _____ Date _____

Witness _____ Date _____

RNM Form HSF No. 3 © 1999 RNM&AI   Ronald N. Morris & Associates, Inc.
Rev. 1/5/2000

APPENDIX 15.5
HANDWRITING SAMPLE FORM (SIGNATURES)

This form appears as an example only. You may download, free of charge, all the evidence collection forms shown in this book at www.academicpress.com/apforensics.

Handwriting Specimen Form

SIGNATURES

↑	↑
↑	↑
↑	↑
↑	↑
↑	↑
↑	↑
↑	↑
↑	↑
↑	↑
↑ Printed name of writer	↑ Date

↑ Writer's signature   ↑ Name of witness

The above is a sample of my normal handwriting

Writing hand: Right (   )   Left (   )

RNM Form HSF No. 5 © 1999 RNM&AI   Ronald N. Morris & Associates, Inc.
Rev. 1/5/2000

CHAPTER 16

WHO DO I SEND THIS CASE TO?

THE QUALIFICATIONS OF THE EXAMINER

How do I select an FDE? Do I just look up handwriting identification in the phone book, see who is listed, and call one of the people listed there? Absolutely not! Whom should I get! How do I know the person is competent, qualified, and ethical? What should I look for in his résumé?

The ultimate goal is to find a qualified, competent, and ethical FDE, not just any FDE. Some of those who are listed in the telephone book, on a web site, or otherwise advertised as "handwriting experts," are FDEs, and there are many who are *not* FDEs. What is the difference between a "handwriting expert" and an FDE? A person listed as a "handwriting expert" may be a graphologist or graphoanalyst who attempts to determine the personality or character traits of an individual based on their handwriting. They are not FDEs who *only* engage in the identification of an individual based on characteristics and features found in their handwriting sample and in a questioned writing being compared with that sample. Further, an FDE is specially trained to examine documents for alterations, the identification of business machine impressions, sequence of writing problems, etc. in addition to his specialized training in handwriting identification.

Before selecting an FDE, there are a number of inquiries that need to be made. Below is a list of some of the questions that should be asked and the verifications.

EDUCATION

What is the educational background of the person I am thinking about retaining? The FDE should have at least a bachelor's or even a master's degree from a fully accredited college or university. There are *no* college degree programs that a person can take as a four- or six-year course of study to qualify him as an FDE.

There are some introductory courses offered at both the undergraduate and graduate level to familiarize the student with some of the basic concepts and things the FDE can and cannot do. These courses are only a semester or two long and constitute a survey type of course. Because of the highly specialized nature of the work, the only way a person becomes an FDE is by completing a two- or three-year apprenticeship program under the direct supervision of a qualified, competent, and ethical FDE after completing his formal college training.

SPECIALIZED TRAINING

What specialized training does he have to qualify as an FDE? Since there are no formal college degree programs, it is important that the FDE receive the type and quality of training necessary to qualify as an FDE. All the training in the world does not amount to anything when it comes to determining whether a person is ethical. It is an individual quality and, frequently, is hard to determine in a first meeting. His reputation derived from those for whom he has worked is sometimes a useful gauge by which his ethics can be measured.

As has been demonstrated in this text, handwriting identification requires a great deal of time to learn its principles and accurately apply them to real case situations. There are no college or university degree programs where a person can receive training in handwriting identification that prepares them to become a competent, qualified, and ethical FDE. An individual seeking a career in this field *must* enter the profession as a trainee, after receiving his college degree, in an apprenticeship program under the direct supervision of qualified FDEs, or in a recognized laboratory having similarly qualified FDEs on staff.

Usually the training program lasts two to three years after completing a college degree program leading to a bachelor's or master's degree. After completing the trainee program, the trainee moves into an apprenticeship situation where he continues to work under the supervision of senior FDEs.

Although not absolutely essential, it is preferred that the candidate for the trainee position have a degree in one of the physical sciences or in a course of formal study where he has been required to learn, and properly apply, the scientific method. It cannot be over-emphasized that even the completion of a graduate degree program in forensic sciences does *not* qualify the individual as an expert in any of them. The graduate must still take part in a trainee/apprenticeship program before he is eligible to qualify as a competent, qualified, forensic expert in any forensic science, especially that of a FDE.

At the conclusion of his trainee program, the new FDE should continue to work daily with competent, qualified examiners for approximately two or more years before being considered senior enough to work independently. Although the length of the training/apprenticeship period may vary by a few months or even a year, this type of learning process is not much different than in any other scientific field.

Confirmation of the validity of the apprentice FDE's work, by those senior examiners under whom he apprentices, is an essential element of the program, and necessary to insure that he is becoming competent and qualified in the learning and proper application of the principles of his profession. There is no substitution for the trainee/apprenticeship period or the desirability of the young FDE to consult with senior FDEs as he continues in his profession.

The amount of information available on handwriting and hand printing identification is extensive, and a central element of the training process is the proper application of those principles in different situations and the subjugation of the subjective element. That is why correspondence programs in handwriting and hand printing identification are inadequate because they do not allow the apprentice an opportunity to work shoulder to shoulder in a full-time laboratory environment with senior, qualified, FDEs on a daily basis. There is no substitute for the fulltime and daily guidance provided by a competent, qualified, and ethical senior FDE.

It has been demonstrated in recent studies that in the identification of handwriting and hand printing, properly trained FDEs are more accurate and will reach the correct conclusion more often than the average person (Kam 1994). An untrained or marginally qualified person has a chance of arriving at the correct answer in any given case, but just because they were lucky enough to get the correct answer in one case does not mean that they are qualified to work the variety of cases that a truly competent, qualified, and ethical FDE is capable of working.

A person wishing to retain the services of an FDE should verify his background, specialized training, and professional associations. What laboratories or professional FDEs offices has he worked in? Was he a full-time trainee or part-time worker? What did his training program consist of? How long was his training program? Whom did he train under, and what are their reputations as FDEs? Were they graphologists or graphoanalysts, whose training and background are in attempting to determine a writer's personality or character, rather than an FDE whose sole purpose is the identification of a writer based on handwriting habits?

CERTIFICATION AND ORGANIZATIONS THAT CERTIFY EXAMINERS

To what professional organizations does he belong? There are many professional organizations for FDEs, just as there are many organizations whose members are graphologists and graphoanalysts. No better description of the differences between the FDE and the graphologist/graphoanalysist and the organizations to which they belong can be found than in the work of Andre A. Moenssens (1997: 332–343). According to Moenssens, there are many professional organizations, regional, national, and international, whose members are competent, qualified, and ethical FDEs. These are some of those professional organizations whose members are engaged "in the traditional work of questioned document examiners . . . ":

ASQDE – American Society of Questioned Document Examiners
SAFDE – Southeastern Association of Forensic Document Examiners
SWAFDE – Southwestern Association of Forensic Document Examiners

Other prestigious organizations that have questioned document sections and whose members are also engaged "in the traditional work of questioned document examiners . . . " (ibid: 332) are: the American Academy of Forensic Sciences, the Canadian Society of Forensic Sciences, the Mid-Atlantic Association of Forensic Sciences, etc. In many instances the membership of these organizations overlaps. FDEs are usually certified by the American Board of Forensic Document Examiners, which is "the principal credentialing body of these organizations . . . " (ibid).

There are other organizations whose membership mostly comprises people whose training is in graphology and graphoanalysis and who are "devoted purely or primarily to handwriting analysis for personality assessment . . . ," or who have members who started "developing their interest in handwriting analysis through graphology or graphoanalysis but who have also branched out into handwriting identification for forensic purposes" (ibid). FDEs generally do not belong to graphology and graphoanalysis organizations. The reason for this is that the training, background, and objectives of their membership is completely different from the professional organizations to which FDEs belong.

What is the American Board of Forensic Document Examiners, Inc.? It is the premier organization for the certification of qualified FDEs in the fields of handwriting and hand printing comparison and all other aspects of forensic document examination. To qualify for certification by this organization, "applicants must be of good moral character, reputation and integrity, and must possess high ethical and professional standing" (ABFDE). To apply for certification, the applicant must show proof of his full-time training for at least two years in a laboratory recognized by the Board. He must also:

- show that he has successfully completed his full-time training program;
- take an examination administered by the Board;
- provide references from three qualified FDE's recognized by the Board who can attest to his training and qualifications;
- be engaged in the full-time practice of forensic document examination;
- provide a record of his involvement in professional activities in the field.

Those examiners who by their training and professional association only examine handwriting and hand printing for identification purposes, or who by their training are FDEs and therefore qualified to examine documents for more than just handwriting identification purposes, are usually the more competent and qualified examiners. They are the ones who should be sought out and retained.

After contacting the FDE, a check of his résumé should be done to determine if:

- his training and background are consistent with his résumé or possibly overstated;
- his membership in any of the organizations described by Moenssens would provide information about his background and qualifications to perform the examination desired;
- there are any questions about his training, the examiners he is affiliated with, or any of his associations, because all questions about his background should be answered satisfactorily before retaining him to perform any examinations.

HOW TO CONTACT AN EXAMINER

There are a number of different sources of information that can be used to contact an FDE. The ABFDE has a web site listing those FDEs who are certified by the Board. The listing is arranged according to the state in which they live or work. Competent, qualified, and ethical FDEs, and some who are not, are also listed in the yellow pages and in other telephone directories; they also send out mailings, have their own web sites, advertise in bar journals, etc.

Most professional FDEs' organizations maintain a directory of their members and their expertise, or the section to which they belong within the organization. These organizations may also have web sites with information for the public on how to contact their central office and obtain information concerning their membership within a certain geographical area. It must be remembered that the organizations are not at liberty to recommend one member over another.

There are also professional referral groups, such as the Technical Advisory Service for Attorneys, which maintain a database of names of experts in many different fields. When contacted for an expert, they provide a list of names to contact about providing the desired services. Referral services do not certify the expertise of its experts. They do require that its experts update their résumés periodically and that they maintain their professional level of expertise.

Ask those who use FDEs on a regular basis for a referral. Contact lawyers and those who retain FDEs for recommendations. Even though they too can be taken in by a person who is not competent or qualified, they are usually the first to find out that the person they hired does not have the training or experience to perform the work. Unfortunately, the bad experience they had with poorly trained, unqualified, or unethical examiners reflects poorly on the competent and qualified FDE; however, over time the latter will establish their credibility and will be called upon in the future to perform the functions for which they have been trained.

SUMMARY

In summary, only an FDE who has the requisite credentials by virtue of his training, experience, reputation, and associations as a competent, qualified, and ethical FDE should be retained to examine and render an opinion in a handwriting or hand printing identification case. Those seeking the services of an FDE should take the time necessary to verify the person's background, contacting references he provided and asking them for other references.

REFERENCES

Kam, Moshe et al. (1994) "Proficiency of Professional Document Examiners in Writer Identification," *Journal of Forensic Science*, 39(5).

Moenssens, Andre A. (1997) "Handwriting Identification Evidence in the Post-Daubert World," UMKC Law Review, 66(2).

American Board of Forensic Document Examiners, Inc. (undated brochure).

CHAPTER 17

SUBMITTING A QUESTIONED DOCUMENT CASE TO THE LABORATORY

WHAT SHOULD BE SUBMITTED TO THE LABORATORY?

This is not an easy question to answer. In fact, the answer depends upon the type of case, the evidence developed in that case, the type of questioned document problems involved in the examination, what the submitter needs to know concerning the document, etc.

Different types of questioned document cases require different approaches. For example, a check case frequently involves the identification of handwriting, possibly ink dating, sequence of writing, alteration or obliteration examinations, etc. Other types of cases can involve the examination of typewritten or printer material, plastic card embosser identification, rubber or steel stamp impressions, etc. The type of examination required has a strong influence on how long it will take to work the case.

Since this book is concerned only with handwriting and hand printing identification, the author does not deal with topics on how to conduct the other types of examinations. However, what is needed by an FDE for any examination is essentially the same, regardless of the type of case.

The best possible evidence is always the original document(s). Some examinations are not possible without them, and some examinations are not complete without them. When conducting handwriting and hand printing examinations, the FDE can occasionally work with good quality copies, usually a first generation copy, and conduct a preliminary examination. Even though some FDEs will identify a writer of written material on copies, usually they reserve the right to change their opinion after an examination of the original. Part of the reason for this will be made clearer in the next section of this chapter.

Some of the suggestions provided here for submitting a handwriting case to the laboratory for examination are also applicable to other types of cases. Enough cannot be said about the importance of collecting and preserving evidence, proper evidence control procedures, chain of custody, and protecting the evidence so that it is not accessible to unauthorized individuals.

ORIGINAL DOCUMENTS v. COPIES

In handwriting and hand printing identification cases, the FDE wants only original documents for complete examination purposes. Copies of documents, as a general rule, do not provide an accurate reproduction of all the features of a writing, and may even contain trash marks or other defects, the presence of which could be misinterpreted.

Whenever a copy is submitted for analysis one of the questions that must be asked is: what generation copy is it? What does this question mean? If an original document is placed on a copier and one copy is made, that copy is the first generation copy. It was made from the original. For a copy, theoretically, this is one of the best possible copies to have because it was made from the original. The quality of this copy is determined by the proper functioning and settings of the copier. Even a first generation copy can have some serious trash marks or other flaws if the copier is working improperly, has something between the document and the glass plate, or has defects on the machine's drum. Examples of this situation will be provided shortly.

If the first generation copy is placed on the copier and a copy made from it, the new copy is the second generation copy because it was made from the first generation copy, which was made from the original document. If the second generation copy is then copied, the new copy will be the third generation copy, and so on. Each time a new generation copy is made, the quality of the new copy is not as good as the copy from which it was made.

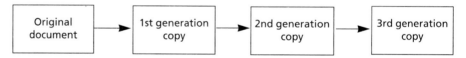

The quality of the copy can also be a function of the color of the ink used to write the original. Usually, blue ballpoint ink does not copy as well as black ballpoint ink. Figure 17.1 shows the original of a document written in both black and blue ballpoint inks, as written on different surfaces as follows. Two sheets of paper were placed together, one on top of the other.

1   The first writing of the word "time," at the top of the columns, was written in both black and blue ballpoint pens, on the top sheet, after placing the package on a desk top.

2   The second was written on the same sheet of paper after removing the bottom sheet and placing the single sheet of paper on the same desktop.

   The remainder of the writings were also written without using a back sheet, as follows.

3   The third word was written with the sheet of paper placed on the rough surface of a carrying case.

4   The fourth word was written with the sheet of paper placed on an oak wood tabletop.

5   The fifth word was written with the sheet of paper placed on a slab of concrete.

The line quality of each writing of the word reflects the different surfaces on which they were written.

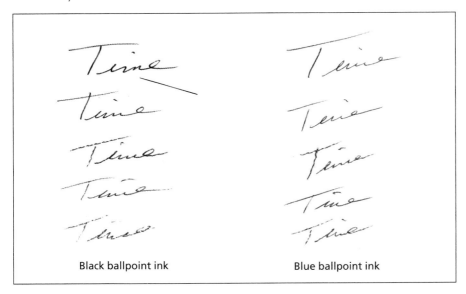

Figure 17.1
The original.

Black ballpoint ink   Blue ballpoint ink

The following guide explains the generation of each copy shown in that figure:

- Figure 17.2 shows a first generation copy of Figure 17.1.
- Figure 17.3 shows a second generation made from the copy shown in Figure 17.2.
- Figure 17.4 shows the third generation copy made from the second generation copy shown in Figure 17.3.
- Figure 17.5 shows the fourth generation copy made from Figure 17.4.

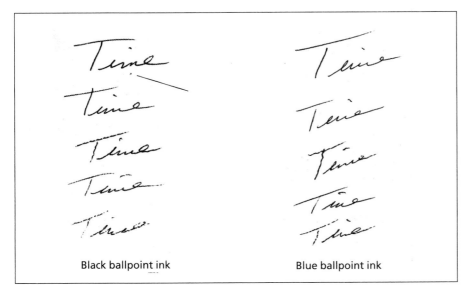

Figure 17.2
First generation copy.

Black ballpoint ink   Blue ballpoint ink

Figure 17.3
Second generation copy.

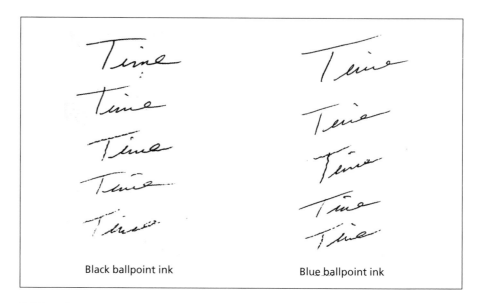

Black ballpoint ink   Blue ballpoint ink

Figure 17.4
Third generation copy.

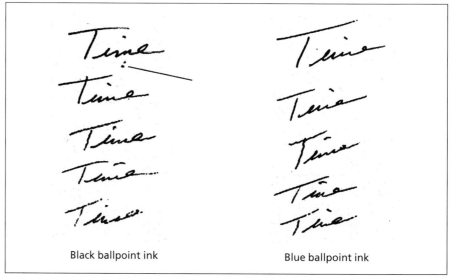

Black ballpoint ink   Blue ballpoint ink

In addition to the degradation in image quality resulting from each succeeding generation of copy, there are defects – trash marks – also appearing on each copy. These were caused by something – whiteout, glue, dust, lint, scratches in the glass, etc. – on the glass between it and the original document.

Referring back to Figure 17.1, there is no mark or spots on the original document located at the end of the line below the foot of the second arch of the "m." Notice on the first generation copy there is a dot at that location, and on the second generation copy there are two dots in that area, on the third generation there are still two dots, the bottom one being darker than the top, and on the fourth generation copy there are three dots in that area.

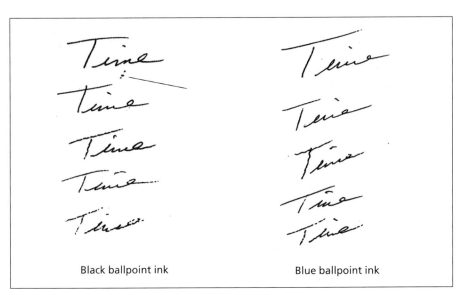

Black ballpoint ink   Blue ballpoint ink

Figure 17.5
Fourth generation copy.

In the case of the first generation copy, based on an examination of the copy, it is not possible to determine whether the dot was on the original document. It would be necessary to conduct an examination of the copier that produced the copy to determine whether or not there is a defect that appears on copies at that exact location. This examination of the machine must be done in a timely fashion before the cause of the dot is removed or the machine cleaned and repaired. (In this case, the author noticed the cause of the dot and removed it from the glass after making the copies. The next person using the machine will not have a spot at that location on any documents copied.) On the second generation copy, besides not being able to tell what generation copy it is, it would be impossible to determine whether the first dot was on the original document being copied, or whether the second dot was caused by the copier being used to make the copy.

Alignment of the document being copied on the glass plate can also affect the location of trash marks on the copy. In this example, let us assume the writer of the material on the original document did not use i-dots when he wrote the letter, but one of these dot defects appeared above the letter's staff on a copy. The FDE might think the i-dot was written by the author of the original material. In this situation, more significance could be attached to the feature than is warranted. The dot in this case would be a feature of writing different from the habits found in the specimens being used for comparison purposes; but it may be considered an accidental feature written by the author of the original document. If the FDE had access to the original document, he would find no i-dot above the staff, consistent with the writer's normal writing habits.

As a further example of problems caused by trash marks or defects, refer to Figure 17.6.

Figure 17.6

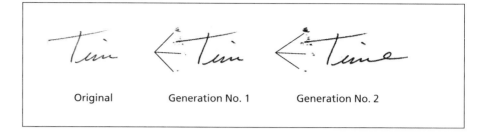

Original   Generation No. 1   Generation No. 2

The original document does not have any of the trash marks shown in the two generations of copies in Figure 17.6. These trash marks were also caused by something stuck on the glass of the copier. The two copies shown in Figure 17.6, Generations No. 1 and No. 2, were made before the author removed the material from the glass, and before the copies shown in Figures 17.2 through 17.5 were made. Notice here, also, that the darkness of the marks on the second generation copy increased, while the pattern of the trash marks remained constant. These examples are but a few of the reasons why it is important to have original documents to work with, and why an FDE usually insists on having either the original or the best available copy (a first generation copy) for examination.

What are some indications of degeneration in image quality with each succeeding generation copy, as shown in Figures 17.2 through 17.5? A couple of examples follow.

- The increasing lack of detail in line quality of the t-cross, particularly the one written on the rough surface, third from the top, written with both the black and blue ballpoint ink.
- The increasing darkness of the copied material, some of which masks the true line quality of the writing.
- Note particularly the tapered t-cross on the second "T" written with blue ballpoint ink.

There are other indications the reader will be able to find as well. Other types of copies, such as carbon copies, carbonless copies, etc., also offer unique problems when conducting a handwriting and hand printing examination. Since a detailed explanation will not be given here for each indicator, it is strongly suggested that readers conduct some experiments of their own.

COMPARABLE SPECIMEN WRITINGS

Although this topic is covered more thoroughly in the chapter on obtaining handwriting samples, here it is re-emphasized because of its importance to the examination process. A meaningful examination is not possible between the names "John" and "Sam" because the same letters and letter combinations found in the one name are not found in the other name. If the questioned material is handwritten cursive, and the specimens are hand printed, again no meaningful examination is possible.

The type of case and writing in question dictates what specimens are needed. Assuming the questioned material is an endorsement area on a check, the investigator should ascertain from the investigation whether the signature only, or the signature, address notation, and account number below it are questioned. If it is determined that only the signature is questioned, because the store clerk or bank teller wrote the address notation, then when a suspect is developed and interviewed, only the appropriate specimens and signatures necessary for comparison purposes would be needed. *All of the writing that is in question should be repeated numerous times in any request specimens obtained for comparison purposes.*

If it is not possible to obtain request specimens that repeat the questioned material, it may be possible to use collected or non-request specimens containing the same letters, letter combinations, numerals, or numeral combinations. Any collected specimens obtained should be sufficient in both quantity and quality to perform a meaningful examination and comparison.

WHAT LABORATORIES ARE AVAILABLE?

There are essentially two categories of laboratories to which an investigator, attorney, law enforcement official, individual, etc. can send a handwriting case for examination. Government officials usually submit cases to a government laboratory at the federal or central government level, a regional or state level laboratory, city or local police laboratory, etc. The federal level laboratories may be operated by a federal law enforcement agency like the FBI, US Postal Inspectors, US Secret Service, etc. Even though some federal agencies have regional laboratories, there are more of them at the state level.

Local police departments, such as New York City, Charlotte, NC, etc., have their own laboratory that usually serves their needs. They also have forensic specialists in a limited number of areas based on the needs of the department. Occasionally, other government agencies, such as the US Internal Revenue Service, Veterans Administration, etc., have their own laboratories.

The second type of laboratory available is the laboratory of the FDE in private practice. Usually, he is retained by attorneys and individuals to conduct handwriting and hand printing examinations, or other questioned document problems, within his range of expertise not discussed in this book. Occasionally he contracts his services to government agencies and works in their laboratory system for a specified time on specific projects.

Private FDEs usually have an established fee schedule detailing the fees they would charge for particular services, their time to examine a case and write a report, and be available for testimony when called upon by the courts. Not all FDEs in private practice charge the same amount for the services they provide. The reader should refer to the chapter on, "Who Do I Send the Case To?" for further details on evaluating an FDE's background, etc.

ASCLAD (AMERICAN SOCIETY OF CRIME LABORATORY DIRECTORS) ACCREDITATION

There is an organization within the US that has established an accreditation program for forensic laboratories. The organization has also accredited laboratories outside of the United States, such as the Hong Kong Government Laboratory. The objectives of ASCLAD are:

1   To improve the quality of laboratory services provided to the criminal justice system.
2   To develop and maintain criteria which can be used by a laboratory to assess its level of performance and to strengthen its operation.
3   To provide an independent, impartial, and objective system by which laboratories can benefit from a total operational review.
4   To offer to the general public and to users of laboratory services a means of identifying those laboratories which have demonstrated that they meet established standards (Cavanaugh 1997: 1; Morris 1998: 281).

A laboratory accredited by ASCLAD has undergone a very stringent examination process to insure the proper handling of evidence and its security while in transit to, in, and from the field. They also do security surveys of the laboratory facilities, and proficiency testing of its staff through a periodic testing program. Usually, private examiners are not accredited by ASCLAD, but there is nothing to prevent their submitting to the accreditation process.

   Although it is not essential that a private examiner have his laboratory accredited by ASCLAD, not doing so should not be a stigma or sign that the examiner and his laboratory are not following accepted practices of evidence handling, or maintaining professional proficiency.

CHAIN OF CUSTODY ISSUES

One of the biggest issues when dealing with documents is insuring the chain of custody of documents while in transit to, while within the laboratory, and when being returned to the submitter. Most evidence handling is nothing more than common sense mixed with a heavy dose of caution. It is vital that evidence sent to the laboratory, while in the laboratory, and when being returned to the submitter, never be in a position where it could be lost, contaminated, or altered. Insuring the integrity of evidence is of prime importance regardless of whether the laboratory is a government or private laboratory.

All documents submitted to an FDE for examination should be sent in such a way that chain of custody is preserved at all times. These are some ways of accomplishing this:

- Certified or registered mail, return receipt requested.
- An overnight shipper requiring a signature at the time of delivery.
- Hand-carrying all items in a sealed envelope or container to and from the laboratory.

Regardless of how the documents are transported to the laboratory, they should be properly packaged to insure that they are not compromised while in transit. Here is one example of what can go wrong in this area. When the author worked in a federal laboratory, an assistant US attorney requested that someone in his office ship newly obtained specimen writing and previously examined questioned documents in a case to the laboratory for examination. The documents were placed in a large brown envelope having a glue flap and sent by regular mail. No special handling was requested, and no signature was obtained at the laboratory to insure its proper chain of custody. The envelope was torn open in shipment and much of the evidence was lost, never to be recovered. This is not the proper method for sending documents in any case.

PRESERVATION AND STORAGE OF EVIDENCE BEFORE SENDING IT TO THE LABORATORY

All documentary evidence should be placed in sealed containers, have a chain of custody form securely attached to the container, and secured in such a way that each time it is given to a person in the laboratory a signature must be obtained. If the container is opened, the evidence should be examined, placed back in the container and resealed, and a complete record of everything done with or to the evidence properly recorded. After examination, the evidence container should be returned to a secured vault until it needs to be removed again. If the FDE keeps the evidence for several days, he should have a secured facility in which to store the evidence when he is not actively working with it.

In the case of private FDEs, they should also provide a secure environment in which the evidence is contained while it is in their control. The transportation of documents to and from their laboratory should also be done using the signed receipt method. All documents should be returned to the submitter as soon as possible.

Frequently, the private FDE goes to the attorney's office where he is asked to conduct a preliminary examination. It may not be possible for the FDE to bring the documents to his laboratory for examination, so the examinations are performed in less than desirable conditions with limited examination aids available to him. He then leaves the documents in the custody of the attorney when he departs the attorney's office. When in his custody at the laboratory, evidence should be secured when it is not being examined.

PREPARING A WORK REQUEST FOR THE LABORATORY

What information should a work request contain? The following is an outline with several examples recommended by the author. Each laboratory has its own policies and procedures for submitting evidence, which should be followed if that laboratory is used.

The work request should consist of the following information:

1   The name, address, and telephone number of the submitter.
2   The reference number assigned to the case by the submitter.
3   A case name or title associated with the assigned reference number should also be given.
4   *Exhibits to be examined:*
    Questioned
    Q-1.
    Q-2.
    Specimens
    S-1.
    S-2.
5   *The problem(s).* What type of examination(s) is being requested on each submitted document or what writing on each document is in question and with which specimen writer should it be compared.
6   *Disposition of evidence.* What disposition of the evidence should be made after the examination? For example, after completing the handwriting examinations should the questioned documents be retained for fingerprint processing or should all the documents be returned to the submitter?
7   When the evidence and report are needed back in the possession of the submitter.

When describing the submitted exhibits, a complete description of each document should be given so that there is never any confusion about which document is Q-1, Q-2, S-1, S-2, etc. The guiding principle is, keep the descriptions concise and complete. When the FDE receives the case with the submitted documents, he should initial and date each one. For example, the notation on

Q-1 written by the FDE would be (Q-1, RNM, 1/5/2000).

As mentioned above, insuring the integrity of evidence being sent to a laboratory for examination is nothing more than common sense with a heavy dose of caution mixed in. To meet the high standards that have been set requires time. It is time well spent because should evidence be lost in transit or contaminated by someone, the whole case could be lost. Should this occur the damage may be irreparable.

REFERENCES

Cavanaugh, M. H. (1997) "Crime Laboratory Accreditation Program," American Society of Crime Laboratory Directors, January.

Morris, Ronald N. (1998) "Evidence," *International Review of Law Computers and Technology*, 12(2): 279–285.

CHAPTER 18

WHAT DOES THE
EXAMINER'S REPORT SAY?

INTRODUCTION

At the conclusion of the analysis phase of his examination, the FDE writes a report that is complete and which its reader should be able to understand. The FDE uses language to accomplish this purpose; however, language is not always precise – the same words can have different meanings, or slightly different meanings, to different people.

Notwithstanding the problems associated with language, the report should be clearly written, concise, and comprehensive. The purpose of this chapter is to assist the reader in understanding the format of a questioned document report and some of the concepts behind the language used to express the different degrees of belief expressed by the FDE.

REPORT FORMAT

Every FDE has a report format and language with which they are comfortable. While there are many report formats, the basic elements of a complete report are as follows:

- A complete description of the document(s) examined.
- A clear statement of the examination(s) requested.
- The use of clearly written and easily understood language and concepts to convey to the reader the result of the examination(s).
- What disposition is made of the submitted document(s) or other remarks.

OPINION TERMINOLOGY – WHAT DOES IT MEAN?

WRITING A CLEAR REPORT

It bears repeating that in every case, the FDE writes a report using language to convey the results of his analysis. Because language is not precise, there is the possibility of confusing the interpretation of the results of his examination. Further complicating the use of language are the legal requirements imposed by the burden of proof and presumption concepts that are a part of the rules of evidence. Although these legal concepts are too broad to cover in minute detail in this work, an overview of the topic is covered later.

Some examiners use a number of qualifying words and phrases when expressing opinions. When multiple qualifying words or phrases are used in the statement of a single opinion, the reader will not have a clear understanding of what the FDE is saying. The clearest statement of an opinion is one that has the fewest qualifying words and phrases. These brief statements are more easily understood by the reader because the writer usually uses words like "wrote," "highly probable," "probably," etc. A reader's understanding of the concepts behind these words and phrases is more easily understood.

The following examples are concise, yet comprehensive, statements expressing the degree of belief the FDE has reached based upon the result of his analysis:

1 It has been concluded that John Doe wrote . . .

2 It has been concluded that John Doe in all probability wrote . . . The phrase "in all probability" can be substituted with the phrases "very probably wrote," or "it is highly probable" that John Doe wrote . . .

3 It has been concluded that John Doe probably wrote . . .

4 There is some evidence to suggest that John Doe wrote . . . Occasionally the phrase " . . . some evidence to indicate . . ." is used.

5 It could not be determined whether John Doe wrote the questioned material.

6 With the material available for comparison, no evidence was found to suggest that John Doe wrote . . .

7 There is some evidence to suggest that John Doe did not write . . . Occasionally the phrase " . . . some evidence to indicate . . ." is used.

8 It has been concluded that John Doe probably did not write . . . .

9 It has been concluded that in all probability, John Doe did not write . . . The terms, "very probable," or "it is highly probable" that John Doe did not write . . . are occasionally used.

10 It has been concluded that John Doe did not write . . .

DEFINING TERMS

What do these statements mean? How should the reader interpret and understand them in the context of a report?

The *first* statement (It has been concluded that John Doe wrote . . .) is unequivocal. It has been said, "There is no stronger opinion given by a document examiner in a handwriting case than a positive identification" (McAlexander 1977). When used, the examiner has no reservation whatsoever about the certainty of his conclusion. He is so certain about his conclusion that for him it is a fact; the writer of the specimens and questioned writing is the same person. Because he can only express an opinion in court, he cannot testify, "it is a fact that the questioned and specimen writings are by the same writer."

What is the standard for such a strong statement of belief? There must be complete agreement in all features of writing important for identification purposes with no significant differences or dissimilarities that could suggest another writer's involvement. The writer of the examined handwriting must have sufficient class and individual characteristics and features in his writing that when taken collectively are in excellent agreement and contain no significant or fundamental differences or dissimilarities in writing habits. There are occasions when a difference or dissimilarity is discovered, but its presence in the writing is far outweighed by the agreement in other equally or more significant features.

The only allowable differences or dissimilarities are those resulting from normal variation in writing. A complete discussion of normal variation in writing is covered in Chapter 4. However, normal variation is expected in every person's writing and is the result of his inability to exactly reproduce writing movements every time he writes the same letter or letter combinations.

The *second* statement (It has been concluded that John Doe in all probability wrote . . .) is used when the evidence falls just short of the requirement for an identification. At times the phrase "in all probability" may be substituted with "very probably wrote" or "it is highly probable" that John Doe wrote . . .

Regardless of the words used, the FDE has some slight reservation and does not want to make a categorical statement at this time. The reason for the slight reservation may be due to questions concerning the quality of the specimens or an absence of features that have significance for identification purposes. When this occurs, additional specimens may be of value in resolving the situation.

If the reason for the qualification was determined to be in the questioned and not the specimen writing, obtaining additional specimens would not be of value. Each situation encountered must be resolved individually based on the evidence available at the time of the analysis. Regardless of the reason for the slight qualification, the FDE selects the language that he uses in his report carefully, because it must reflect his degree of belief based on his analysis of the specific available evidence.

The *third* statement (It has been concluded that John Doe probably wrote . . .) is used when the evidence points rather strongly toward the specimen writer, but still falls short of the requirements for a less qualified opinion. Even though there are significant similarities present in the questioned and specimen writings, also present are irreconcilable differences not explainable by the available writing.

These irreconcilable differences may have varying degrees of significance attached to them. For example, if the questioned or specimen writing is a photocopy and the examiner is not able to determine stroke direction or line quality characteristics, etc. sufficiently, he might express his degree of belief by using this statement. Having said this, the determination of stroke direction or line quality for every feature of the writing can be outweighed by the collective significance of other qualities and features present in the writing. These other qualities and features may be as equally important for identification purposes. The evidence in each situation must stand on its own merit.

When the word "probable" is used instead of the words "highly probable," there is by definition a greater likelihood that someone other than the specimen writer wrote the questioned material. However, in this situation, the evidence is still pointing rather strongly in the direction of the specimen writer. Most people believe that when the word "probable" is used, it means a slightly better than 50% chance of some event occurring or not occurring. That meaning does not apply here.

The Random House Webster's *Electronic Dictionary and Thesaurus*, College Edition, has this definition for probable: " . . . having more evidence for than against, or evidence that inclines the mind to belief but leaves some room for doubt" (Random 1992). This definition is closer to what the FDE is saying when he uses the word "probable" to express his degree of belief. What is he saying? "There is more evidence to suggest that this specimen writer wrote the questioned material than there is to suggest he did not write the questioned material."

The *fourth* statement (There is some evidence to suggest, or to indicate, that John Doe wrote . . .) is used when there are a few handwriting features in agreement, some having more significance than others for identification purposes.

When this opinion is given, the FDE is saying to the reader: "Keep this writer in mind." Although there is not a sufficient amount of evidence to say he probably wrote the questioned material, there are some qualities and features of the writing in agreement which *suggest* he has the skill and ability to write this way. The significance of those features, though, is limited. Later, another writer could be "identified" as the writer of the questioned writing; and this would not be inconsistent with this degree of belief.

The *fifth* statement (It could not be determined whether John Doe wrote the questioned material) is used when the examiner is not able to determine whether the specimen writer wrote the questioned material.

At the beginning of his analysis, the FDE does not know whether the specimen writer wrote the questioned writing. He must begin his work from a neutral position. The purpose of his analysis is to try to determine whether the specimen writer wrote the questioned material.

There are some occasions when, after his analysis, he still does not know whether the writer of the specimen writing wrote the questioned writing. In other words, he has made his analysis and there is insufficient evidence present to make even a qualified statement concerning authorship.

These same general principles apply as well to the degrees of belief expressing negative opinions. As with positive opinions, in many cases, the evidence varies in significance *against* common authorship and the same language described above can be used to express the possibilities that the writings are not of common authorship.

An elimination opinion, "the writer of the specimens did not write . . . " is harder to reach than an identification opinion, and there are technical reasons for such a strong statement. However, when an FDE says that a writer "did not write" something, he is as certain that this person in fact did not write the questioned material as he is if he had said the person did write the questioned material.

THE EXAMINER TESTIFIES

DEFINING LEGAL TERMS

Legal requirements are placed on counsel concerning the "burden of proof" standard they have to meet when trying a case in court. Over time, the courts have established these standards as they relate to both criminal and civil litigations. One explanation of the standard is: "The duty of a party in a lawsuit (is) to persuade the judge or the jury that enough facts exist to prove the allegations of the case. Different levels of proof are required depending on the type of case . . . The burden of proof always lies on the party who takes the affirmative in pleading" (Lectric, "Burden of Proof").

To meet this standard imposed on him, legal counsel presents evidence to the court establishing his position and refuting that of the other party. The evidence submitted falls into two very broad categories relevant to this discussion, "direct" and "opinion" evidence. Direct evidence is: "Direct proof of a fact, such as testimony by a witness about what that witness personally saw or heard or did" (Lectric, "Evidence, Direct"). Opinion evidence is: "Testimony from persons (Expert Witnesses) who, because of education or experience, are permitted to state opinions and the reasons for their opinions" (Lectric, "Evidence, Opinion").

Qualified expert witnesses are permitted by the court to present opinion testimony concerning their examination and analysis of evidence. What qualifies them as an expert is determined by a combination of their education, experience, and work in their profession, and the judge's recognition of their expertise based on their qualifications.

Rule 702 of the Federal Rules of Evidence reads: "If scientific, technical, or other specialized knowledge will assist the trier of fact to understand the evidence or to determine a fact in issue, a witness qualified as an expert by knowledge, skill, experience, training, or education, may testify thereto in the form of an opinion or otherwise" (Law, Cornell . . .). Federal Rules of Evidence Nos. 702, 703, 705 and the decisions handed down by the court in Frye v. US, 293 F.1013 (D.C.Cir.'23) combined to become the test by which reliable expert testimony was allowed in the courts. In the case of Daubert v. Merrell Dow Pharmaceuticals, Inc. 509 US 579 (1993), the Supreme Court narrowly defined what constituted scientific knowledge – the admissibility of expert evidence based on the courts determination of the relevance and reliability of that evidence under Rule 702. At this point the author is not going to enter into a discussion of this topic because he is not qualified to do so. Rather, the reader is directed to the works of Moenssens (1997) and numerous other sources of information on this subject, some of which can be found at the web sites listed at the end of this chapter. The publications and members of FDE organizations, such as the American Society of Questioned Document Examiners (ASQDE) and the American Academy of Forensic Scientists (AAFS), are a valuable resource of information on this topic. Since 1993 there have also been numerous court decisions concerning the Daubert challenge to Rule 702 and what was known as the Frye test.

The burden of proof requirement legal counsel must meet has an impact on expert witnesses. Frequently, legal counsel expects the expert witness to state his opinion in language that corresponds to the legal standard applicable to the relevant burden of proof. These standards are, for example:

- *Beyond a reasonable doubt:* The level of proof counsel must establish in a criminal case, based on all the evidence he presents, must show that beyond a reasonable doubt the things he said happened, happened. "Beyond a reasonable doubt" is "the highest level of proof required to win a case" (Lectric, "Beyond a Reasonable Doubt"). Reasonable doubt is: "The level of certainty a juror must have to find a defendant guilty of a crime. A real doubt, based upon reason and common sense after careful and impartial consideration of all the evidence, or lack of evidence, in a case.

  "Proof beyond a reasonable doubt, therefore, is proof of such a convincing character that you would be willing to rely and act upon it without hesitation in the most important of your affairs. However, it does not mean an absolute certainty" (Lectric, "Reasonable Doubt").

  In a civil case there are two levels of proof counsel may be required to meet: "clear and convincing evidence" and the "preponderance of the evidence."
- *The clear and convincing standard:* "The level of proof sometimes required in a civil case for the plaintiff to prevail. It means the trier of fact must be persuaded by the evidence

that it is highly probable that the claim or affirmative defense is true. The clear and convincing evidence standard is a heavier burden than the preponderance of the evidence standard but less than beyond a reasonable doubt" (Lectric, "Evidence, Clear and Convincing").

- *The preponderance of the evidence standard:* "The level of proof required to prevail in most civil cases. The judge or jury must be persuaded that the facts are more probably one way (the plaintiff's way) than another (the defendant's)" (Lectric, "Preponderance of the Evidence").

The language the FDE uses in his report does not have to mirror the burden of proof terminology established by the courts. When he testifies, the testimony he gives concerning his analysis is only one part of the whole case. If the whole case, when presented, does satisfy the court standard, the evidence testified to by the FDE is not going to help, regardless of how strong his opinion. The FDE is not, nor should he be, required to word his report or give testimony using consistent language with the burden of proof standards.

Sometimes counsel tries to persuade the expert witness to express his opinion in percentages, through the use of a scale from 1 to 100, or by some other illustrative means. By doing this, counsel is trying to show that the testimony of the expert should be given more weight because it conforms to the burden of proof standard he, the counsel, must follow. The expert witness is, and should be, very cautious when using any analogy, scale, or other reference system to establish the degree of certainty he has concerning the results of his examination. The content of his report should stand on its own merit as he provides the judge and/or jury with information they need concerning the results and procedures of his analysis.

SUMMARY

The FDE, at the conclusion of his analysis, should write a clear, concise, and comprehensive report concerning the evidence he examined, what examinations he performed, the results of his analysis, and the disposition of that evidence. When called upon to testify in court, he should remember that he is presenting opinion testimony concerning his work, and is not an advocate for either side. His testimony will either support or not support the position of either side or counsel. Since he is not an advocate for either side, he should not word his report or testify in any manner that makes it appear that he is conforming to the burden of proof standards imposed on legal counsel. Those standards apply only to all of the evidence presented, not just to his testimony. A competent, qualified, and ethical examiner always remembers the role he has in assisting the court and jury in reaching a verdict based on all of the evidence presented.

HOW DOES THE FORENSIC DOCUMENT EXAMINER TESTIFY IN COURT?

Before testifying in court, the FDE has a lot of pretrial preparation to do. In fact, there is a lot to do before he meets with counsel for a pretrial conference. The amount of time spent in trial preparation can be almost as much as the time necessary to examine the case when it came into the laboratory. What are some of the things the FDE must do in preparation for trial?

1 He has to review all the exhibits he examined when working the case. Usually there is some lapse of time between working the case and the trial. The FDE should completely re-examine the case as if it just arrived in the laboratory for the first time. There are several reasons for this, but the main one is that he must be familiar with the exhibits he examined previously so that he knows the exact reasons why he wrote the report. He must know where each feature of writing is located that led him to the conclusion or opinion he rendered, and he must be prepared to point those features out when he testifies.

Further, it may be necessary for him to prepare photographic enlargements of portions of the documents to use as an illustrative aid when testifying. These photographic enlargements should contain representative samples of the writings examined and be arranged in such a way that he, counsel, the judge, and the jury may be able to easily follow and understand his explanation in support of his findings. The findings or conclusions he reaches are never based on the illustration he prepares for court purposes, they are *always* based on the sum total of all the evidence he examines before the illustration is ever needed.

2 He has to prepare the enlargements. Some FDEs use 35 mm cameras to photograph exhibits, but a few still use 4X5, or some other size, sheet negatives. With the advent of computer imaging, more FDEs are using digital imaging technology in conjunction with presentation software, such as Microsoft PowerPoint™.

Regardless of what presentation method he uses, the FDE must assure himself that the final product is a fair and accurate reproduction of the actual evidence, with the possible exception of size and color. Any illustration or visual aid used in court must faithfully reproduce the original document(s) or the impression could be given that the witness is trying to hide something from the trier(s) of the case.

What should a handwriting illustration look like? While no two examiners would probably ever agree on exactly what type of illustration to use, there is a consistent format that seems to be recognized as the universally accepted format for a court illustration. The sample in Figure 18.1 is offered as an example.

If there is too much on the illustration, it has a cluttered or busy appearance and will be hard to use and understand. The purpose of the illustration is to assist in the explaining of some of the reasons for the opinion(s) expressed in his report. The illustration should never be a hindrance.

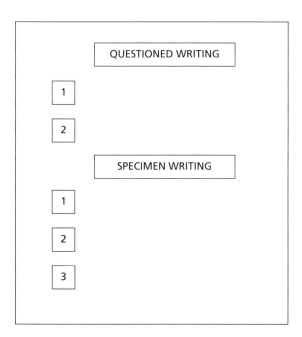

Figure 18.1

The basic format for a handwriting illustration chart used in court to assist the FDE when explaining some of the reasons for his opinion. As a general rule, there should be no more than two questioned signatures and six to eight specimen signatures, plus one or two examples of individual letters, such as initials, on an illustration chart. There are exceptions to this guideline, but the important thing to remember is to keep the illustration simple and easy to present and understand.

The illustration should *never* contain specimen writing of two – or more – different writers, unless there is some compelling reason for doing so. When more than one specimen writer is the focus of the FDE testimony, separate illustrations for each specimen writer should be used even if the same questioned writing is used on both illustrations.

3   The FDE may find it necessary to prepare a special report for use at the pretrial conference to assist counsel in understanding the examination process and the exhibits examined. As an example, one case on which the author worked involved over 50 writers and 500 questioned documents. It was concluded that a significant number of the specimen writers wrote the signatures and other material on the questioned documents. In preparation for trial, and to assist counsel, I prepared a special summary of the results based on the information in my report. The purpose of the summary was to help counsel, judge, and the jury understand the significance of the results of my examinations. This supplemental document also proved to be of assistance to the defense attorneys and their clients because all of their clients pleaded guilty after inspecting the illustrations and supplemental document. It is essential that counsel " . . . completely understand the full significance of the technical evidence" (Hilton 1982: 401). It is equally important for the judge and jury to understand the full significance of the technical evidence.

The FDE usually has a pre-trial conference with counsel. If he practices in a federal or state crime laboratory, the attorney he usually works with is known as a prosecutor. Occasionally he will work with a defense counsel because his findings may actually assist the defendant. As stated above, it makes no difference which counsel the FDE works with; if he is truly an impartial expert he could be called by both sides to testify. If the FDE is in private practice, the attorney he works for could represent either the plaintiff or defendant. In either case, it is vital that he has a pre-trial conference with counsel. These are several reasons for having the pre-trial conference:

Preparation

The purpose of a pre-trial conference is to prepare both the witness and counsel for what is about to take place in the courtroom. This is a critical part of the case, especially for the counsel who will be questioning the witness. What does this mean?

During the pre-trial conference, counsel and the FDE have the opportunity to become familiar with each other, review evidence examined by the FDE, and, for counsel, to determine how his witness will testify at the time of trial or the deposition. Legal counsel also wants to know how this witness will appear on the stand. If the witness does not make a good impression with the jury, the attorney's case can be jeopardized. The jury hears what the witness says, but they also consider how his body language supports or refutes what he says.

Review of the FDE background

A review of his background is critical because counsel must be certain that the FDE has the necessary qualifications to examine the evidence in his laboratory, and to present the results of his work in court. This is particularly important if they have not worked together before.

No one is more familiar with the FDE's background than he himself. He may have done many different things in his life that assists him when working questioned document cases. However, it is not necessary for him to recount all of those accomplishments, every training session he has attended, or cases he has worked (document case(s) he has worked), etc. in order to testify in court as an expert. A review of some of the necessary qualifications is discussed next.

Review the FDE's qualifying questions

The FDE usually has a prepared list of qualifying questions for counsel that he may wish to use. Who knows the FDE background better than himself; his education and training, the professional associations he belongs to, etc. Some counsel, though, would rather use their own list of questions; however, when they do they run the risk of asking a question the answer to which they do not want to hear. That is why wise counsel will ask the FDE for, and work with, his list of suggested qualifying questions.

When an FDE is being questioned on his background, training, and other qualifications that prepared him for this profession, the questions he is asked should be designed to show that he possesses the necessary knowledge and skill to perform the examinations that were necessary to arrive at the correct conclusion(s). What questions best fulfill this obligation? A list of suggested questions is provided here:

- *Please state your name.* For the record, it is important that the court record accurately identify the name of the witness.
- *What is your professional title?* If the witness is a full-time stockbroker who only does this type of work as a hobby, they should not be allowed to testify. If the witness is a full-time FDE, Examiner of Questioned Documents, Document Analyst, or a Forensic Document Consultant, etc. then he should be qualified.

  There are some people who study handwriting in an attempt to determine the writer's personality or character, a task not entered into by the FDE. Individuals who study handwriting for this purpose are usually referred to as "graphoanalysts," and their work "graphology" or "graphoanalysis." Graphology is defined as: " . . . the study of handwriting, esp. when regarded as yielding clues to the writer's character" (Random 1992). FDEs *do not* engage in this area of work. Individuals who engage in graphology or graphoanalysis may not be very different from the FDE and may not be qualified to testify in court concerning questions involving altered documents or the forensic identification of handwriting. The judge as "gate keeper," under the new rules of evidence based on recent court decisions involving the admissibility of scientific evidence, must determine whether a graphoanalyst is qualified to testify.

- *By whom and where are you employed?* The purpose of this question is to try and determine whether the witness actively works in the profession, just as his job title provides information about his full-time employment. If he works for "Joes Brick Yard" full-time and says he is a full-time FDE, there may be a problem. Additional questioning will be necessary to resolve some of the apparent differences.

- *How long have you been an FDE?* If the witness has been practicing for three years, then it is safe to assume that he is either an advanced trainee or has just completed a basic training program. If the witness is in any of these categories, he is still working under the direct supervision of one or more senior examiners, or should be, to properly improve his skills and knowledge. There is nothing wrong with this. Every competent, qualified, and ethical examiner must make that first appearance in court as an expert witness. If this person is still working with senior examiners daily, counsel can be a little more comfortable that the witness has also received numerous hours of training in courtroom etiquette and demeanor. Regardless of his limited experience, this witness is far more qualified than the individual who has taken a correspondent course or has read a few books without being under the direct supervision of senior examiners and in a structured apprenticeship program. Of course, it may be better to have a FDE who has been practicing for 15 years.

- *What training have you had to qualify you as an FDE?* Here the witness should give an overview of his qualifications that he has received the proper training under the direct supervision of competent, qualified, and ethical examiners is critical. So is the continuation of that training throughout the remainder of his career.

Since there are no college degrees given in Questioned Documents, it is important that a trainee's apprenticeship program be regimented and strictly controlled by the senior examiners under whom the trainee is working and in a recognized forensic document laboratory. His training program should consist of study, research, and experimentation assignments. He should be applying the principles learned in the cases worked by the senior examiner(s), and his work should be reviewed for completeness, accuracy, and the proper application of the principles the trainee has been learning. The length of time required for a complete and comprehensive training program is approximately three to four years' duration.

When responding to this question, it is not necessary for the witness to list every book or technical paper he has studied, every scientific seminar or college course he has attended, or every technical organization in which he holds membership, etc. He is only required to summarize this information to demonstrate that he has the requisite training and background required to be proficient at his work and to qualify in court. Too often witnesses try to impress the court and jury by taking a lot of time to regurgitate material that they know nothing about. The true professional lists only those items from his background that are most relevant to the current situation, and is prepared to respond to further questioning, if necessary.

- *How many times have you testified as an expert?* This question is designed to give some information on whether or not the witness has been accepted in court as an expert. A follow-up question is usually: in what courts have you testified? Counsel does not want to know how many times in federal, state, and local courts; he wants to know if the witness has testified in any of these.
- *What makes handwriting identifiable?* The purpose of this question is to provide the court and jury with information they will find useful in the evaluation of the witness's testimony. It is not intended to make them experts in the field of handwriting identification. The court and jury are the ultimate trier of facts. If a basis for understanding the scientific testimony about to be heard is provided to them, not only do they appreciate it, the information helps them to establish the witness's credibility.
- *What steps did you follow in conducting your examination(s) and what are some of the things you considered?* This question brings the court and jury directly to the case they are hearing. The witness verifies that he has followed established procedures in his examination and evaluation of the evidence and, in doing so, arrived at the proper conclusion.

What other topics should be discussed at the pre-trial conference?

- A survey of the findings in the report. Assuming the FDE's report is organized and well written, that it contains easy-to-understand concepts and language, this part of the conference should be relatively brief. The most important thing is that at its conclusion, counsel fully understands the technical aspects of the FDE's testimony as it relates to the particular case.

- How the evidence will become part of the court record. What documents will be handed to the witness for identification and an opinion, based on the results of the laboratory examination, while he is on the witness stand? At the time of his examination, the FDE should write, in small letters and numerals, the date he examined the document(s), the number he assigned to the document(s) that will be used in the report, and his initials. Other reference numbers, such as case number(s) or chain of custody document number(s), should also be written on each document. By doing this, the FDE can easily refer to his notes and locate the document being referred to if a question is asked about the document and he is not able to answer it without that referral.

   At the time of trial the FDE should know for each document what examinations were requested and the results of those examinations. However, some cases involve too many documents for him to remember what was said about each one. If there are a large number of questioned writings and suspect writers who have written multiple entries on each document, he will want to refer to his notes to refresh his recollection. Each case is different and there is no hard and fast rule about what is proper procedure, except to say, if possible, the FDE should not refer to his notes any more than is absolutely necessary.

   Items given to the witness should be presented in an organized manner so the court and jury understand their importance and relevance. This is the responsibility of counsel. The witness should be prepared to respond in an accurate manner to any question presented by counsel. For example, if counsel has not given the witness all of the specimen writing that was used in the examination, the witness should say so. If the witness is handed a document that does not contain his initials, he should point that out because it may have been handed to him by mistake. Accuracy in recognizing documents he examined is a very important part of the FDE's testimony. In the pre-trial conference, these issues should be resolved so that there are no mistakes in front of the court and jury.

- Issues such as the authenticity of specimen writing used for the examination should also be discussed at this time. In reality, it should have been discussed before the FDE begins his laboratory examinations; however, events between the time of the examination and trial may make it impossible to get certain writing admitted into evidence. If counsel is not able to enter some of the specimen writing into evidence, the FDE will have to conduct a re-examination of the material and, in all probability, he will arrive at a different conclusion. If this occurs, opposing counsel must be notified in a timely fashion of the change based on the new examination.

- A discussion of the questions to be asked on direct, possible cross-examination questions and re-direct is an essential part of the pre-trial conference. As stated above, under no circumstances should the FDE be instructed or told, by counsel or anyone else, what to say when he testifies. If counsel attempts to instruct the witness on what to say in response to any question, the FDE should remember that he is totally impartial regardless of who called him to be their witness. The author has had counsel try to instruct him on what to say in response to a question while on the witness stand. In one instance the counsel wanted testimony that did not accurately reflect the evidence or opinion given. I refused to do as was requested and testified in accordance with the standards required of my profession. Remember, the FDE's testimony should be accurate, fair, impartial, and, most important of all, in his own words. He should always answer questions from either counsel the same way, with the same inflection in his voice, not behaving defensively or seeming to show favor to either side, etc. Most counsel respect the witness's impartiality; however, there are a few who do not.

■ A discussion about how to question an opposing expert could be part of the pre-trial conference. Occasionally, the FDE finds that he is going to be opposed by another examiner. This opposition may take the form of a conclusion that is completely different from his, or the opposing expert may just take issue with his examination methods, or the significance he attached to various features of the writing, etc. Hilton takes a rather strong position about opposing experts. "If the identity of an examiner who has examined the papers for the opposition is known, his technical ability and ethical standing should be discussed. In a vast majority of cases testimony against the facts are given by poorly qualified or unscrupulous 'experts'" (Hilton 1982: 401). Hilton's position is not entirely without merit. Unfortunately, there are examiners who are either "poorly qualified or unscrupulous," and, even more unfortunately, there is very little that can be done to prevent them from examining cases or testifying in court.

Many other items may be discussed during a pre-trial conference. It is not possible to explore each possibility at this time. The most important thing the FDE must remember is to be prepared, to know what was done and how he did it in this particular case, and why he arrived at the conclusion he did; he must also be prepared to testify truthfully and accurately in court.

REFERENCES

Beggs, G.J. (n.d.) *Novel Expert Evidence in Federal Civil Rights Litigation*.

Hilton, Ordway (1982) *Scientific Examination of Questioned Documents*, revised edn, New York, NY.

Law, Cornell, at http://www2.law.cornell.edu/cgi-bin/folioc . . . 27rule701!27)/doc/{t209}/pageitems={body}?Topic: – "Federal Rules of Evidence."

The Lectric Law Library™ Reference Room, at http://www.lectlaw.com/ref.html (date of search 10/22/98). Topics: "Burden of Proof," "Evidence, Direct," "Evidence, Opinion," "Beyond a Reasonable Doubt," "Reasonable Doubt," "Evidence, Clear and Convincing," and "Preponderance of the Evidence."

McAlexander, Thomas V. (1977) "The Meaning of Handwriting Opinions." A later version of this paper has been published in the *Journal of Forensic Sciences.* Over the many years of our association and working in the same laboratory, Mr McAlexander has written numerous papers and articles on this topic. While the wording of this material is largely mine, if there is any commonality between this material and his, credit for that commonality should go to Mr McAlexander.

Moenssens, A.A. (1997) "Handwriting Identification Evidence in the Post-Daubert World," *UMKC Law Review*, 66(2).

Random (1992) *Random House Webster's Electronic Dictionary and Thesaurus*. College Edition, Reference Software International.

www.wcl.american.edu
www.lectlaw.com/ref.html
www.cornell.edu

AUTHOR INDEX

SUBJECT INDEX

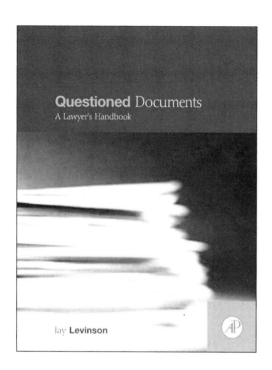

DATE DUE